Social Psychology Across Cultures

Analysis and perspectives

PETER B. SMITH
University of Sussex

MICHAEL HARRIS BOND
Chinese University of Hong Kong

HARVESTER WHEATSHEAF

New York London Toronto Sydney Tokyo Singapore

First published 1993 by
Harvester Wheatsheaf
Campus 400, Maylands Avenue
Hemel Hempstead
Hertfordshire, HP2 7EZ
A division of
Simon & Schuster International Group

Designed by Claire Brodmann.

Typeset in 10/12 pt Palatino
by Mathematical Composition Setters Ltd, Salisbury, Wiltshire.

Printed and bound in Great Britain at
the University Press, Cambridge

British Library Cataloguing in publication data

A catalogue record for this book is available from
the British Library

ISBN 0-7450-1170-5 (hbk)
ISBN 0-7450-1171-3 (pbk)

1 2 3 4 5   96 95 94 93 92

In science, novelty emerges only with difficulty, manifested by resistance, against a background provided by expectation.

Thomas Kuhn, *The Structure of Scientific Revolutions* (1962)

Contents

Contents

Acknowledgements

We should like to acknowledge helpful assistance in our preparation and revision of this book from Svend Borge Andersen, Tomohide Atsumi, Bob Baron, Anne Cathcart, Tim Church, Andrew Colman, Richard DeRidder, Helga Dittmar, David Dyker, Alan Page Fiske, Arlene Franklyn-Stokes, Bill Gabrenya, Howard Giles, Ana Delgado Gonzalez, Bill Gudykunst, Mike Hogg, Nick Hopkins, Geert Hofstede, Barbara Krahé, Mansur Lalljee, Kwok Leung, Barbara Lloyd, Walt Lonner, Jodi Lynn, Janak Pandey, Mark Radford, Laura Sidorowicz, Ted Singelis, Toshio Sugiman, Anti Uutela, Katsuya Yamori and Alistair Young. We are also indebted to the Canon Foundation in Europe for the award of a fellowship to the first author. This support facilitated the writing of a substantial part of this book.

We are grateful to the following publishers and authors for permission to reproduce the tables and figures listed: Figure 3.2 by permission of Academic Press and Shalom Schwartz; Figure 3.3 by permission of Shalom Schwartz; The New Guinean faces in Figure 4.1 by permission of Paul Ekman; Figure 4.2 by permission of Ype Poortinga; Figure 6.1 by permission of Duke University Press; Table 6.1 by permission of David Trafimow; Figures 6.2, 7.1, 9.1 and 9.2 by permission of Larry Feign; Box 7.1 by permission of Pergamon Press; the Table in Box 8.4 by permission of Miriam Erez; Box 9.1 by permission of Stephen Bochner; Boxes 3.1, 10.1, 10.2 and 10.3 by permission of Sage Publications Inc.

ONE

Introduction

Psychology has had a long past but only a recent history.

(Ebbinghaus, 1908)

The task of this book is simply stated. We wish to examine the prospects for a social psychology whose findings are known to be valid in all parts of the world. Social psychology has through most of its history been a predominantly North American enterprise. Within the USA and Canada there exists a great diversity of cultural groups, so it is entirely possible that research undertaken there will prove to reflect the cultural variability to be found in other parts of the world. However, we can only be sure that this is so if we make thorough tests in which the different cultural groups involved in particular studies are clearly and separately identified.

An example of how this is a strategy which pays off is given by recent work on gender differences. Only when researchers started to make systematic comparisons of men's and women's responses to situations did a picture start to emerge as to how gender roles are socialized and what are the cultural factors acting in society to sustain and to change them. Before we shall be in a position to address such issues, we need to lay out some brief understandings of the history and geographical dispersion of social psychology. In Chapter 3 we shall then consider what we mean by the word 'culture'. By the time we reach Chapter 11 we will feel better able to return to the issue of how the conclusions we shall draw about culture relate to the differences found *within* a culture, between subgroups such as those based upon gender and race.

There are a number of reasons why attending to culture is a particularly timely task. For example, increasing travel and communication links among countries and continents impose limits on interest in studies of social behaviour which might be found to hold true only in one or another country. The populations of many countries are also asserting their

1

heterogeneity more energetically, and we need to be able to understand what processes come into play when they meet and interact with one another. In addition, we must consider the possibility that the ways in which people relate to each other in different cultural groups differ sufficiently that the same study will yield different results, depending on where the study is done.

The world-view of the social psychology textbook

We shall start with a brief survey of the current situation. Research into social psychology is undertaken in many parts of the world and the results are published in numerous technical journals. The results of these studies are then transmitted to a wider audience through the medium of student textbooks. Let us compare two recent introductory textbooks: Baron and Byrne (1986, 1991), which is the best-selling US text; and Hewstone, Stroebe, Codol and Stephenson (1988), which is the best-known European text. We find that each of these cites around 1,600 references to published works in social psychology. However, Baron and Byrne are US authors, whereas Hewstone *et al.* edited a text written by 25 different European authors. An analysis of where the studies were done which are selected for inclusion by these authors shows some interesting patterns, as can be seen in Table 1.1.

Of the studies cited by Baron and Byrne (1991), 94 per cent had first authors who were from North America, while just 6 per cent were drawn from the whole of the rest of the world. In Hewstone *et al.*, about two-thirds of the references are to North American work and 32 per cent to the

Table 1.1 Coverage of social psychology textbooks

		References cited from studies done in:				
Authors	Country	North America	Europe	Australasia	Authors' own country	Rest of the world
Baron and Byrne (1991)	USA	1,668	37	15	(1,668)	47
Baron and Byrne (1986)	USA	1,550	17	8	(1,550)	27
Hewstone *et al.* (1988)	Europe	1,100	489	20	(489)	12
Pandey (1981)	India	368	19	0	115	0
Furuhata (1980)	Japan	195	9	0	19	0
Rodriguez and Seoane (1989)	Spain	1,037	304	0	70	0
Strickland (1984)	USSR	34	22	0	191	4

Note: Overall figures are only approximate, as some studies were done in more than one country. We took first author's location as the basis for classification.

rest of the world. Of these 521 references, however, almost all refer to work done in Europe, leaving rather over 2 per cent from the rest of the world. These figures are only approximately accurate, since a number of studies were done jointly by authors in Europe and North America. We should also note in passing that there is nothing unique about these two particular texts in this respect. Similar figures would most likely emerge had any other US or European texts been used. As the table also shows, Baron and Byrne (1991) have responded to increasing recent interest in cross-cultural issues by doubling the number of non-American studies compared to the previous edition of their text.

We cannot be sure that where a study was done necessarily tells us what cultural groups were represented among the participants in the study. But looking at textbooks written in other countries does show us whether the origins of the social psychological studies put before students are or are not the same ones around the world. Table 1.1 shows what we find if we look further afield, or at texts written in languages other than English. The table shows the details for Pandey's (1981) Indian survey of social psychology, Furuhata's (1980) Japanese text, the social psychology volume of the Spanish language *Handbook of General Psychology* (Rodriguez and Seoane, 1989) and a volume of papers by Soviet social psychologists edited by Strickland (1984). The figures illustrate several points. First, they show the strong influence of North American sources, even in texts published in languages other than English. The Soviet work shows a lesser preponderance, but it was not written as a text designed to represent social psychology as a whole.

Frequent citation of US studies is no doubt partly attributable to the fact that there are a great many researchers into different aspects of social psychology in North America. Just how many there are in relation to other parts of the world is very hard to estimate. One possible way is to examine the American periodical *Psychological Abstracts*, which surveys English language publications from around the world. During three months in 1991, it published abstracts of 301 publications in the fields of social psychology and personality. Of these, 77 per cent were from North America, 13 per cent from Europe and the remaining 10 per cent from the rest of the world. If we were to make the crude assumption that on average all social psychologists publish English language articles at the same frequency, this suggests that about three-quarters of the social psychologists in the world are North Americans. Such an estimate could well be inaccurate, but it is not too far out of line with the finding of Rosenzweig (1992), who reports that of the 56,000 researchers in the entire field of psychology world-wide, 64 per cent are Americans.

The figures in Table 1.1 also make clear that the studies cited in each textbook are strongly influenced by the authors' nationality. Substantial numbers of well-conducted studies published in Europe, Australia, India,

Japan and elsewhere are discussed only in the texts published locally. A third point only emerges when one returns to the texts and scans those studies which are referenced from outside of the authors' own region. In some cases the reader is not told that the study being reported was in fact done in another country. Of the studies reviewed in Baron and Byrne's text, for example, the locations of the 99 studies cited from outside North America are mentioned in just 46 cases. These 46 references are of particular interest to our theme in this book. In 24 of them, Baron and Byrne address directly the question of whether the findings obtained are similar to or different from those which had been obtained in the USA. In eight cases they report that the studies did show various kinds of difference, whereas in the remaining 16 the results were found to be similar to US results. This sampling thus suggests that around two-thirds of studies do yield similar findings when done outside North America. We shall review this conclusion as we examine these 24 studies and many others in the course of this book.

Lonner (1989) has surveyed 33 US textbooks in general psychology and found a similar predominance of North American citations. The question we must now address is whether this focus upon North American studies is problematic or not. If we were discussing textbooks on physics from different parts of the world, it is quite possible that we would find a similar distribution of researchers' locations. After all, as with physics, most of the best-known and most able researchers in social psychology are located in North America, and it need be no surprise that textbooks give their work deservedly substantial coverage.

It is not, however, very likely that studies in physics give different results simply because they are conducted at different locations. When we are concerned with social behaviour, there is a much stronger possibility that different results might be obtained. Researchers in the USA have been as alert as those in other countries to such possibilities, and some of them have been in the vanguard of social scientists who examine whether or not studies done in one country are replicable elsewhere. Our purpose here is thus not to make some kind of ethnocentric criticism of North American social psychology, but rather to explore the work of those researchers from all countries who have sought to broaden the data base upon which our subject rests.

We cannot hope in a work of this length to give a full account of contemporary social psychology. This book is therefore written on the assumption that you, the reader, have already read or have access to a social psychology textbook available in your country. In the next chapter we shall start to look in more detail at some of the evidence stemming from studies which have been repeated in more than one country. In later chapters we shall continue so far as possible to focus upon studies which have been conducted in two or more countries.

Box 1.1   *What is a considerate supervisor?*

A recent study surveyed leadership behaviours in electronics assembly plants in four countries (Smith *et al.*, 1989). The plants were in the USA, Hong Kong, Japan and Britain. In all the plants studied, supervisors who were considerate towards members of the work team were positively evaluated. The focus of the study, however, was on what the supervisor actually has to do in order that he or she is perceived as considerate. Workers in the plant were asked to indicate how often their supervisors performed a variety of different behaviours. It was found that 'considerate' supervisors have to do rather different things in order to earn that label in each of the different countries. For example, one question asked about what the supervisor might do if a member of the work team is experiencing personal difficulties. Workers in Japan and in Hong Kong responded that to discuss the matter with other members of the work team in the person's absence would be a considerate behaviour. In contrast, workers in the USA and in Britain evaluated such public discussion as an inconsiderate thing to do. Thus the study illustrates how a specific action may have quite different meanings attributed to it depending upon the cultural context within which it is performed. In Japan and Hong Kong greater value is attached to indirect communication as a form of tactfulness, whereas in Britain and the United States higher value is given to directness. We explore more fully why this difference exists in Chapter 8.

Before we start on our main task, let us look at what happens when two people from different parts of the world interact with one another. By looking at failures in their attempts to communicate, we can gain some further ideas as to the issues which might lead research studies done in different parts of the world to have different outcomes.

An instructive cross-cultural episode

Chan Chi Lok, a Chinese freshman at a Hong Kong university, has taken a course in Business English from Mrs Jean Robertson, a British teacher recently arrived from Scotland. Mr Chan has failed his final exam and Mrs Robertson has made an appointment to meet him at 12 o'clock to discuss his poor performance. She has a 12.30 lunch date with the department chairman, George Davis.

Chan arrives at 12.20, knocks on Mrs Robertson's door and enters without waiting for a response. Mrs Robertson looks up in surprise. Chan approaches her chair and stands right beside her, smiling. 'Have you had your lunch yet?', he asks.

Mrs Robertson replies sternly, 'Chan, sit yourself down over there', pointing to a chair positioned about six feet from her desk. 'I doubt you are twenty minutes late', she complains.

'Pardon?' Chan asks.

Mrs Robertson repeats herself slowly.

Chan pauses. 'Well, ah, the train was delayed', he lies, looking down, 'and I couldn't get on the school bus, so I walk all the way to your office', he explains, telling the truth.

'Did anyone ever tell you that you are a wee bit slippery, Mr Chan?'

'Huh?'

'Never bother', she retorts. 'Your final exam mark was none too good. What way have you done so poorly?'

Chan sneezes twice.

'Do you have a cold?', asks Mrs Robertson.

'No, teacher – you stink', Chan explains, referring to her perfume.

Mrs Robertson's mouth drops.

Chan responds to her apparent distress by switching back to her earlier question and explains, 'I don't know. But I tried very hard and re-read the book four times before the exam. All we found your test very difficult', Chan continues, referring to his classmates.

'It's no good hiding behind the others: you must stand on your own two feet', Mrs Robertson challenges. 'And effort is not enough for a pass.'

'But my English has improved so much from you. Your teachings are so good. I have to pass out from this course for being promoted.'

'I'm not caring about any of that, Mr Chan. What is at issue is your ability at English. And it wasn't helped by your frequent absence from class.'

'My mother was in the hospital during this term time. I had to visited her every day.'

'Your first responsibility is to your studies, Mr Chan. You could well have visited your mother fine in the evenings.'

'But who watches after my sister?' Chan retorts.

'You don't get it, do you?' Mrs Robertson sighs.

'Yes', answers Chan, puzzling his teacher further.

'Mr Chan, I'm away now, as I have a previous appointment.'

'Couldn't you just give me a compassionate pass, teacher? I really need to pass out of your course.'

'What?! A *compassionate* pass? I've never heard of the like! Anyway, I've got to run. Phone me for an appointment if you want to have a wee word about retaking the exam.'

Mrs Robertson then goes to the door and holds it open, as Mr Chan walks out, eyes downcast.

'Don't be late next time, Chan. If you can't get here on time we'll never get anywhere.'

Aftermath

This encounter between Mr Chan and Mrs Robertson was the culmination of a term's interaction as student and teacher in a small class. It had been Chan's first opportunity to interact with a foreigner and Robertson's first term of teaching Chinese students. Unfortunately, little light was shed by the sparks which they generated from one another, and their time together merely served to strengthen the stereotype Chan has about western women and Robertson has about Chinese persons.

When Mrs Robertson meets her departmental chairman for lunch, she responds to his 'How are your classes going?' by complaining that she is very angry with impolite, irresponsible and illogical students. For his part, Chan later responds to his sister's concern about his depressed mood by stating that his teacher is 'a little bit' unsympathetic. Furthermore, she is 'slightly' aggressive when problems arise and legalistic about grades. His sister is not surprised to hear this criticism about a woman who lunches alone with a male colleague! She is, however, surprised at her brother's certainty of judgement, because he has frequently told her that he does not understand half of what his teacher says anyway.

A typical result?

We do not intend our case study to imply that the transactions between Mrs Robertson and Mr Chan are a product of their specific gender, age or cultural backgrounds. Nor do we underestimate the real difficulties of teaching and learning English. But unfortunately, unhappy outcomes such as occurred in this case are the norm rather than the exception in many cross-cultural encounters. They continue because each party to the encounter provides the other with important services – Mrs Robertson with a well-paid job in an exotic setting, Mr Chan with access to a native speaker of English, the language 'of wider communication'. Nonetheless, they do not enjoy the process and are often puzzled, frustrated and angry with one another. The delights and possible synergy to be derived from bridging the cultural divide escape them.

As we will discover, a little cultural knowledge would go a long way towards improving the outcome of such cross-cultural encounters. We would like this book to serve that end, for the twenty-first century will bring more not fewer such exchanges across cultural lines, as our planet continues to shrink into a 'global village'. Our increasing interdependencies will require us to 'hang together, or else we shall surely hang separately', to quote Patrick Henry. This 'hanging together' could be achieved with more enthusiasm and appreciation if parties to the exchanges anticipated and understood the likely problems.

We will refer to the exchange between Mr Chan and Mrs Robertson throughout this book, to give concrete illustration to the issues which we shall be discussing. We shall pay attention in particular to the way in which their cultural backgrounds led each of them to adopt different values, different styles of communication, different ways of showing emotion and different ways of negotiating. If you, the reader, wish quickly to satisfy your curiosity as to how we perceive what went on between the two of them, you will find our fullest analysis at the end of Chapter 9. However, our own cultural backgrounds, English male and Canadian male respectively, may have led us to miss other aspects which are apparent to you. If so, we should be happy for you to let us know. We too are working to broaden our cultural sensitivities!

TWO

The world of social psychology

If a man does not keep pace with his companions, perhaps it is because he hears a different drummer. Let him step to the music he hears, however measured or far away.

(Henry Thoreau, *Walden*, 1854)

Before we look in detail at the concepts which cross-cultural social psycho-logists find most useful in guiding their studies, we need to place social psychology as a whole into some kind of social and historical context. This will be the task of the present chapter. First we shall look at the way the subject has developed over the past century. Having documented the manner in which social psychology became most firmly rooted in North America by the middle of the century, we next take nine of the best-known US studies and review what happened when they were repeated in other countries. Finally, we shall need to think through more carefully the issues which emerge from this survey, especially how best to interpret variations in findings from around the world.

The where and when of social psychology

The issues of importance to social psychologists have been debated throughout recorded history. To a surprising degree, we find that the points of greatest disagreement at the present time were already sketched out by the ancient Greeks. For instance, is it more fruitful to study social behaviour by focusing on individuals and their motivations and cogni-tions? Or do we learn more by examining social structures and the way in which they mould our behaviours and thoughts? Aristotle would have a clear preference for the first strategy, while Plato's thought fits the second option more closely.

Beginnings

The origins of contemporary social psychology are usually traced to the Germany of around a century ago. Although Wilhelm Wundt is best known for establishing the first psychology laboratory in the world, and for work in psychophysics, between 1900 and 1920 he also published 10 volumes on what he termed '*Völkerpsychologie*'. This term does not translate readily from the German, but his approach included material which would these days be classified as social anthropology or sociology as well as social psychology. He stressed the role of society in defining our cultural and social context. In terms which became widespread later, he was a sociological social psychologist. Other writers in Germany at around the same time laid more stress on the individual, but their work was and still is much less well known.

By the early twentieth century, both the sociological and the more individual-centred or psychological approaches were well established in North America and in Europe. Of the first two English language textbooks published, one fell into either camp. McDougall (1908) stressed the individual's instincts, while Ross (1908) stressed uniformities in behaviour resulting from the social influences of others. During the next few years, the development of behaviourist psychology encouraged the view that, if social psychology were to become a science, it must develop precise ways of measuring behaviour and experimental methods of testing its determinants. This trend was particularly strong in the United States, as exemplified by Floyd Allport's (1924) experimentally oriented text and the great attention given subsequently to the development of valid measures of attitudes, which were conceptualized as the individual's predispositions to behave in particular ways. However, the stress on experimentation did not occur solely in the USA, and in fact the first text on experimental social psychology was that of Moede (1920) from Germany. In other European countries such as France and Britain, sociology and social anthropology developed more strongly.

Probably the most important figure in the development of contemporary social psychology was the German, Kurt Lewin. Lewin's interest in the study of perception moved during the 1930s to the area of social behaviour. His emphasis upon the interrelatedness of different elements in what he called the individual's life-space meant that he was sympathetic to those who thought we should study social systems as well as individual processes. He saw less value in abstracting one or another fragment of social behaviour and studying it in isolation. Additionally, he encouraged the use of the experimental method. He thus provided a potential bridge across the widening gap between sociological social psychologists and psychological social psychologists. He also promoted cultural integration. For instance, during the early 1930s he developed links with social psychologists not only in Europe and the USA, but also in Japan and India.

The move to America

With the rise to power of Hitler in 1933, Lewin and many other prominent Jewish social scientists fled from Germany, most of them going to the USA. Working first at Iowa, then at MIT, Lewin undertook classic studies in the fields of leadership and group decision, studies which we shall discuss shortly. More important in the long run, he trained a succession of researchers, many of whom became key figures in the post-war flowering of American social psychology. Festinger, Kelley, Cartwright, Deutsch, Schachter, French and Thibaut were among his students. Each of these researchers developed distinctive programmes of experimental work, but it is notable that, after Lewin's death in 1947, the emphasis on social systems as a whole was gradually reduced. Gaining adequate control of the experimental environment was seen as the first priority, and if that meant the use of increasingly simplified settings, the gain in precision was thought worth the sacrifice.

The subsequent explosive growth of North American social psychology is well known. It should be noted, however, that while psychological social psychology has become dominant, there continues a rather separate tradition of sociologically oriented social psychology in the USA, a tradition which works mostly within the non-experimental methods established by, for example, Mead, Goffman and Bales (see Hewitt, 1991).

Spreading the word

After the Second World War, social psychology outside North America sank to a low ebb. It was estimated that in the late 1950s, there were more social psychologists at the University of Michigan than in the whole of western Europe! Naturally, when social psychology was gradually re-established in universities and research institutes around the world, it was done in the spirit then firmly rooted in North America. Psychology laboratories were established and experiments conducted, as though there were no important differences dependent on where in the world a laboratory was located.

The impact of social psychological theories originating in North America around the world continues to be strong to the present day, as we can deduce from the survey of textbooks in Chapter 1. The most notable exception to this trend has been in the former Soviet Union. There, the implicit individualism of US theories was for a long time considered unacceptable, and distinctive theories were developed instead around the concept of the collective (Andreeva, 1979; Strickland, 1984). Such theories should not be seen simply as something imposed by the former Soviet political system. They belong in the tradition of a more sociological approach to psychology, as exemplified by the early Russian work of Vygotsky with children, and are compatible with the collectivist values of Soviet scientists and people. As we shall discover in the next chapter, they are also compatible with concepts developed recently by cross-cultural psychologists.

A number of other concerns arose as social psychologists attempted to use methods developed by North Americans in their own countries. In developing countries, a frequent complaint has been that the available theories do not address the issues which are most urgent. Social psychologists in these countries have found it desirable to contribute directly to national development and to create theories and methods which are relevant to these development issues (Blackler, 1983; Sloan and Montero, 1990). Misra (1981) describes how, as a US-trained social psychologist, he began work in India on attribution theory, but ten years later was engaged in studies of effective salesmanship. Sinha (1986) likewise abandoned his commitment to experimental method and became a leading exponent of the 'indigenous psychology' movement, which proposes that distinctive theories will be required for each cultural context that is studied. Marin (1983) reports a similar trend in Latin America, with social psychologists active in community development programmes. A recent issue of the journal *Applied Psychology* (Wilpert, 1991) surveys the uses of social psychology in community development projects in Brazil, Chile, Colombia, Mexico, Puerto Rico and Venezuela. The common thread in all these Third World projects has been a move from what Moghaddam (1990) calls a 'modulative' orientation toward a 'generative' orientation. In other words, social psychologists in these countries have become less concerned with describing and analyzing the status quo, and more concerned with generating positive social changes.

A different problem, more frequently voiced by social psychologists in western Europe and other industrialized countries, was that when they attempted to replicate North American studies, they quite often obtained different results. Sometimes also they found it difficult to set up experiments in a way which their subjects found plausible. These difficulties provide the principal starting point for the rest of this book, and we shall look at examples shortly.

The worries of the western Europeans were, however, not solely empirical. They were concerned also that the strongly individualist manner in which many US theorists conceptualized social behaviour ignored the context in which that behaviour took place. Their view that it is the context which gives behaviour its meaning is, of course, connected to the preoccupations of earlier European theorists from Wundt onwards. The flavour of their critique is suggested by the pointed title of Tajfel's (1972) watershed paper, *Experiments in a Vacuum*.

This quick overview of the history of social psychology has necessarily given a somewhat stereotyped view of the state of the subject in this or that country. Making generalizations about whole countries is something that social psychologists should be more cautious about than most. However, we generalize in the manner of an artist, who lays down a broad brush outline for more detailed work later. It is now time to consider what happened when some well-known studies washed up on foreign shores. If these studies are unfamiliar to you, you may well find it useful to read fuller descriptions of them in a social psychology text. We start with studies that look at rather basic aspects of social cognition, and work towards those involving more complex social behaviours.

How well do the classic studies replicate?

The effects of mere exposure

One widely replicated US study in the field of social cognition is that first reported by Zajonc (1968). He proposed that the more often we are exposed to a stimulus, the better we like it. Repeated exposure to, for example, Chinese characters and to nonsense words has shown that US subjects liked better the things they had seen more often. This has led some commentators to point out that repeated exposure of ourselves and those around us may provide the basis for positive feelings about oneself and form the basis on which friendships could arise. Findings of this type have been obtained in 20 or 30 published American studies.

Replications of the mere exposure study have been reported from only two countries, Brazil and Belgium. Vanbeselaere (1983) had considerable difficulty in obtaining findings similar to those of Zajonc. In an extended series of studies, the usual relation he found was curvilinear, as shown in Figure 2.1. His Belgian student subjects evidently liked objects which they had seen a few times less well than those which they had seen only once or even not at all. Rodrigues (1982) reports that his Brazilian results support Zajonc, but as can be seen in the figure, his results also showed little or no increase in liking until after the first few exposures.

Vanbeselaere is unable to provide an explanation of why his results differ from the US ones. Since they are well replicated, and to some extent are echoed by Rodrigues' results, a cultural explanation is a possible candidate. It could be the case, for example, that Americans focus more immediately on the stimuli provided, whereas Belgians and Brazilians

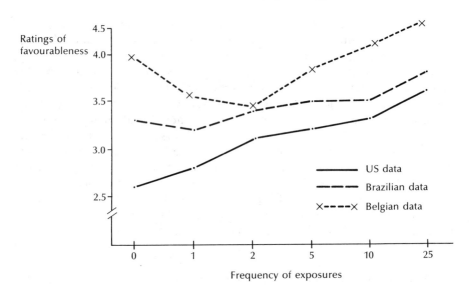

Ratings of favourableness

Frequency of exposures

US data
Brazilian data
X----X Belgian data

Note: Zajonc and Rodrigues both used the same set of Chinese characters as stimuli. Vanbeselaere used a set of nonsense syllables. Vanbeselaere also had some difficulty in finding the best translation of Zajonc's experimental instructions. The graph above was obtained when he translated Zajonc's instruction to 'guess' the attractiveness by the Flemish word for 'judge'. When he translated 'guess' literally, there was no increase in attraction with increased exposure at all. The translation difficulty illustrates the problems of carrying out exact cross-cultural replications.
Source: Modified after Rodrigues (1982).

Figure 2.1 Frequency of exposure and liking for the stimulus

usually take more time attending to the context of the experiment, and only start noticing which stimuli are being repeated after a few have already gone by. This explanation would account for two experimental conditions under which Vanbeselaere did get results like the US ones.

He found that he could obtain a steadily rising graph like those reported in the USA, if he offered his subjects money to guess whether supposedly Turkish adjectives (actually nonsense words) had a positive or a negative meaning. His second 'successful' procedure was to allow his subjects to look at all the words together, after they had been exposed to some more than others, but before they made their ratings. These are situations in which subjects are encouraged to attend more closely to the stimuli. Under these conditions, the overall result of greater liking for the most frequently seen stimuli may hold good for all three cultural groups. Why it might take Belgians and Brazilians longer to attend closely to the target stimuli will, of course, need to be studied further.

Social loafing

At least since the work of Allport (1924), there has been interest among social psychologists in the effect of the presence of others on an individual's behaviour. Allport was interested in whether people worked harder or less hard in the presence of others. One of the more recent series of such experiments concerns what has become known as 'social loafing'. This phrase describes a behaviour pattern based upon the fact that, when several people are performing a task together, any one person may feel that he or she does not need to exert maximal effort. Indeed, in what was effectively the first recorded social psychology experiment, conducted in the 1880s, a French engineering professor named Ringelmann showed that three men did not pull on a rope three times as strongly as did one man (Kravitz and Martin, 1986). This study occurred well before what is usually said to be the earliest social psychology experiment, the US study on a similar topic by Triplett (1898).

The more recent work of Latané, Williams and Harkins (1979) concerned how loudly people shouted or clapped in groups of differing sizes, compared to when they are alone, and demonstrated similar reductions in average output. Latané's shouting experiment has been repeated using schoolchildren in India, Thailand, Taiwan and Japan, university students in Malaysia and Japan, and junior managers in Japan (Gabrenya, Wang and Latané, 1985). In all these cases, some evidence of social loafing was found. However, Shirakashi (1984–5), who also used Latané's procedures, found no evidence of social loafing among Japanese students. Furthermore, subsequent studies in the USA have shown that social loafing is reduced or eliminated where the task is seen as important and where group members believe that their performance is under surveillance by other members. We might therefore predict that the social loafing phenomenon would be absent from cultures where these factors are more generally salient. In order to test this speculation, more meaningful experimental tasks are required.

Gabrenya *et al.* (1985) compared US and Taiwanese school children on a task involving the counting of tones heard over headphones. Subjects worked either individually or in pairs. They found that in this situation, social loafing was present among the US children, but the Taiwanese children actually performed *better* when working in pairs. The effect was particularly strong among ninth-grade boys.

In a similar vein, Earley (1989) compared the performance of 96 managers from the USA and China on an 'in-basket' simulation of work. During a one-hour period, they had to attend to a set of work items including prioritizing interviews, filling out requisition forms, and rating job applications. They were told that they were working either alone or in groups of ten. Those working alone were advised that they should complete at least

20 items. Those in groups were advised that 200 items would be needed and that only the total number of items completed by members of the group would count. The results showed clear evidence of social loafing among the US managers, whereas the Chinese managers worked harder in the group condition than when alone. More recently, Earley (in press) has reported a similar difference between US and Chinese managers based upon ratings made of their actual performance at work, under individual and group working conditions.

The likelihood that this difference in findings between the USA and China is due to cultural factors is raised by two related studies involving Japanese subjects. Matsui, Kakuyama and Onglatco (1987) found that in Japan each person in two-person student groups worked harder on average than did individuals on a number-counting task. Yamagishi (1988) made a comparative study between Japan and the USA. Subjects in this study were informed that they were working in groups of three, but that they would not be able to monitor how much work the other members of the group were putting in. Rewards were based upon the group's productivity on a letter-matching task, but on each trial members were given the chance to opt for an individually based reward instead. Yamagishi found that the Americans were inclined to opt for the individual reward when the penalties for doing so were low, but not when they were high. However, the Japanese frequently chose the individual reward even when the penalties for doing so were high. Yamagishi concludes that the Japanese did this because they wished to avoid the situation where they had no information on how hard the others in the group were working. By opting for the individual reward they could be certain that they would not be penalized by any social loafing which was occurring.

The range of countries from which studies have been reported is not wide, but it appears that social loafing can be considered a universal phenomenon only when detected through the most trivial types of experimental task. Where the task becomes more important and meaningful, it becomes possible to differentiate cultures from one another. In later chapters we shall advance theories which attempt to show why these differences occur.

Conformity and independence

The most widely replicated social psychology experiment of all time is Asch's (1951) study of conformity, of which there are at least 24 published non-US replications, from 13 countries. In this study a naive subject is repeatedly asked to judge which of three lines matches another line, in the presence of several other people who frequently all give the same *wrong* answer. The replications show widely differing rates of conformity and independence in the different countries, and we shall examine possible reasons for this variation in some detail in Chapter 8.

Aside from the differences found in the results from this experiment, there is another issue of interest here. The Asch experiment is almost invariably described as a study of conformity, even though the original study showed that two-thirds of the judgements made by subjects were independent of the pressure upon them to give the wrong judgement. Friend, Rafferty and Bramel (1990) examined reports of the Asch studies in 99 US social psychology texts. They found an increasing trend over time to concentrate upon the fact that one-third of the judgements were erroneous, and to use this as evidence of how widespread is the process of conformity in society. Friend *et al.* point out that this interpretation is precisely the opposite of what Asch was trying to show, and indeed succeeded in showing: namely, that his subjects were not entirely conformist and that most judgements were entirely correct. One can only speculate as to why this interpretation of Asch's findings occurs.

This type of reinterpretation of results is not an isolated instance. The findings of other classic studies, such as Milgram's work on obedience, to be discussed shortly, are often also reported as though all subjects succumbed to social pressures. One possibility is that writers of texts – including us, the writers of this one – are seeking to persuade you, the reader, that social behaviour is understandable and predictable. To assert that people sometimes, even often, act independently of those around them might seem to undermine the case for a social psychology, and encourage instead the study of personality.

But we are straying a little from our main theme. The value of Friend *et al.*'s critique for our purposes is that it alerts us to the fact that we cannot judge whether 37 per cent of conforming responses and 63 per cent of independent ones are *high* or *low* figures until we can compare them with figures from other cultures. In a society which values independence and initiative as highly as do many Americans, we might expect that any evidence of conformity would be interpreted negatively. In a cross-cultural context, we have to entertain the possibility that a 37 per cent conformity rate is relatively low, as Asch believed, and not high as many of the textbook writers assert.

What happens to social deviates?

Another classic study concerning conformity was the one reported by Schachter (1951). Schachter set up group discussions, in which accomplices were briefed to take up particular positions. In different conditions of the experiment the accomplice was either to take up and keep to a deviant position ('deviate'), or to take up a deviant position but gradually be won over by the group ('slider'), or to agree with the average of group opinions from the start ('mode'). In the USA, Schachter found that the deviate quickly attracted a lot of attention, which tailed off as his opinions were found inflexible and he was rejected. The slider received continuing attention as he moved toward a more conforming position.

A rather similar study was undertaken by Schachter *et al.* (1954) in seven different European countries. In this case, the subjects were 11-year-old boys invited to join a model aeroplane club. Asked to select which of several model aeroplanes to build, the experimenter's accomplice consistently chose a rather boring glider in preference to a choice from several other more attractive possibilities. The results proved much more complex than the experimenters had expected, making it difficult for them to test the complex set of Lewinian hypotheses which they had formulated. The basic problems were three. First, not all groups reached agreement in the time allotted. Second, some groups reached agreement by agreeing with the supposedly deviant accomplice and did not reject him, as had occurred in the US study. Third, where there was a deviate, he was more strongly rejected in some countries than in others. Each of these effects occurred to a different extent in the various countries, as can be seen in Table 2.1.

In Britain, Germany and Belgium, the groups were less likely to oppose the deviate, less critical of him even when they did oppose him, and more likely to be persuaded by him. De Monchaux and Shimmin (1955), who conducted the British part of the experiment, suggested that by expressing their preference consistently, the supposed deviates may in fact have become leaders in some groups. It could be that, in ways unintended by the experimenters, the deviates used in some countries behaved in ways that were more attractive than those in other countries. We shall see in Chapter 8 that research into influence by minorities has become a favoured topic among quite a few European social psychologists, and this study appears to have stumbled upon an early experimental instance of its occurrence.

Table 2.1 Deviance and rejection in seven European countries

	Percentage of groups agreeing against the deviate	Percentage of groups agreeing with the deviate	Percentage of groups not agreeing at all	Mean attractiveness of deviate
France	95	0	5	6.00
Norway	80	3	17	5.09
Holland	75	12	13	3.47
Sweden	66	9	25	4.50
Belgium	63	3	34	3.88
West Germany	50	18	32	2.01
England	37	20	43	3.04

Source: Adapted from Mann (1980).

Even if this analysis is correct, we still do not have a satisfactory explanation of why there was more minority influence in some countries than others. The countries in which there was some minority influence also appear to have been the ones where there was more argument, since a larger proportion of their groups failed to agree. It could be that in some countries the group members deferred more to authority than others, but there is no way of knowing whether this is because of some type of cultural difference, or simply because the experimenters or their accomplices in each country behaved in slightly different ways. At the very least, we must conclude that an experimental procedure designed to study social deviance in one country can elicit behaviours more usually thought of as examples of leadership or minority influence when used elsewhere.

Obedience to authority

Among the most controversial and widely discussed studies reported by social psychologists is Milgram's (1974) study of obedience to authority. In this study, Milgram found that around 65 per cent of his American subjects accepted orders to give electric shocks to other people in the course of a 'learning' experiment. This result occurred despite the fact that information was clearly visible to subjects that each shock was stronger than the last and that dangerously high levels of shock were being administered by the subject before the experiment terminated. Although the experiment was, of course, based upon deception and no shocks were actually administered, it was convincingly staged, with tape recordings being played of the protests and screams of the supposed victim.

Milgram's goal was to determine whether or not we are predisposed to obey an authority figure, even when that figure makes unreasonable demands and provides no reasons for doing so. A number of critics within the USA (e.g. Baumrind, 1964) suggested that such experiments are unethical, in so far as they stress and potentially humiliate the experimental subject. Despite this ethical outcry, researchers in at least eight other countries have attempted to repeat Milgram's procedures, and these studies provide us with an opportunity to review whether the findings are replicable within other cultural settings.

The results obtained are shown in Table 2.2. Several researchers included different variations in their experimental designs, as indeed did Milgram's original series of studies. The figures given in the table show the percentage of subjects who continued to administer shocks right up to the maximum level of 450 volts under what Milgram called his 'baseline' experimental condition. In the Italian study the maximum shock level was only 330 volts, at which level Milgram found 73 per cent obedience.

Table 2.2 Studies of destructive obedience to authority

Study	Country	Subjects	Percentage obedient
Milgram (1963)	USA	Male general population	65
		Female general population	65
Rosenhan (in Milgram, 1974)	USA	Students	85
Ancona and Pareyson (1968)	Italy	Students	85
Mantell (1971)	Germany	Male general population	85
Kilham and Mann (1974)	Australia	Male students	40
		Female students	16
Burley and McGuiness (1977)	UK	Male students	50
Shanab and Yahya (1978)	Jordan	Students	62
Miranda et al. (1981)	Spain	Students	over 90
Schurz (1985)	Austria	General population	80
Meeus and Raaijmakers (1986)	Holland	General population	92

It can be seen that the Australians and the British were rather less obedient than the Americans, the Jordanians were close to the US level, and the Spaniards, Austrians, Germans, Dutch and Italians were somewhat higher. However, we cannot be very confident that the differences found tell us much about cultural differences unless we can first rule out all other differences among the ways in which the experiments were staged. In the case of experiments on shock, this comparison is particularly difficult, since in each one a particular experimental accomplice is used, and some of these confederates may have been perceived as more vulnerable or more deserving of shocks than others. For instance, one of the 'victims' in Milgram's study was a smartly dressed businessman, whereas in the Australian study a 'long-haired' student was used.

Many other differences among the studies are also likely to have contributed to the variations in results obtained. For instance, the Dutch experiment was not actually concerned with giving shocks, but instead used a similar task where the subject was instructed to harass and criticize someone filling out an important job application form. Another difference may explain why Australian women were much less willing to give shocks than Australian men, even though Milgram found no gender difference in the USA. This difference could have arisen because the Australian women were asked to give shocks to a female victim, whereas the victims in Milgram's studies were all men.

A more useful way to learn from this batch of studies is to examine what factors caused changes in levels of obedience *within* each country and then compare these results *across* countries. Milgram found that levels of obedience in his studies varied from 0 per cent to 92 per cent. Some of the largest variations occurred when additional accomplices were introduced into the experiment. In one version of the study, this extra accomplice was the person who actually administered the shocks, when instructed to do so by the naive subject. As in the standard study, the naive subject had already been instructed by Milgram that shocks should be given whenever the 'learner' made mistakes. Thus the only difference from the 'baseline' conditions is in who actually presses the shock button. Under these conditions, obedience rose to 92 per cent. In the Australian study, obedience also increased when the subject was transmitting the instructions to give shocks to someone else. In this case obedience rose to 68 per cent among men and 40 per cent among women.

In another of Milgram's variations, when extra accomplices refused to carry out their part in administering shocks, the proportion of obedient subjects fell to just 10 per cent. In Holland it fell to 16 per cent, and in the German study, when subjects saw another subject refusing, their obedience level showed a more modest decline to 52 per cent. These studies thus show that in these four countries, the actions of additional people within the experimental setting can raise or lower obedience levels considerably. In deciding whether or not to obey, learners evidently take account of the social context around them, not just the demands of the authority figure. This particular series of studies does not give us enough data to know whether this happens more in some countries than in others.

A different type of variation in experimental procedure was also included in the same four countries. In each of these studies, the experimenter reminded the experimental subjects that they were responsible for their own actions. In the USA, Australia and Germany this was done by telling subjects that they could choose what level of shock to administer. In Holland they could choose how much to harass the job applicant. In all four countries, this reminder reduced the number of subjects inflicting maximum harm to virtually nil.

The obedience experiments tell us two things. First, they make clear that substantial numbers of people in a variety of countries will carry out orders from authority, even when this compliance will harm others. The countries in which these studies have been reported are, with the exception of Jordan, all advanced industrial countries, so we should hesitate before concluding that we have identified a universal aspect of social behaviour. We shall return in Chapter 8 to the question of whether similar obedience to leaders would be expected from other countries.

Second, these studies suggest that in none of the countries studied is obedience to authority the kind of blind process which some interpreters of Milgram's work have implied. Levels of obedience can and do vary greatly, depending on the social contexts which define the meaning of the orders given. The importance of context may also vary from country to country.

Box 2.1   *Mrs Robertson and Mr Chan: Teacher and Learner*

> The obedience studies supposedly concern a teacher and a learner,
> though the teacher is required to use methods which are, to say the
> least, unorthodox. Our case study of Mrs Robertson and Chan Chi Lok
> also focused on the teacher–learner relationship. The misunder-
> standings between them illustrate some of the ways in which, although
> both accepted that it was Mrs Robertson's job to instruct, they had
> different ideas as to what exactly was the nature of Chan's expected
> performance. Mrs. Robertson, for example, stressed time-keeping,
> grades and regular attendance, while Chan assumed that evidence of
> effort and (Chinese) politeness was more important.

Leadership style

One of the earliest experiments reported by Lewin's research group in
Iowa was a series of studies of the effectiveness of different styles of
leadership in youth clubs (Lewin, Lippitt and White, 1939). As with some
of the other studies reviewed in this chapter, the results are sometimes
inaccurately quoted in texts. Lippitt and White had the youth club leaders
adopt an autocratic, a democratic or a *laissez-faire* role in each club. Each of
these roles and the leaders playing the roles were rotated among the clubs.
The researchers concluded that the democratic leaders were the most
popular with club members and that morale was highest in the democratic
condition. However, when they measured how many aircraft models the
clubs had made – a task in which the clubs had been engaged – the autocratically run groups were more productive. The researchers also noted that,
when an autocratically run club was left unattended for a while, members
broke up some of the models, while in the democratic clubs they continued
their work. The *laissez-faire* clubs were both dissatisfied and unproductive.

   The Lippitt and White studies were carried through at the time of the
Second World War, when feelings about autocratic and democratic leadership were running particularly high. Lewin felt that it would be good to
replicate the project in nations seen at that time as highly autocratic. After
the war, he therefore contacted Japanese social psychologists whom he
had known in the 1930s. The resulting studies (Misumi and Nakano, 1960)
showed that Japanese children's preferences and level of performance
varied, depending upon how complex the task was. With more difficult
tasks they preferred autocratic leaders and did more work for them, but
with easier tasks they preferred democratic leaders and were also more
productive with them.

Meanwhile, in Germany (actually, the former East Germany), the principal other defeated nation of the Second World War, Birth and Prillwitz (1959) reported results essentially similar to those of Lippitt and White. However, Meade's (1967) study in India found that the boys in his clubs preferred autocratic leadership, were less often absent and worked more productively under it. Leader styles do thus show differing effects in differing countries, but the results did not match up with Lewin's expectation that the Second World War enemies of the USA (Germany and Japan) would favour authoritarian leadership. However, youth clubs provide a rather narrow base upon which to generalize, and we shall return to a broader range of studies of leadership in Chapter 8.

Group decision

Another well-known series of experiments involving Lewin were those in which he compared different ways of encouraging people to change their dietary habits during the Second World War. These showed that American housewives were much more willing to change their behaviours after group discussion than after receiving a lecture (Lewin, 1947). The behaviours changed included serving unusual cuts of meat, and having children drink more milk, cod-liver oil, orange juice and so forth. Similar studies were conducted in the USA involving work groups in factories deciding how new changes might be accomplished. Lewin argued that group discussion methods were effective because they provided a way in which group norms about what behaviours are desirable or undesirable might be 'unfrozen' and then 'refrozen' into a new pattern.

There is clearly a good deal in common between the enthusiasm of the Lewin group for democratic leadership and their subsequent work on group decision. However, studies of group decision in other countries have given results as mixed as did those of democratic leadership. Numerous studies have been reported from Japan (e.g. Makita, 1952; Misumi and Haraoka, 1958, 1960), all of which have shown that change following group discussion was greater than after lectures. This is consistent with the group-oriented nature of Japanese society. We saw above that under some circumstances Japanese children preferred autocratic leaders, but this apparent inconsistency can be explained through closer analysis of how hierarchy and participation are linked in Japanese society. We shall look at this relationship in Chapter 8. In more recent times, the introduction of changes in Japanese factories through the use of discussion groups called 'quality circles' has become very widespread indeed.

Attempts to introduce changes through group discussion in factories in some other countries have been much less successful. French, Israel and Ås (1960) used group discussion to introduce changes in a Norwegian shoe

factory. Many of the workers did not perceive group discussion as a legitimate way to introduce change and they responded no more positively than
did those in the control condition. This negative result may have arisen
because they believed the groups to be bypassing their commitment to
trade unions, or because they thought it was the role of management to
propose changes.

Still less successful was an attempt to introduce group participation in a
Puerto Rican garment factory (Marrow, 1964). The use of groups was seen
by workers as evidence that management did not know how to manage,
leading them to think the firm would soon be out of business. A number
of workers left their jobs and joined other firms as a result!

Juralewicz (1974) also studied group decision in a Puerto Rican garment
factory. He found no benefit from having the whole group participate in
decisions, but when the groups put forward representatives to discuss the
changes, the groups' subsequent response was significantly better.

These findings suggest that the meaning of group participation, like that
of leader style, varies substantially in different countries. Indeed, research
has also suggested that response to group participation varies substantially
within the United States. We turn next to a further series of studies
concerning group decision, which have been conducted in a rather more
tightly structured format.

Group polarization

One particular type of group decision making has been very frequently
studied: namely, the making of choices involving risk. This enthusiasm followed Stoner's (1961) initial discovery that the groups which he assembled
tended to make decisions which were more risky than the average of the
views of the group members. Further research both in the USA and in
France (Moscovici and Zavalloni, 1969) revealed that such 'risky shifts' are
not universally found, but that group decisions do tend to polarize towards
one or the other extreme on scales measuring members' opinions.

Several factors are thought to contribute to this phenomenon. First, it is
proposed that where risk taking is highly valued, individuals may be
persuaded towards greater risk taking by comparing their preferences with
those of others and discovering that some people favour greater risks.
Conversely, where caution is valued, the discovery that some group
members are more cautious than oneself could be influential. Second, it is
thought that group decision provides opportunities for more persuasive
arguments to be brought forward, at least some of which any one
individual might not have considered. Finally, these studies have usually
been conducted with groups of people who are initially strangers, so that
the shift could have something to do with their getting to know one

another and defining their own and the group's identity by taking a more extreme collective stand.

In theory, studies of polarization from other parts of the world have considerable potential in helping to clarify which of these explanations has greatest generality. In practice, there are some difficulties in realizing this outcome. Table 2.3 shows studies of group polarization that used a format which was at least similar to the original design devised by Stoner. Significant average shifts towards risk after group discussion have been reported from six countries other than the USA, whereas no overall effect occurred in the studies from Germany, Uganda and Liberia. However, as was also found in the USA, the average shift is misleading, because certain discussion items regularly produced a shift toward caution rather than risk. The table shows that, in those studies where separate means for each individual item are given, some significant shifts towards caution were also found in the results from other countries.

It is notable that, with the exception of the two African studies, all of these findings were obtained in some of the more industrialized countries of the world. Researchers in these countries have proceeded more recently to debate alternative explanations of why polarization occurs in groups. For our present purpose it is important to reflect upon the circumstances in which these findings were obtained. All but one of these studies were

Table 2.3 Studies of group polarization

Study	Country	Subjects	Mean shift per item	Items with Shift to risk	Items with Shift to caution	Total items
Original Stoner items						
Rim (1964)	Israel	General	0.6	4	2	6
Bateson (1966)	UK	Students	0.4	–	–	5
Kogan and Doise (1969)	France	Students	0.5	–	–	5
Lamm and Kogan (1970)	Germany	Students	0.2	–	–	6
Jamieson (1968)	New Zealand	Workers	0.6	8	3	12
Bell and Jamieson (1970)	New Zealand	Students	0.5	–	–	12
Vidmar (1970)	Canada	Students	1.4*	–	–	10
Carlson and Davis (1971)	Uganda	Students	−0.2	0	2	11
	USA	Students	0.6	3	1	11
Semin (1975)	UK	Students	0.9	6	0	11
Jesuino (1986)	Portugal	Students	0.4	9	2	11
New Items						
Fraser *et al.* (1971)	UK	Students	0.5	3	1	8
Gouge and Fraser (1972)	UK	Students	0.3	1	2	8
Gologor (1977)	Liberia	Students	0.0	3	3	6

* Vidmar omitted both the items which usually move towards caution.

based on *ad hoc* groups of college students, working without appointed leaders. Even the workers in Jamieson's (1968) study were strangers to one another attending evening classes. Many of the risky situations portrayed in Stoner's questionnaire are characteristic of American culture, and less likely to have meaning the further one moves from populations who are familiar with aspects of US life. Even in the studies of students, researchers frequently chose to drop some of the questionnaire items since they would not be meaningful locally.

This problem is most acute in the two African studies. These were both conducted with school children. In Liberia there was some definite evidence of polarization, whereas in Uganda there appears to have been little movement in either direction. This difference could have arisen because in the Liberian study locally meaningful items were specially constructed, whereas the American items employed in Uganda may well have been of lesser meaning or interest.

We have very little knowledge of whether polarization occurs within groups which have a more established structure. In parts of the world where social groupings are less fluid, and hierarchies more firmly established, we might expect quite other processes to come into play, as may have been the case in the African studies, and in some of the studies of group decision reviewed earlier. Studies from within the USA (Wehmann, Goldstein and Williams, 1977) and from Portugal (Jesuino, 1986) suggest that, where a leadership structure is provided, polarization is much reduced. Polarization may thus be something which occurs in groups when they first form, or when they are developing attitudes towards new events. As such, it may be more frequent in cultural settings where group memberships are fluid and transient.

Group conflict and co-operation

In a series of field studies, Sherif *et al.* (1953; 1961) explored the dynamics of conflict and co-operation between groups. They did so by assembling summer camps of young boys in remote settings, and implementing an elaborate experimental design over several weeks. Basically this design required the creation of randomly composed groups, which were then set in competition with one another. When a situation of some hostility had been engineered between the groups, Sherif *et al.* were able to test their hypothesis that, by providing shared 'superordinate' goals on which the whole camp needed to work together, the conflict and mutual prejudice which had built up could be resolved. The Sherifs and others have used this model to suggest that similar principles could be used to understand and work on a variety of real world social conflicts. Critics have doubted whether such a model is valuable in analyzing larger-scale or longer-term conflicts (e.g. Billig, 1976), but we shall focus here upon the prior question of whether boys' camps in other countries behave in similar ways to those which the Sherifs studied.

The complexity of these impressive experiments has ensured that not many researchers have been able to replicate them. However, Tyerman and Spencer (1983) in Britain, Diab (1970) in Lebanon, and Andreeva (1984) in the Soviet Union have done so. Tyerman and Spencer argue that many of the Sherifs' findings were a consequence of the temporary nature of the groupings they created. They therefore conducted a study of a boy scout troop on their regular summer camp. The four patrols in the camp initially showed the same level of in-group favouritism as was reported in the Sherif studies. However, even though the patrols had segregated quarters and engaged in a programme of competitive activities, just as occurred in the Sherif camps, no increase was found in inter-patrol hostility or stereotyping. Late in the camp it was found possible to increase intergroup co-operation by a lecture from the camp leader, a procedure Sherif had reported to be ineffective. Tyerman and Spencer conclude that behaviour within their camp was regulated by a long-established set of social norms, which were largely unchanged by the two-week camp.

Diab's camp in Lebanon mirrored Sherif's procedures more precisely. He recruited ten Christian and eight Muslim 11-year-old boys and reported that initial friendship patterns were *not* wholly along religious lines. After two random groups had been composed, they developed very different cultures. One group named themselves 'The Friends' and established a warm and co-operative climate. The other group named themselves 'Red Genie' and were highly aggressive and competitive. They stole things both from one another and from members of the Friends. During competitions, Red Genie were mostly ahead, but in the final stage the Friends passed them and took the overall prize. It proved impossible to continue the camp into the 'co-operation' phase, since the reaction of Red Genie to their defeat included stealing knives, threatening others with them, and attempting forcibly to leave the camp.

The sample of subjects in this study is small, so one should probably resist the temptation to see parallels between it and the tragic exacerbation of intercommunal conflicts which has occurred for prolonged recent periods in Lebanon. However, it does illustrate a point also made by Tyerman and Spencer, that the culture of each specific group will depend not just upon externally imposed incentives of competition or co-operation, but also upon established traditions and local cultures which form a background to specific events within each group.

Of the replications of the Sherif studies, the only one which offers unambiguous support, is Andreeva's (1984) Russian study. As Sherif would predict, Andreeva found that, while Pioneer youth camps were engaged in competitive sports, in-group favouritism increased; but when they switched to helping on agricultural collectives, in-group favouritism declined again. From the studies available, it appears that Sherif's findings are most clearly upheld in temporary settings, where other longer-term preoccupations are less troublesome. We shall see at later points in this book that time perspective is much longer in some parts of the world than others. Even within the USA, there is of course substantial attention to longer-term time perspectives. If we are to understand longer-term conflicts between groups then, we shall need to take account of the processes that come into play as the time perspective of the relations between groups is extended.

Some second thoughts on replication

This completes our survey of attempts to replicate some of the best-known American studies in different countries. The results appear rather discouraging. The only topics on which there is much evidence for successful replication are the studies of obedience and of mere exposure. There is some suggestion that social loafing and group polarization are general phenomena, but in both cases, where more realistic experimental designs are used, the results from different countries start to diverge. In the case of leadership, conformity, group decision and intergroup relations there are rather more marked differences in results.

We find ourselves in a situation a bit like that of Chan and Mrs Robertson. Our anticipations about how people will behave do not seem to be very accurate, but it is difficult to be sure why. Faced with this difficulty, we may well, like them, fall back on our existing preconceptions. Depending upon where we come from, we may account for the non-replicability of studies in different ways. An American social psychologist might point to the methodological rigour of modern US studies and the demanding standards of major US journals, and suggest that studies elsewhere may not have been conducted with quite such care. This line of reasoning could be pursued through the use of statistical techniques such as meta-analysis, which enable the pooling of the results of a series of similar studies, yielding estimates of whether variations in experimental design or the location of the study can better account for the differing results obtained. However, such meta-analyses have not been reported for the research fields upon which this chapter has focused.

A European might lay more stress upon the traditions of sociological social psychology and suggest that tight experimental designs often wholly or partially distort the phenomena which we ought to be studying anyway. A social psychologist from a more hierarchical culture might conclude that westerners know best how to do social psychology and feel that locally done work was unworthy of comparison and so could be ignored. Finally, a social psychologist from a developing country could argue that it was more important to develop themes relevant to local problems and practices rather than to follow the precedents of established social psychology.

A closer look at the problem

If we are to avoid such prejudices, we need to establish ways of judging what is a good cross-cultural social psychology study. Such criteria are likely to include prescriptions about method and formulations of relevant theories. Let us first consider methods. Many of the studies touched on so far in this chapter were done in a single country, by different investigators. They were done because a particular US study had become well known, and others wished to see whether they could get similar results. However, it is very difficult for different experimenters working in different countries at different times to design and carry through studies that are closely similar. For this reason, one can never be sure whether a successful replication (or a failure to replicate) is actually due to similarities or differences between the two countries in which the studies were done. Often it could just as likely be due to differences in the samples of subjects studied, or differences in questionnaire translations or other local variations unrelated to the original experimenter's concerns. Such issues are important within countries too, but they become more acute in cross-cultural work.

There are ways in which these methodological problems can be reduced, and some of the studies already considered did employ them. For instance, it is beneficial for the same group of researchers to conduct a concurrent study in two, and preferably more than two, countries using closely similar methods and subjects, as was the case in the Schachter *et al.* (1954) study of social deviance reviewed earlier. The larger the number of countries involved, the better is the chance of understanding why the results come out as they do. Where only two countries are involved there are invariably several possible explanations of differences obtained, and no clear basis for choosing between them.

It is also good scientific practice not only to translate questionnaires into a form which is locally understandable, but then to have someone independent of the study translate the questionnaire back into the first language, to check that there have been no mistranslations (Brislin, Lonner and Thorndike, 1973). However, even where these and the other sound practices outlined in Box 2.2 are followed, demographic differences between subject populations in the various countries and different nuances of language meaning will ensure that the matching of neither subjects nor measures will be exact. Doing cross-cultural social psychology can never be like reading a thermometer in different countries.

Box 2.2 *Equivalence problems in cross-cultural social psychology*

Scientific logic requires that cross-cultural comparisons be made across groups that are equivalent in all respects *except* their cultural backgrounds. If these groups are different in any other ways, then alternative explanations, called 'plausible rival hypotheses', may be advanced to explain the resulting difference. Of the many potential sources of inequivalence in cross-cultural research (see Brislin, Lonner and Thorndike, 1973), the major ones are as follows.

Translation
Subjects are instructed by spoken or written word, and often their spoken or written responses constitute the measures of interest in the research. These instructions and responses must be faithfully rendered into the language of comparison used in the research.

The method of back-translation (Brislin, 1970) is most often used to establish linguistic equivalence.

Manipulating variables
Social psychology experiments involve the operational manipulation of some construct, like loss of face, through various procedures, like insulting the subject. This manipulation must, however, have the same meaning or impact in the cultural groups involved. For example, a collective insult like 'All you Sicilians (Canadians) are prejudiced' would probably be perceived as stronger in a collectivist than in an individualist culture (Semin and Rubini, 1990) and hence would not constitute an equal loss of face.

The solution to this source of inequivalence is to consult carefully with bicultural collaborators to establish functional similarity in the manipulations used. Once established, these manipulations must then, of course, be delivered by local experimenters speaking the native language of the subjects.

Subjects
The respondents in our research may play identical social roles in their cultures – for example, university students, political party members or participants in a training course – but have very different backgrounds within each cultural group. In some cultures university students are carefully selected on the basis of highly competitive exams, religious orthodoxy, family position, tribal affiliation or other criteria. It is difficult to compare them with university students in the West where access to education is less restrictive and generally determined by a broader range of academic achievement.

The solution to this problem is to look beyond socially equivalent labels to the actual background of the subjects, and equate for key variables other than culture. Where strict comparability is impossible, choose measures and examine variables unaffected by the non-cultural differences. Alternatively, take responses from a variety of people in each culture and use statistical procedures to partial out the influence of the other confounding differences, such as educational level or religious affiliation. Obviously, the characteristics of our cross-cultural samples must be carefully described and the use of imprecise ethnic labels (e.g. Asian-American) avoided (Trimble, 1990).

Scale usage
Verbal measures of the Likert or 'yes–no' format are often used to collect data in cross-cultural research. The interpretability of scores may be confounded, however, by culturally different ways of responding to such scales. Response sets (e.g. Hui and Triandis, 1989), such as generalized acquiescence or moderation tendencies, may interact with scale content to render outcomes non-comparable.

Various procedures, such as within-subject standardization (Bond, 1988b), elimination of scale mid-points and reduction of scale steps, have been advanced to overcome this problem.

The research tradition
Many people grow up in cultures where political polls, consumer surveys, Kinsey-type interviews and subject-pool requirements are taken for granted, along with the assurance that response confidentiality will be honoured. Neither this research tradition nor the guarantee of anonymity can be presumed to obtain in most cultures. Social science may not be practised at all, or may be highly politicized.

As Jahoda (1979) and others remind us, this fact of cultural difference brings the 'normal' enterprise of social psychology into question. As a result, innovative methodologies must often be used to replace laboratory experiments and questionnaires, relationships with cultural informants must be discreetly nurtured, and careful training of subjects must precede data collection. In all cases, the cultural context of 'doing social science' must be thoughtfully assessed by the social scientist to ensure that the outcome of the resulting research has a claim to validity.

In order to take account of this inevitable variability, cross-cultural social psychology needs theories. These theories should not just be consistent with existing social psychology; they should also propose explanations as to why social processes might operate differently in different parts of the world. If we have available a theory which can account for the different effects found in the differing samples, we shall have a much more secure basis both for social psychology and for cross-cultural study. We shall begin the search for such theories in the next chapter. But first we should look at two programmes of research which help to define more precisely the nature of the problems to be solved.

Systematic programmes of replication

Amir and Sharon (1987), who are Israelis, attempted to define how large was the problem of cross-cultural replicability. They point out that studies such as those discussed in this chapter are selectively sampled, in this case because they happen to be well-known studies. Amir and Sharon therefore reviewed studies published in four major US social psychology journals over a two-year period, and selected six where they saw a good possibility that the variables which had been investigated in the USA would have a similar meaning in Israeli society. They then replicated each of these studies twice in Israel, first with a population similar to that used in the US study, and second with a different population. In each case this meant that they did one study with university students and one with high school students.

The original six US studies reported a total of 64 significant main effects and interactions. Amir and Sharon's 12 replications generated 30 significant effects. Of these, 24 replicated the US findings either in the comparable Israeli sample or in both samples. While this result may sound like substantial evidence of replicability, the more important figure is that none of the remaining 44 significant US findings was found in the Israeli studies, and six significant Israeli findings were not found in the US originals! Amir and Sharon note that almost all of the findings which did show some replicability were main effects rather than interactions.

Amir and Sharon's findings suggest that the replicability problem is substantial. We shall review studies in Chapter 3 which suggest that the USA and Israel are by no means the most dissimilar countries in the world. The differences in replicability found might be even greater between more dissimilar pairs of countries. One weak link in the chain of reasoning of Amir and Sharon is that their studies were conducted about ten years after the US studies which they were replicating. However, if one believes that the processes studied by social psychologists are basic to social interaction, one should not expect major changes to occur over such a time period. Another minor irony is that they apparently failed to notice that one of the six 'US' studies which they chose to replicate was in fact an Australian study.

The only other replication project of comparable scope is that carried through by Rodrigues (1982) in Brazil. Rodrigues provides brief details of attempts by himself and colleagues to replicate 15 published US studies during the preceding decade. Rodrigues concludes that in only about half of them were the US findings upheld.

A theory-driven programme of research

If we accept that the replication problem is quite severe, then this accentuates our need to find theories to account for why the difficulty arises. An early example of the way in which this may be done is provided by the work of Berry (1967). He studied the degree to which individuals differentiated themselves from their context in subsistence societies. The particular aspect of his ambitious project which is of interest here is how open to influence from other people these individuals were. His reasoning was that the degree of influence found would depend upon the culture of the different societies he studied. In particular, members of societies based upon hunting do not have great need to co-ordinate their actions with one another. On the other hand, societies which practise farming require that all members co-operate in planting and harvesting at certain times of year, and that agreement is maintained over the safe storage of food through lean times, since these matters are crucial to survival. Openness to influence should therefore be greater in agricultural than in hunting societies.

To test his hypothesis, Berry devised a procedure reminiscent of the Asch conformity studies. He asked his subjects to match a line against any one of eight other lines of varying length. However, he went on to point out to his subjects that most people say that the sixth line is the closest in length (which it was not). Berry found that over a series of trials, members of food-accumulating societies accepted the experimenter's 'help' much more than did members of hunting societies. These findings were replicated among cultures ranging from the Eskimo to various societies in Africa, New Guinea and elsewhere.

Surprisingly, however, Berry and Annis (1974) did not find the predicted differences in response to experimenter 'help' among various north-west American Indian groups. Since these cultural groups were not so diverse as those studied earlier, the later study was a more severe test for Berry's theory. Berry warns that no one theory can be expected to account for all the variations in social processes. What we must search for are theories having a relatively broad range of validity. Berry's series of studies provides one step in that direction, but a wider search will be needed.

THREE

Culture: the neglected concept

Every man is in certain respects
a) like all other men, b) like some other man, c) like no other man.

(Kluckhohn and Murray, 1948)

The whole of psychology can be said to be concerned with the consistency and the variability of behaviour. All that divides cross-cultural psychologists from other psychologists is their interest in studying variability in behaviour among the various societies or cultural groups to be found around the world. While an interest in such issues has long been central to the practice of social anthropology, most psychologists have assumed that the processes they study are in some way more fundamental. Fundamental processes are not necessarily invariant, but psychologists have most typically sought to explain variations in behaviour by reference to more accepted influences, such as the individual's genetic make-up, specific life experiences or environmental pressures.

What is culture?

In order to understand how the concept of culture may prove helpful to social psychology, we need a clear definition. Segall, Berry, Dasen and Poortinga (1990) present the view that culture comprises 'the man-made part of the environment'. Thus culture entails not only material man-made objects, such as houses, methods of transport and implements, but also social institutions, such as marriage, employment, education and retirement, each of them regulated by a host of laws, norms and rules. Such a definition provides a first approximation, but it does not help us to decide, for example, how to draw boundaries among cultures. How much

difference must there be between two populations before we say that they
are different cultures?

There are no agreed answers to this question. Rohner (1984) sees culture
as an organized system of meanings which members of that culture attribute to the persons and objects which make up the culture. This definition
implies that the concept of culture should be restricted to *what things mean*
to a group of people. Most anthropologists have argued that the physical
objects found within a culture are also elements to be included within its
definition. Jahoda (1984), for example, asserts that while the meanings
which we ascribe to, for instance, the houses that we live in are important,
the very existence of houses in a culture also contributes to the way in
which members of that culture think about other aspects of their lives.
Those who are nomadic or homeless will put a different set of meanings
upon events in their daily life.

The debate as to whether human artefacts generate meanings which are
salient in a culture, or whether a culture creates artefacts which represent
the types of meaning it gives to events, is reminiscent of other long-
running controversies in psychology. For instance, the relative potency of
environment and heredity in determining behaviour has been fiercely and
endlessly debated. Ultimately, such controversies are not resolvable, since
they pose as opposing causes factors which are in practice interwoven. For
our purposes the more important aspect of a definition of culture is that a
culture is a *relatively organized* system of shared meanings.

Rohner (1984) also proposes that we should distinguish between the
concepts of culture and of social system. He defines a social system in
terms of the behaviours found within a culture. This is in contrast to his
emphasis upon defining culture in terms of the shared meanings which are
given to events. Social psychologists have repeatedly found that the
behaviours of individuals are not always consistent with their espoused
attitudes, and Rohner's distinction parallels these findings. However, it is
not easy in practice to draw a sharp line between culture and social system
thus defined. Theorists such as Ajzen (1988) have shown that apparent
inconsistency between attitudes and behaviour will often be explicable
because several different attitudes held by the individual concurrently are
all relevant to a particular behaviour. Apparent inconsistencies between a
social system and the culture in which it is embedded may prove explicable
in similar ways. For instance, the celebration of Christmas festivities which
currently occurs in some non-Christian countries is most likely explicable
in terms of the attractiveness of 'modern' commercialized systems of gift
exchange, rather than in terms of the religious significance given to them
by Christians.

Rohner also discusses the concept of society, as widely used by sociologists. He defines a society as *the largest unit of a territorially bounded, multi-
generational population, recruited largely through sexual reproduction, and*

organized around a common culture and a common social system. The concept of society thus acknowledges the degree to which culture and social system are interwoven. Rohner notes that in many parts of the world the concept of society has become synonymous with that of nation. The power of modern governments to legislate combined with increased speed of communication and of travel have made it more likely that nations will become societies. This is not to deny that within many nations there will persist clearly separable subcultures. These may be demarcated, for instance, primarily by religion as in Northern Ireland, by language as in Belgium, by race as in Malaysia and Singapore, and by class or by education as in many countries.

National cultures

It was suggested above that no definitive agreement is possible as to how to distinguish one culture from another. Our further discussion has brought us to the point of acknowledging that the history of the world over the past century has created increasingly powerful nation-states, which are certainly societies within Rohner's definition, and which may for many purposes be considered as cultures. Much of the research to be discussed in this book reports little more detail about the sample of respondents studied than the name of the country in which the study was done. For practical purposes we are therefore restricted to using distinctions based on what we shall call 'national cultures'.

In doing so, we need to bear in mind two major penalties which we incur on the way. First, when we compare national cultures, we can lose track of the enormous diversity found within many of the major nations of the world. We should bear in mind that differences found between any two countries might well also be found between carefully selected subcultures within those countries. Second, we risk implying that national cultures are unitary systems free of confusion, conflict and dissent. Within any national culture there will be all manner of divergences in the experiences of the individuals constituting that culture. We shall need to be very careful to avoid implying homogeneity in the life experiences of any two members of a given culture. These points will be explored more fully in the next section.

Nations and cultures

As we saw in Chapter 2, numerous studies have been completed around the world which attempt to repeat studies originally conducted in the United States. As the results of these studies accumulate, it becomes increasingly urgent that we have some conceptual framework which will help us to understand why one replication might 'succeed' where another 'fails'. In other words, of all the existing differences between national cultures, which are the ones upon which we as social psychologists could most usefully focus in attempting to explain the different results of studies?

Hofstede's classic study

A major step forward on this front was accomplished by the publication of Hofstede's (1980) book, *Culture's Consequences*. Hofstede had access to morale surveys conducted by a large, American-owned multinational firm, to which he gave the pseudonym Hermes. Comparable samples of employees in all the countries where Hermes was represented were asked to complete the survey, which was administered twice, in 1967 and in 1973. This yielded no fewer than 117,000 responses! The items contained in the questionnaire concerned various aspects of employees' work experience, and were not formulated originally with any intention of contributing to psychological theory.

Hofstede's approach was to analyze data from this data bank in such a way that he was able to make comparisons among *countries*. The size of his sample therefore became not 117,000 but 40, since the criteria which he developed revealed that he had adequately large samples from each of 40 countries. However, the mean scores on each questionnaire item which he had for each country were, of course, based on a substantial number of respondents from within that country. He also used a variety of complex statistical procedures to equate differences between the samples on factors such as age, gender and type of work.

When he made a factor analysis of these mean scores for the 40 countries, Hofstede found that he could classify the countries along four dimensions. These dimensions were named as 'power distance', 'uncertainty avoidance', 'individualism–collectivism' and 'masculinity–femininity'. Table 3.1 shows which questionnaire responses were most useful in defining the meanings of each of these dimensions, including examples from both ends of the masculinity–femininity dimension. Hofstede discusses power distance in terms of the amount of respect and deference between those in superior and subordinate positions. Uncertainty avoidance is thought of as a focus on planning and stability as a way of dealing with life's uncertainties. Individualism–collectivism has to do with whether one's identity is defined by personal choices and achievements or by the character of the collective groups to which one is more or less permanently attached. The masculinity–femininity dimension refers to the relative emphasis on achievement and interpersonal harmony which characterizes gender differences in some national cultures.

Table 3.1 Hofstede's four dimensions of culture – related values

Value	Questionnaire item	Response
Power distance	How frequently, in your experience, does the following problem occur: employees being afraid to express their disagreement with their managers?	(Frequently)
Uncertainty avoidance	Company rules should not be broken, even if the employee thinks it is in the company's best interest	(Strongly agree)
	How long do you think you will continue working for this company?	(Until I retire)
Individualism	How important is it to you to have a job which leaves you sufficient time for your personal or family life?	(Very)
	How important is it to you to have considerable freedom to adapt your own approach to the job?	(Very)
Femininity	How important is it to you to have a good working relationship with your manager?	(Very)
	How important is it to you to work with people who cooperate well with one another?	(Very)
Masculinity	How important is it to you to have an opportunity for high earnings?	(Very)
	How important is it to you to get the recognition you deserve when you do a good job?	(Very)

Hofstede's study thus provides us with one possible way of classifying the differences found among the 40 national cultures represented in his sample. Subsequently, he further enlarged his sample to cover a total of 50 national cultures and three 'regions', for each of which he pooled the data from adjacent countries that he deemed to be culturally similar (Hofstede, 1983). The rank orders of the scores received by each of the countries in his sample are shown in Table 3.2. The range of countries included is impressive indeed. The most striking omissions are the former Communist bloc and most of Africa. Hofstede's study has been criticized in a number of ways which will be considered shortly, but it is clear that in terms of global coverage it was, and still is, unrivalled.

Hofstede also notes, as can be seen from Table 3.2, that although the dimensions of individualism–collectivism and power distance were treated by him as separate factors, they are negatively correlated with one another. One group of mostly European and North American countries emerge as high on individualism and low on power distance, whereas another group of mostly Latin American and Asian countries emerge as low on

Table 3.2 Rankings of national cultures using Hofstede's classification

Country	Power distance	Uncertainty avoidance	Individualism	Masculinity
Africa (East) region	22	36	34	39
Africa (West) region	10	34	40	30
Arab region	7	27	26	23
Argentina	35	12	22	20
Australia	41	37	2	16
Austria	53	24	18	2
Belgium	20	5	8	22
Brazil	14	21	26	27
Canada	39	41	4	24
Chile	24	12	38	46
Colombia	17	20	49	11
Costa Rica	43	12	46	48
Denmark	51	51	9	50
El Salvador	18	5	42	40
Ecuador	8	28	52	13
Finland	46	31	17	47
France	15	12	10	35
Germany (West)	43	29	15	9
Great Britain	43	47	3	9
Greece	27	1	30	18
Guatemala	3	3	53	43
Hong Kong	15	49	37	18
Indonesia	8	41	47	30
India	10	45	21	20
Iran	29	31	24	35
Ireland	49	47	12	7
Israel	52	19	19	29
Italy	34	23	7	4
Jamaica	37	52	25	7
Japan	33	7	22	1
Korea (South)	27	16	44	41
Malaysia	1	46	36	25
Mexico	6	18	32	6
Netherlands	40	35	4	51
Norway	47	38	13	52
New Zealand	50	40	6	17
Pakistan	32	24	47	25
Panama	2	12	51	34
Peru	22	9	45	37
Philippines	3	44	31	11
Portugal	24	2	34	45
Singapore	13	53	40	28
South Africa	35	39	16	13
Spain	31	12	20	37
Sweden	47	49	10	53
Switzerland	45	33	14	4
Taiwan	29	26	43	32
Thailand	22	30	40	44
Turkey	18	16	28	32
United States	38	43	1	15
Uruguay	26	4	29	42
Venezuela	5	21	50	3
Yugoslavia	12	8	34	48

Source: Adapted from Hofstede (1983).

individualism and high on power distance. Distinguishing national cultures on the basis of their scores on individualism–collectivism has attracted many cross-cultural researchers in recent years and we shall refer to it frequently in the remaining chapters of this book. In doing so we shall need to remember its close linkage with the power distance dimension. The remaining two dimensions group countries in ways which may well be important, but which are less consistent with previous results and theorizing. Perhaps for that reason, other researchers have made less use of them to date.

Evaluating Hofstede

It is time to evaluate Hofstede's contribution. His definition of culture is quite compatible with that of Rohner (1984). He defines culture as *the collective programming of the mind which distinguishes the members of one group from another* (Hofstede, 1980, p. 21). In other words, cultures are conceptualized in terms of meanings, and it is quite appropriate to study them by assessing the values of representative samples of members from each culture. However, Hofstede is particularly careful to avoid what is known as the *ecological fallacy*. As applied to the study of cultures, this fallacy would be the mistaken belief that, because two cultures differ, then any two members of those cultures must necessarily also differ in the same manner. For instance, someone might expect that, because America scores higher than Guatemala on individualism, then a particular American is bound to be more independent or individualist than a particular Guatemalan. This is not so, as the frequency curves in Figure 3.1 indicate. The mean score for a national culture within Hofstede's study will be the *average* of the

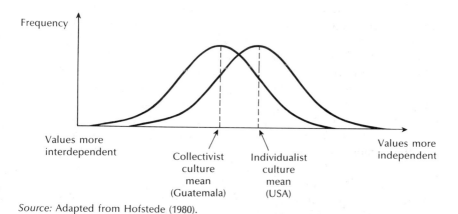

Source: Adapted from Hofstede (1980).

Figure 3.1 Hypothetical distributions of independent/interdependent value scores in an individualist and a collectivist national culture

scores of those who responded to the questionnaire. Within each national sample there may be wide variations, so that it is perfectly possible to come across a Guatemalan who is more individualistic (further to the right in Figure 3.1) than a particular American. It is for this reason that Hofstede conducted his factor analysis upon mean scores for national *cultures*, rather than upon the scores for individual respondents. The benefit provided by the huge sample size is that it raises the likelihood that the country means are reliable estimates of the values prevailing in the national cultures sampled.

One might argue that the task of social psychology is to predict how individuals behave in their social context. If Hofstede's mean scores for countries cannot do this, of what use are they? The implicit flaw in this line of questioning is that social psychologists rarely attempt to predict the behaviour of a *specific* individual. What they do is to attempt predictions about how populations of individuals will behave. Thus, provided that a study done in a particular country is based upon an adequately representative sample, knowledge of the Hofstede scores for that country may be helpful in interpreting the average results from people in those countries.

This statement assumes that Hofstede was entirely successful in the representativeness of his own sampling within the countries he studied. There are several obvious limitations to his sampling, however. First, all respondents were employees of Hermes. Hermes is a very well-known US corporation, which is frequently said to have a distinctive culture of its own. The fact that Hofstede found national culture differences *despite* this unifying influence could be counted as a strength of his project. It remains undeniable that his sample was predominantly male, that it was drawn only from the marketing and service divisions of Hermes and that the data were all collected at least 20 years ago. The only way to test whether these sampling limitations are important is to compare the results with those obtained by subsequent researchers and we shall do this shortly.

The title of Hofstede's book is *Culture's Consequences*, thereby implying that culture can act as a causal factor. When he reports, as he does, that the individualism scores of the countries in his sample correlate +0.82 with their gross national product per head of population, it is very tempting to infer that rich countries are rich because they have individualist cultures. To do so would be hazardous indeed, as with all correlational data. An equally plausible hypothesis is that western national cultures are mostly individualist *because* they are relatively rich. The rapid economic growth of Japan, Hong Kong and other non-individualist Pacific Rim countries provides further reason for doubting that individualism by itself provides the path to riches. What we should be watching for is whether rising affluence in collectivist countries is followed by rising individualism. We shall examine the evidence on this point in Chapter 11.

Box 3.1 *A taste of collectivist decision making*

Chuck and Mary Hooley from Toronto had recently arrived in Brazil, where they were to spend a holiday. After a few days relaxing at the beach and in their hotel, they were delighted to be invited for an authentic local meal in a restaurant with some Brazilian acquaintances. When they were seated, the waitress soon came to the table and gave a single menu to one of their Brazilian friends, who proceeded to study it. Chuck and Mary both felt it important to take care as to what they ate, so they signalled to the waitress that they would like more menus to look at. They could see that the one their host had was in English as well as Portugese. However, she responded only by saying that the menus were all the same. Soon, the Brazilian with the menu began to make some suggestions as to what he was sure they would like to try. Chuck and Mary began to feel frustrated. They did not want to offend their host, but they did need to know what the choices were.

Meanwhile, their Brazilian colleague was puzzling as to why Chuck and Mary seemed so reluctant to accept his carefully selected recommendations. After all, in this situation the cultural norm would be for him to point out the best choices for the members of his group, and the waitress had correctly inferred that, as the senior member of the group, it would only be he who needed to see the menu.

Source: Freely adapted from an original episode described by Brislin *et al.*, *Intercultural Interactions: A practical guide.* © 1986 Sage Publications Inc. Reprinted with permission.

We have discussed Hofstede's study at some length, since it has a key place in the contemporary development of cross-cultural social psychology. The dimension of individualism–collectivism in particular has attracted a good deal of subsequent interest. Triandis (1989, 1990) has summarized a great variety of ways in which social behaviours differ between people in individualist and collectivist national cultures, and Box 3.1 gives an example of what may happen when members of nations varying on these dimensions meet up. However, before we can be sure that these are indeed useful concepts for our purpose, we need to review related studies.

Further studies of values

A group of researchers describing themselves as the Chinese Culture Connection (1987) investigated the possibility that Hofstede's study might be biased towards western values, simply because it derives from a questionnaire designed by various westerners. Hofstede himself freely acknowledges that no study can hope to be entirely value-free, and disarmingly includes in his book two pages describing his own personal values, so that the reader may form a view of the author's own possible biases. The Chinese Culture Connection started its work by asking Chinese informants to list Chinese values of fundamental importance to their culture. These were then used to construct a value survey which was ultimately administered to 100 university students in each of 23 national cultures. Analysis of these data in the same manner employed by Hofstede again yielded four factors. The ordering of countries along these dimensions was then compared with the ordering of the same countries which had been obtained by Hofstede.

As Table 3.3 shows, three of the four factors showed substantial overlap. The importance of this finding is considerable. The two studies used measures with quite different cultural origins, were done at different times, and were directed towards quite different samples within each national culture. Yet, they supported the view that power distance, individualism–collectivism and masculinity–femininity describe dimensions of variation in values which are relatively culture-robust. They also suggest that uncertainty avoidance and Confucian work dynamism are less universally accessible values, though they may well still be important. Putting the results of the two studies together, we might conclude that we should add Confucian work dynamism to Hofstede's four dimensions if we wish to classify cultures in the most valid way possible. Hofstede (1991) himself accepts this conclusion, but prefers a different name for the fifth dimension. He points out that all the Confucian values clustered together emphasize the virtue of taking a long-term perspective, while those who are low on this dimension focus more on the present and the past.

A further large-scale study of values has been undertaken by a team organized by Schwartz in Israel (Schwartz and Bilsky, 1987, 1990; Schwartz, 1992; Schwartz, in press). These researchers made a detailed review of earlier theory and studies of values from both western and non-western sources. They identified 56 values and constructed a questionnaire in which respondents were asked to indicate how much each of these was

Table 3.3 Equivalence of factors obtained by Chinese Culture Connection and by Hofstede

Chinese Culture Connection	Hofstede
Integration	Collectivism
Human-heartedness	Masculinity
Confucian work dynamism	———
Moral discipline	High power distance
———	Uncertainty avoidance

'a guiding principle in my life'. Responses were obtained from 25 countries, from most of which there were two samples, students and secondary schoolteachers. The countries sampled included at least one from each continent.

The data were analyzed by the statistical procedure known as smallest space analysis. This locates the means for each item in a multidimensional space, in a manner which represents how close each item is to each of the others. This procedure tells us which questionnaire items cluster together, but it does not tell us which values were most important within each national culture. Separate analyses of this type were made for each of nearly 60 samples. The results showed remarkable consistency, with possible minor exceptions from China and Zimbabwe. Schwartz and Bilsky found that the spatial relationships of the means within two dimensions could be summarized as falling within ten regions, as shown in Figure 3.2. Each of these regions was given a name which summarizes the points which typically fall within it.

The strength of this project is that it included a very thorough sampling of values which might be important to those in various national cultures. It therefore provides a check on whether or not the earlier studies had significant omissions. The resultant ten value-types are clearly more numerous than those identified by Hofstede (1980) and the Chinese Culture Connection (1987). However, an examination of these values indicates that they represent a refinement rather than a contradiction of

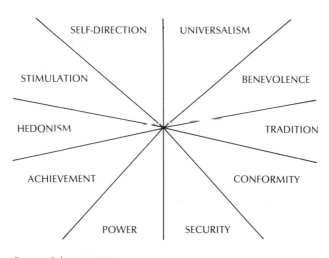

Source: Schwartz (1992).

Figure 3.2 Summary diagram showing value configuration typically obtained in Schwartz and Bilsky's smallest space analyses of individual-level data

earlier work. On one side of Figure 3.2 lie values which would fall within Hofstede's concept of individualism, such as self-direction, stimulation and hedonism. On the opposite side lie central components of collectivism, such as security, tradition and conformity. Masculinity–femininity reappears as achievement opposed to universalism, and power distance as power opposed to benevolence.

The method of data analysis employed initially by Schwartz differs from those used by Hofstede and by the Chinese Culture Connection. Data from his samples have typically been analyzed separately, using individuals as the unit of analysis. Nevertheless, similar dimensions of valuing emerged. The two major surveys of values published since Hofstede's project have thus sustained and amplified his conclusions rather than contradicted them. It is time to consider their implications.

Culture as a theoretical cure-all

Having discussed what we mean by national culture, and shown that there is some defensible evidence that one can classify national cultures in terms of the importance attached to different values, we are now in a position to confront some of the central dilemmas of cross-cultural research. We shall examine three. First, should we be looking for universal aspects of social behaviour: in other words, those which transcend national cultures? Or is it more valuable to try to understand the variations, which as we have already seen in Chapter 2 do occur? Second, how can we think clearly about causation? In what sense could we say that a national culture causes the social behaviour of its members? Finally, do values provide us with the most useful basis on which to classify national cultures?

The search for universals

Whether one sees it as important to establish the universals of human social behaviour may depend partly upon the academic discipline in which one was trained. As Lonner (1980) points out, social anthropologists have spent a good deal of time attempting to identify universals. This no doubt stems from the daunting diversity of the societies which they have studied. For them, the identification of universals is a prerequisite to any type of comparative theorizing. In contrast, most psychologists have assumed that the processes which they study are universal. Work has been centred in relatively few and somewhat similar national cultures, in fact in the high individualist, low power distance cultures identified by Hofstede. This geographical fact about the doing of psychology has made easier the assumption that what is true locally must be true everywhere.

Given this assumption, the logical extension to social psychological studies first done in the United States has been to repeat them elsewhere. As we saw in Chapter 2, this procedure has given mixed results. One type of response to this confusion is to sort the studies which do replicate from those which do not and infer that the successful ones will contribute to generalizations about universals. The alternative, which we favour, is to focus on the ones which do not, and to develop theories as to the ways in which variation may point towards universals which are not immediately apparent.

The emic–etic distinction.   Several such theories have been put forward. Berry (1969, 1989) makes use of a distinction first made by linguists, between phonetics and phonemics. While phonetics has to do with the universal properties of spoken sound, phonemics concerns the ways in which such sounds are formulated within the context of particular words and languages. In a similar way, Berry argues that 'etic' analyses of human behaviour are those which focus on universals. For example, we all eat, we (almost) all have intimate relations with certain others and we all have ways of greeting strangers. An 'emic' analysis of these behaviours, on the other hand, would focus on the different, varied ways in which each of these activities was carried out in any specific cultural setting.

Berry argues that many of the attempts to replicate US studies in other parts of the world can be classified as 'imposed etic'. In other words, the measures used assume that the situation being studied has the same meaning to the new participants as it did to those in the setting where the measures were originally devised, and that therefore responses will have an equivalent meaning. Consider, for instance, the California F scale, a measure of intolerance towards minority groups developed by Adorno *et al.* (1950), and widely used subsequently in the USA and elsewhere. Kagitcibasi (1970) reported that, when the scale was used in Turkey, responses to the items did not correlate with one another at all well, as they had done with the original American subjects. In Turkey, the same scale items tapped several different concepts. In another study, Pettigrew (1958) used the same scale among South African whites. He found that scores on the F scale there did not correlate with anti-black prejudice in that setting, as they had with American subjects. The use of such imposed etic measures could be a major contributor to replication failures.

Berry acknowledges that cross-cultural psychologists mostly wish to finish up by being able to discuss generalizations which are etically valid. In place of the use of imposed-etic measures, he outlines a strategy for reaching a more valid set of 'derived-etic' generalizations. These are to be arrived at by conducting parallel emic studies within a series of national cultures. By allowing measures to be constructed separately in each national culture studied, we do not force them into equivalence. If we nonetheless do find some convergence between the results obtained within each culture, we can be more confident that we have identified processes which are equivalent, and we are in a position to make derived-etic generalizations at least about the range of cultures we have sampled.

While only a few of the studies discussed in this book have followed this procedure in full, rather more have moved some way towards it, compared to the procedures used by earlier researchers. Schwartz's work on values provides an excellent example. His list of 56 values was not originally constructed for use within any particular specific culture, and drew upon non-western sources such as the Chinese Culture Connection survey as well as western ones. Although the value list was not constructed separately in each country, researchers at each site were able to insert additional values if they sensed the need. Few did so. Furthermore, Schwartz's data analysis has been conducted, at least initially, separately for each country-sample. The results therefore provide independent tests of the way in which the meanings given to values within each sample cluster together. What Schwartz has accomplished is thus a parallel series of emic studies within different cultures. The remarkable convergence of his results from almost all samples provides a result which is not imposed-etic, but which gives an increasingly firm base for general theorizing about the structure of human values at the etic level.

We can also test the probability that the studies of values have identified a validly etic set of concepts by comparing them with classifications derived from separate sources. Fiske (in press) reviews a broad range of sociological and anthropological studies, and draws from them the proposition that there are just four elementary forms of social relations. He names these as 'communal sharing', 'authority ranking', 'equality matching' and 'market pricing'. The first two of these are defined in ways which are very close to Hofstede's conceptions of collectivism and of power distance. The remaining two dimensions are less obviously related to Hofstede's other concepts, but we need to exercise care in determining whether or not concepts identified by different researchers overlap simply on the basis of the names assigned to them.

Fiske's definition of equality matching is in terms of a relationship within which the parties are separate but relate on the basis of equal contribution. Market pricing, on the other hand, refers to relations where people seek to achieve a profit over one another through competitive advantage. Table 3.4 suggests ways in which Fiske's dimensions and the classifications of values by Schwartz and by Hofstede may be reconciled. In seeing possible parallels, we should bear in mind that the goals of these authors are not the same. Schwartz and Hofstede have been trying to develop etically valid classifications of the salient values of different cultural groups. Fiske is trying to classify different dimensions of social behaviour, all of which may well occur within any particular cultural group. For instance, a member of

Table 3.4 Possible relations between the concepts of Hofstede, Fiske and Schwartz

Hofstede	Fiske	Schwartz
Individualism	Low communal sharing	Affective individualism
Collectivism	High communal sharing	Collectivism
High power distance	High authority ranking	Hierarchy
Low power distance	Low authority ranking	Social concern
Low uncertainty avoidance	———	Intellectual individualism
Masculinity	Market pricing	Mastery
Femininity	Equality matching	Harmony

Note: The Schwartz concepts in this table are those derived from his country-level analyses (see p. 51).

culture X might relate to blood relatives on the basis of communal sharing, to a boss at work on the basis of authority ranking, to a friend on the basis of equality matching and to a shopkeeper on the basis of market pricing. Equally, of course, a member of culture X might espouse individualist values at work and collectivist values at home. If the concepts in Table 3.4 do show some convergence, that adds strength to the argument that they are encompassing a good deal of what is important about social behaviour both within and between cultures.

Cultural causation of behaviour

This brings us to the second of the dilemmas listed at the beginning of this section. The issue of whether culture can ever legitimately be considered to be a cause of social behaviour is debated by Rohner (1984). The definitions which we have discussed for culture, social system and society rest upon analyses of the beliefs and actions of their members. Consequently, if we claim that culture can explain behaviour we are formulating a tautology: we are saying that something may be explained by itself. However, if we claim that individualism or some other specific value can explain some aspect of social behaviour, we are then on rather firmer ground. We have then abstracted what we regard as a key element of culture and proposed that it can explain other aspects of culture.

Levels of Analysis. Unfortunately, this still does not completely solve the problem, as we must also address the question of levels of analysis. Many of the studies to be discussed in this book will compare characterizations of particular national cultures with the behaviour of a small sample of subjects drawn from within those cultures. In other words, we may find ourselves asserting that the collectivism of, say, Indonesian national culture *causes* a group of Indonesian students to make certain attributions about their work on a questionnaire. When expressed like this it is easy to see that the implication of causality is too strong to be plausible. We may in a general sense expect Indonesian national culture to be expressed in the educational system of that country, the type of students recruited, the type of teaching and the type of assessment. But if we want to make a firmer test of causal links, we should be better off knowing how collectivistic the specific group of Indonesian students in the study actually were. In other words, the measures of independent and dependent variables in a study should be assessed at the same level of generality.

Culture-level measures can best be used to explain culture-level variation. Individual-level measures can best be used to explain individual-level variations. Since most social psychological research is conducted with individuals rather than cultures, there is a pressing need for more researchers to use such individual-level measures, rather than relying on culture-level characterizations such as those provided by Hofstede. The alternative strategy of analyzing the properties of cultures as a whole, using culture-level concepts, is of course also possible (Leung, 1989), and we shall be considering a few such studies. The fact that so few studies have been conducted with culture-level concepts is probably itself a reflection of the dominance of individualist values in the countries where most social psychology has been undertaken.

Triandis, Leung, Villareal and Clack (1985) proposed that, in order to avoid confusion between analyses conducted at the level of cultures and analyses based at the level of individuals, we should use different but related pairs of concepts. Their suggestion was that we use the term 'allocentric' to describe a member of a collectivist culture who endorses collectivist values. Similarly, they suggest the use of 'idiocentric' to describe a member of an individualist culture who endorses individualist values. The proposal is a good one, but the terms are sufficiently novel that they have not been adopted by other researchers. In this book we shall follow Markus and Kitayama (1991) by using the terms 'interdependent' and 'independent' to identify persons who endorse collectivist and individualist cultural values respectively. We hope these terms are a little more user-friendly.

Unfortunately, many published studies do not provide us with the necessary data to make such distinctions, but we can be more confident of the conclusions of those which do. Leung and Bond (1989) have devised statistical procedures which enable individual-level scores to be computed in ways which are not overlaid by differences in means between different country samples. When this method was used upon the data assembled by the Chinese Culture Connection (1987), the conclusions relating to the main first factor found in that study were unchanged (Bond, 1988b).

Similar procedures have been used by Schwartz (in press), so that he could reanalyze his data bank, using suitable standardized means for each value within each sample for each country as the unit of analysis. When compared with his previous individual-level analyses, a rather similar pattern is found, organized into seven culture-level value-types, as can be seen in Figure 3.3. The words written in each segment of the figure indicate the actual values which serve to define each value-type. As with the Chinese Culture Connection results, these results provide some reassurance that, providing the data are analyzed in appropriate ways, fairly similar results emerge from individual-level and culture-level analyses. This gives us an additional reason to be confident of the findings from the series of cross-cultural studies of values.

As Figure 3.3 shows, Schwartz's most recent analysis suggests that it would be fruitful to subdivide Hofstede's concept of individualism into what he calls 'affective individualism' and 'intellectual individualism'. Whether or not this and the other revisions to the Hofstede model implied by the figure are to prove helpful will depend upon whether the additional distinctions proposed do clarify why different empirical results are

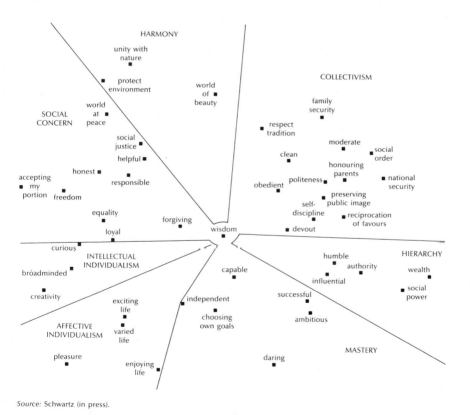

Source: Schwartz (in press).

Figure 3.3 Configuration of values obtained in Schwartz's country-level analysis

obtained from the national cultures which would be separated out by the Schwartz classification. Table 3.5 shows which of Schwartz's samples scored highest on each of his seven dimensions of cultural values. It is particularly interesting to note that, in contrast to Hofstede's results, the strongest individualists were Europeans rather than North Americans. The American student samples scored higher on the dimensions of hierarchy and mastery.

Values and behaviour

The final question posed at the beginning of this section was whether classifications based on people's values provide us with the firmest basis upon which to rest cross-cultural comparisons. Many psychologists choose behaviour as the bedrock upon which their discipline rests, and there are examples aplenty of people behaving in ways apparently at odds with their values. In order to resolve this impasse, we need to reflect upon what we mean by values and what we mean by behaviour. Values are universalistic statements about what we think is desirable or attractive. Values do not ordinarily contain statements about how they are to be achieved. Behaviours are specific actions, which occur in a particular setting, and may be observed at a particular time.

When we think about these definitions it is apparent that they have something in common with the emic–etic distinction. Schwartz and others have found that there is some etic validity to his generalizations about the range of values which humans espouse. It is hard to imagine how a similar project could be successful if it were focused upon behaviours, because the meaning of a behaviour is the meaning of the behaviour *in its context*. The wave of a hand or the planting of a kiss has no clear meaning until we

Table 3.5 Samples scoring highest on each of the Schwartz country-level value domains

Value	Highest scoring samples
Collectivism	Estonians and Malays
	Teachers from Taiwan, Turkey and Poland
Harmony	Teachers from Italy and Finland
Social concern	Teachers from Germany and Spain
Intellectual individualism	Students from Holland and Italy
Affective individualism	Students from England, New Zealand and Australia
Mastery	Students from USA
	Teachers from China
Hierarchy	Teachers and students from China and Zimbabwe
	Students from USA

specify a context. The expression of specific behaviours can perhaps best be thought of as an emic reflection of the participants' various values.

There are *some* behaviours whose meaning is relatively invariant. Bond (1991a), for instance, has conducted a culture-level analysis of death rates from various types of illness and compared these with value classifications derived from the Chinese Culture Connection study. His analysis controlled statistically for level of economic development, which does of course also strongly affect the incidence of illness and death. He found, for instance, that deaths from myocardial infarctions were very much higher in cultures which valued reputation more highly than righteousness.

However, it is not essential that we should base cross-cultural psychology on either a classification of values, or a direct study of behaviour. There are further options. Leung, Bond and Schwartz (1991) reported a series of comparative studies from Hong Kong and Israel. They proposed that differences in subjects' behaviour would be better accounted for by their *expectancies* about the outcomes to others' behaviour, rather than by the subjects' own values. The prediction was strongly upheld. One's embeddedness in national culture is thus likely to be not just a matter of having a particular set of values, but equally (or even more) a matter of knowing how people's various actions are likely to be received. Of course, one's estimates about this will be strongly affected by knowledge as to what are the dominant values of most people in the local culture, so personal values and expectancies are likely to be intertwined. Indeed, it has recently been shown that there are cultural differences in the degree to which people expect values and behaviour to be consistent. Kashima *et al.* (1992) found that Australian students were much more likely than Japanese students to expect that a person's behaviour would be a true reflection of his or her values.

Teasing apart the interrelation of values, expectancies and behaviour is a task for the future. In the next chapter we shall look at the outcomes of a variety of studies where researchers have investigated whether or not they can identify relatively universal aspects of social behaviour. If it proves to be the case that they cannot, the case is strengthened either for concentrating upon emic analyses, or else for analyzing the differences found, using such derived-etic frameworks as those which the values researchers have thus far provided.

FOUR

The search for universals of social behaviour

No man is an island entire of itself.

(John Donne, *Meditations*)

We noted in the previous chapter that psychologists have often seen their task as the identification of processes which are fundamental and universal. In this chapter we shall examine some aspects of personality and social behaviour which have been rather thoroughly examined from this etic perspective, and then draw some conclusions as to how successful this approach has been.

Gender relations

The question as to whether there are any universal differences in the social behaviour of men and women has excited controversy, at least since the time of the classic anthropological studies of Margaret Mead (1935). Her studies showed wide differences in gender roles across the three primitive societies which she studied in New Guinea.

Uniformities or differences?

A great many relevant studies have been completed since then, so that we now have a very substantial data base against which to test propositions. Buss and his collaborators (1990), for example, conducted a study of mate preferences in 37 national cultures, with a total sample of almost 9,500. Each respondent was asked to rate how important or desirable was each of 18 qualities and to rank order a further 13 criteria which could be used in choosing a mate. Examples of the qualities included were dependable character, chastity and good health. The results are reported by gender (Buss, 1989) and by culture (Buss and 49 co-authors, 1990).

The paths by which these two sets of findings were published provide an interesting example of the way in which psychology is often much more interested in universality than in variability. The variation in mate preferences accounted for by gender amounted to 2.4 per cent of the total variance. The variation accounted for by culture averaged 14 per cent. The analysis by gender was published in the widely read journal *Behavioral and Brain Sciences*, in which a sociobiological theory is advanced to account for the way in which gender differences may arise through natural selection. The theory advanced was commented upon by 27 well-known discussants. It is also one of the studies featured by Baron and Byrne (1991), in fulfilment of their intention to increase coverage of cross-cultural issues. The analysis by culture, accounting for *seven times* as much variance, was published in the *Journal of Cross-Cultural Psychology*, which is read by many fewer readers.

The gender differences found were that men tended to evaluate potential mates on the basis of youth, health and beauty, while women tended to pay more attention to earning capacity, ambition and industriousness. Buss proposes that this is because men seek women who are best able to reproduce, while women seek men who will be best able to care for them and their children. While these findings do certainly account for a small but significant proportion of the variance, focusing upon them takes attention away from the fact that in the sample as a whole men and women placed exactly the same four attributes highest on their preference list – mutual attraction, dependable character, emotional stability and maturity, and pleasing disposition. Their rankings of qualities also placed the same four items at the top – kind and understanding, intelligent, exciting and healthy.

In contrast to these uniformities between genders, there was much more substantial variance in the preferences across different national cultures. The greatest variation was found in the emphasis given to premarital chastity. Some 37 per cent of the variance on this measure was accounted for by culture. Buss *et al.* used multidimensional scaling techniques to clarify which national cultures had similar patterns of preferences. The clearest dimension to emerge was labelled by them as 'traditional' versus 'modern'. They suggest that it overlaps substantially with the Hofstede (1980) dimension of individualism–collectivism.

Another study which favoured universality was that by Byrne and seven co-authors (1971). They showed that in India, Japan, Mexico and the United States, people are attracted to others who have similar attitudes to themselves. No gender differences were found. This study was based upon showing people a completed attitude questionnaire purportedly filled out by someone else and asking how much they are attracted to this person.

These findings do not necessarily contradict those of Buss. It is possible, indeed likely, that those who favour, for instance, premarital chastity in a partner would also accept that it was desirable for themselves to be chaste as well. In this way the more abstract concept of similarity provides a possible universal, which when examined more closely proves to be based on a variety of differences in specific preferences between one national culture and another.

Gender stereotypes

A series of studies complementary to those of Buss have been made by Williams and Best (1982, 1990, 1992), who explored gender stereotypes in 30 different national cultures. One hundred male and female students in each country were asked to indicate whether each one of a series of adjectives on a checklist was considered in their culture to be associated with men, with women or with both equally. They found a substantial world-wide consensus about different gender roles. Men were believed to be higher on dominance, autonomy, aggression, exhibition, achievement and endurance. Women were believed to be higher on abasement, affilia-tion, deference, succorance and nurturance. Williams and Best (1990) also found that these generalizations held true when people were asked to describe *themselves*, rather than to describe men and women thought to be typical in their culture, as they had been asked to do in the earlier study.
   However, the degree of consensus about these stereotypes varied from one culture to another. Williams and Best (1992) related these findings to the Hofstede rankings of national cultures. They found a strong correlation between individualism and low consensus about gender stereotypes. In other words, in more collectivist cultures there is more consensus about the roles of men and women, whereas in individualist cultures there is more disagreement. This variability in individualist cultures is probably an accurate reflection of smaller gender differences, associated with the greater legal protections accorded to women's rights there. Thus we find again that what appears to be a reliable cross-cultural universal does have some variability which can be meaningfully interpreted in terms of cultural variation.

Generalities or detail?

The studies of gender differences illustrate a principle which will recur in other material that we shall review shortly. If we wish to make statements about universal or etic aspects of social behaviour, they need to be phrased in highly abstract ways. Conversely, if we wish to highlight the meaning of these generalizations in specific or emic ways, then we need to refer to more precisely specified events or behaviours. In this way we can find some possibility of etic statements about gender role differentiation and about similarity as the basis for attraction. But we also find frequent examples of the ways in which these generalizations are expressed in quite different ways in different national cultures. The more detailed the description of behaviour, the greater becomes the likelihood of finding significant variation.

For instance, the Buss study found that the second most highly desired attribute of a mate, world-wide, was dependable character. However, Christensen (1973) found very large variations in attitudes to marital infidelity in nine national cultures. The percentage of students disapproving of infidelity varied from 10 per cent in the Danish sample to 90 per cent of mid-Western Americans. Presumably the way in which Buss's and Christensen's findings are to be reconciled is to say that infidelity is thought of as being a sign of undependability in some cultures but not in others. However, this line of reasoning can be further extended – what specific behaviour is it that is thought of as amounting to infidelity? Buunk and Hupka (1987) compared reactions to various forms of sexual behaviour by one's partner toward a third party in each of seven national cultures. It was found that in Hungary, kissing and hugging evoked strong jealousy, while dancing together in Russia, flirting in Yugoslavia and having sexual fantasies about another in the Netherlands were reported to be the most upsetting. If one looks at behaviours in this degree of detail, it could turn out that almost every national culture gives unique meanings to general principles.

Emotional expression

A number of researchers using procedures popularized by Ekman have found that photographs of faces carefully posed to depict different social emotions can be interpreted accurately by people from many parts of the world. In the early studies (reviewed by Izard, 1980), subjects were shown a series of photographs and asked to choose which of a list of emotions each face portrayed. Results from 12 countries showed that at least six emotions could be reliably discriminated in all countries. Examples of the emotions portrayed in this type of study are shown in Figure 4.1. The 'universal' emotions proved to be enjoyment, sadness, anger, disgust, surprise and fear.

Ekman, Sorenson and Friesen (1969) provided the most stringent test of the durability of these findings, by repeating them among pre-literate societies in New Guinea. They found that the results held up, even when Americans judged New Guinean faces and New Guineans judged American faces. Ekman et al. (1987) improved their design even further by

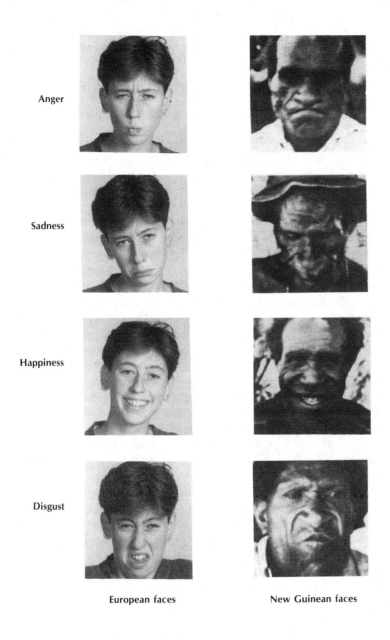

Anger

Sadness

Happiness

Disgust

European faces   New Guinean faces

Source of New Guinean faces: Ekman *et al.* (1969). © Paul Ekman, 1972.

Figure 4.1 Some faces used in studies of emotional expression

asking for ratings of the intensity with which each emotion was portrayed. Sampling across ten countries, they again found high consensus on which of the six emotions was being portrayed. They also found agreement on which emotions were the most intense, and on variations in the intensity of each emotion separately.

Decoding emotion

These studies are frequently cited as an instance of a universal ability to decode emotions in the same manner. Some caution is required before such a conclusion could be accepted, however. First, in these studies subjects were provided with a list of names for emotions from which to choose. Furthermore, the list of named emotions all derived from English language names for emotions, translated into the subjects' languages. Although the results show that choices are far above the level which would be achieved by guessing randomly, the 'imposed-etic' provision of the names for emotions makes the task very much easier. Izard (1971) also used photographs, but asked subjects in the USA, Britain, France and Greece to describe the emotions portrayed in their own words. The percentages of responses which the researchers judged to be correct in these circumstances were very much lower, and they varied sharply among the different emotions. Joy and surprise were consistently recognized, while interest and shame were the least identifiable. Boucher and Carlson (1980) obtained a similarly low rate of 'correct' responses, comparing American and Malay judgements of both US and Malay photographs. Markus and Kitayama (1991) report studies made in Japan in which subjects were asked to rate the similarity between all possible pairs of 20 different emotions specified within the Japanese language. While the majority of emotions could be mapped in a manner which replicated the relations found in similar English language studies, some could not. These were emotions which were differentiated along a dimension measuring engagement versus disengagement in a social relationship. In generalizing about the recognition of emotion, then, we should bear in mind the likelihood that we are speaking only about the recognition of those emotions which prove to have relatively high cultural generality. As Russell (1991) emphasizes, both the labelling of emotions and the very representation of emotions as entities may vary substantially between cultures.

Matsumoto (1989) reanalyzed the results of several of the early studies of facial emotion recognition, in a way which relates them more closely to the theme of this book. He computed correlations between the percentage of subjects in each of 15 countries correctly identifying each emotion, and scores for those countries on Hofstede's (1980) four dimensions. He found that happiness was more readily identified in national cultures which are high on individualism and low on power distance. Sadness, on the other hand, was more identifiable in collectivist cultures. Once again, we discover that the variability within a generalization may itself be explicable.

Displaying emotion

Matsumoto (1989) was not able to provide a clear explanation of why this particular pattern of differences should be found, although one could speculate. However, in a further study he compared the ability of US and Japanese judges to recognize six emotions. He used faces of both nationalities and both genders, showing real rather than posed emotions. His American subjects proved significantly better at identifying anger, disgust, fear and sadness, whereas both nationalities did equally well at recognizing happiness and surprise. Matsumoto concludes that the Japanese were less good at identifying negative emotions because it is socially less desirable to express such emotions in Japan than in the USA. The Japanese judges did better at judging female faces than male faces, which is consistent with somewhat more tolerance for the expression of emotion among Japanese women than men.

This research points the way toward more fruitful research in this area. Rather than considering solely the recognition of facial expressions across cultures, what is needed is a careful comparison of each of the stages entailed in the experience of an emotion in different cultures (Mesquita and Frijda, 1992). We must consider what triggers the emotion, how it is experienced and whether or not it is shared with others. What the early studies established is that there is considerable generality in the manner in which certain facial emotional expressions can be *decoded* in different cultures. Of equal or greater interest is the question of whether there are differences in the frequency with which these emotions *are actually experienced and displayed* in different national cultures. While the decoding studies can tell us something about universal, biologically rooted processes which may underlie certain types of emotion, studies of experience and display can tell us in what ways culture may channel these processes.

Scherer and others undertook a survey of reported emotions in 27 countries (Wallbot and Scherer, 1986). In each country, students and young professionals were asked to report on naturally occurring emotions. In the sample as a whole it was found that anger and joy were consistently reported as the most frequent emotions. However, there were significant variations across samples in the frequency, intensity and duration of reported emotions.

Scherer, Wallbot and Summerfield (1986) report that differences between the eight European countries included in the overall study were less than expected. The differences found are reported qualitatively and not related to theoretical models such as that of Hofstede. However, Gudykunst, Ting-Toomey and Chua (1988) reanalyzed some of these findings in terms of Hofstede scores for the relevant countries. They examined the situations in each national culture which were most frequently reported to trigger the emotions of enjoyment, sadness, fear and anger. Even within the relatively homogeneous sample of European data, substantial differences were found. Fear, for example, was associated with *novel situations* in cultures which were high on masculinity but low on power distance and uncertainty avoidance. Gudykunst *et al.* argue that this finding is consistent with the Hofstede perspective, since cultures which are high on power distance and uncertainty avoidance will have developed well-established procedures which would reduce the fearfulness, indeed the likelihood, of novel situations.

A comparison of the American and Japanese data deriving from this same project is reported by Matsumoto, Kudoh, Scherer and Wallbot (1988). They found that, compared with Japanese students, US students reported emotions which lasted longer, were more intense, and were accompanied by more bodily symptoms. The US students also described themselves as reacting more positively to the emotions they described, and as expressing more verbal reactions to them. In contrast to the European study, these findings suggest not only that different triggers to emotion occur in different cultures, but also that Americans actually react more emotionally than do Japanese, in general. Whether or not one accepts such a conclusion must depend upon whether one thinks the Americans and Japanese were equally forthright in describing their emotions. In cross-cultural comparisons, it is difficult to disentangle reports of emotions from cultural display rules as to what emotions may be expressed and when, even to supposedly neutral researchers.

The 'inscrutable oriental'

Westerners have long stereotyped Japanese and other east Asians as 'inscrutable'. A much discussed but unpublished study by Friesen (1972) illustrates how the results of Matsumoto *et al.* might be explained. Friesen showed short films to Japanese and American students, either when they were on their own, or when there was a 'scientist' present. The film presented was either a stress-inducing film about body mutilation or a neutral film. The reactions of the film watchers were themselves filmed as they watched. When they viewed the films alone, both Japanese and Americans registered similar reactions of disgust as they watched the body mutilation film. However, when the scientist was present, the Japanese no longer indicated disgust, but were found to smile more instead. Display rules about how to behave in the presence of an authority can thus override

Box 4.1 *A clash of display rules*

In the interchange between Chan and Mrs Robertson, Chan gave very little direct expression to his feelings in Mrs Robertson's presence. When talking to his sister, he expressed rather more, but the reaction was still fairly muted by western standards. In contrast, Mrs Robertson did express some of her irritation directly, both by way of what she said, and also through tone of voice and various sighs and facial expressions. However, she was much more forthright when discussing the episode afterwards with her department chairman. Both parties had adhered to their respective sets of display rules, and most probably neither knew how distressed the other was. Chan's feeling was more likely shame; Robertson's, anger.

more spontaneous emotions. It is possible that the reports of emotions by the Japanese in the Matsumoto *et al.* study were affected by similar factors. In other words, we still have only rather partial evidence that persons in some countries *experience* more emotion than others, but we have much stronger evidence that display rules vary from culture to culture.

Gudykunst *et al.* (1988) undertook further reanalyses of the European data which bear upon the matter of display rules. They found that both verbal and non-verbal reactions to experienced emotions were significantly stronger in national cultures high on individualism. This finding is consistent with the Matsumoto *et al.* finding, since Hofstede rates the USA much higher on individualism than Japan. In a similar way, Argyle, Henderson, Bond, Iizuka and Contarello (1986) found that rules restraining the social expression of anger and distress were more strongly endorsed in Japan and Hong Kong, which score higher on collectivism, than in Italy or Britain, which score higher on individualism.

The data on emotional expression are thus rather clear. The decoding of emotional expressions has rather high generality, but when and how we express our emotions is much more culturally bounded. Individualist, low power distance cultures may be more expressive because in such cultures there is a greater need for such cues in guiding our reactions to one another. In collectivist cultures, role and context will provide a greater share of the necessary cues.

Personality traits

A variety of personality researchers have considered the question of whether particular personality traits or groups of traits are found universally. This has frequently involved taking a personality measure first developed in the United States and testing whether it has predictive validity elsewhere. For instance, Kelley *et al.* (1986) compared those who scored high and low on Rotter's (1966) external locus of control scale. This measure assesses the degree to which one believes that various types of event are outside one's personal control. Those who believe in an external locus of control have been found also to score high on a chronic self-destructiveness scale. In the USA, high scores on this scale are found to go along with heavy drinking, excessive smoking and dangerous driving. Kelley *et al.* asked students in Hong Kong, India, Venezuela and the USA to complete both questionnaires. It was found that in India and in Hong Kong, but not in Venezuela, those scoring high on external control also scored high on chronic self-destructiveness. However, no check was made on whether chronic self-destructiveness scale was a valid predictor of behaviour outside the USA, so it is difficult to interpret the result of this imposed-etic study.

A clearer result was obtained by Evans, Palsane and Carrere (1987), who used the measure of Type A personality (Glass, 1977). This identifies the type of person who is competitive, aggressive and compulsively active. They found that in India as in the USA, Type A bus drivers had more accidents. In India, Type A drivers also blew their horns more often, overtook more often and braked more frequently. This illustration of cross-cultural predictive validity despite the use of an imposed-etic measure is encouraging, but we need to look at more systematic tests done in a wider range of countries.

Extraversion–introversion

Eysenck and Eysenck (1982) put forward the view that their personality model has cross-cultural validity, on the basis of the use of their personality questionnaires by many researchers in 25 countries. The Eysenck model specifies three personality dimensions – 'introversion–extraversion', 'neuroticism–stability' and 'psychoticism' – for each of which they argue for a biological basis. The first of these is a particularly interesting personality dimension from our point of view, since we might expect that an introvert would tend to stay with established membership groups and hence endorse interdependent values, while an extravert would enjoy meeting new people and hence endorse independent values. However, no cross-cultural tests of such hypotheses are available. The evidence for cross-cultural validity put forward by Eysenck and his associates is based upon the results of separate factor analyses of responses to his questionnaire in each country. They report that closely similar factors emerge in all the countries where it has been used.

Eysenck's conclusions have been challenged by Bijnen, van der Net and Poortinga (1986), who argue that the statistical tests used to judge the similarity of factor structures are unreliable. Bijnen *et al.* were able to show that they could in some cases detect an equally high level of similarity between sets of numbers which had been generated randomly by a computer. Eysenck (1986) contested this conclusion, citing further statistical analyses, but Bijnen and Poortinga (1988) cast doubt on these also. It appears that the tests used continue to show an apparently 'good' match between two data sets even when up to 18 out of 21 questionnaire item responses have been replaced by random data.

The doubts cast upon Eysenck's analyses do not, of course, imply that extraversion or other personality traits do not have some etic generality. This remains perfectly possible, but alternative research methods are likely to be needed to test whether or not they do. The Eysenck Personality Questionnaire was originally devised in Britain and its use in many other countries falls into Berry's (1969) category of imposed-etic. The data from other countries are tested to see whether they fit the original British pattern. Munro (1986) summarizes a decade of research with the Eysenck Personality Questionnaire and other personality tests such as the Rotter scale in Zimbabwe. He found that in his samples some questionnaire items correlated poorly with the intended dimensions. Munro concludes that a better strategy is to start by building an emically valid questionnaire within any one national culture, and then examining convergences with western-based personality theories. This is the same strategy as that followed by the Chinese Culture Connection researchers discussed earlier.

Starting from the emic

A series of studies from the Philippines shows how fruitful this strategy can be in the field of personality research. Church and Katigbak (1988) asked Filipino students to provide descriptions of the qualities they would expect to find in healthy and unhealthy persons. A scale on which to describe one's own personality was constructed from the items provided. This scale was then presented to further students along with several well-known US personality measures. It was found that the responses to the scale did not correlate too well with the US measures, and furthermore that the items on the US scales did not cluster together for Filipino students in the way that they had done for American students.

Thus far we have a somewhat dispiriting set of results, which might imply that all we can hope to do is to make emic studies within cultures and give up on trying to find dimensions with etic validity. However, Church and Katigbak (1989) report further analyses which were based upon a thorough implementation of Berry's view as to what is the appropriate way to link emic and etic findings. They argue that, rather than use the same standard questionnaires in each country, one should first look at the interrelations *among* the emic data set from within each culture. The interrelations found can then be compared with proposed etic generalizations derived from broader theorizing. In this case the etic generalizations which they drew on were the proposal of McCrae and Costa (1987) that the various traits proposed by western researchers can be reduced to five major dimensions of personality. These are identified as 'extraversion', 'agreeableness', 'will to achieve', 'emotional stability' and 'openness to experience'.

Using the character traits provided by their Filipino subjects, Church and Katigbak (1989) tested whether these traits also would be clustered by Filipinos into similar groupings. Several tests were used, in one of which subjects were asked to sort the traits into groups of those that 'go together'. In a second study, subjects were asked to rate their fellow students, and their ratings were then factor analysed. Each of these methods supported the cross-cultural validity of the McCrae and Costa 'Big Five' personality dimensions. It is interesting to note that Eysenck's dimensions do themselves overlap with the Big Five (McCrae and John, 1992). The Church and Katigbak study thus supports Eysenck's views but it does so through a more cross-culturally sensitive research procedure. In a parallel series of studies, Yang and Bond (1990) found that the five imposed-etic dimensions of personality as measured by Norman (1963) correlated well with four of five factors derived from Chinese person perception scales. The fifth dimension appeared functionally similar to the American, but required assessment in an emically sensitive manner. Studies supporting the generality of the Big Five factors have also been reported from Israel, Germany and Japan (Digman, 1990).

Evaluating the Big Five

This series of studies suggests that there is some cross-cultural generality in the way in which personality traits are clustered together by subjects who are asked to make judgements about their own or others' personality. This need not surprise us, since as we saw earlier there is also some generality in ability to recognize expressed emotions, which presumably provides the basis for many personality judgements. However, just as we found that variations in emotional display rules can overlay uniformities in emotional expression, so it may be that there are cross-cultural variations in the circumstances under which people are willing to make trait attributions to themselves or others. We shall review evidence that this is in fact so in the next chapter.

Church's series of emic studies of Filipino personality also led him to discuss which personality concepts were most central to Filipino culture. The concept of *pakikisama*, which translates as 'going along with or conceding to the in-group', has often been identified as particularly important. Church points out the similarity between this concept and emic concepts reported by other researchers into societies which are as highly collectivist as are the Philippines. He notes in particular the concept of *sympatia*, which is given great importance in many Hispanic cultures, and *philotimo* within Greek culture. In a similar way, Filipino emphasis on dependence and loyalty to superiors has parallels with the Japanese concept of *amae*, which describes the process of being nurtured by a powerful superior and being reciprocally obligated to him (Church, 1987). Thus while Church's results indicate that Filipinos are able to perceive one another in ways which are consistent with an etic formulation of the Big Five personality traits, they may give more importance to one of those traits, namely agreeableness. Members of many other high collectivist, high power distance cultures may do likewise, as Bond and Forgas (1984) found when comparing Australians and Hong Kong Chinese. This difference in which personality dimensions are salient in particular cultures parallels the manner in which Schwartz finds that, while the structure of values is invariant across cultures, there are differences in how strongly each value is endorsed within a culture.

If the Big Five personality traits do underlie personality judgements in a wide variety of national cultures, then it becomes important to examine how far the Big Five correspond with the dimensions of values identified by Schwartz which we have been using to support Hofstede's characterization of different cultures. Presumably one's values reflect one's needs, which in turn arise from the socialization process in each cultural group. These socialization processes 'educate our attention' (Zebrowitz-McArthur, 1988), so that members of that culture are relatively sensitized

Table 4.1 Possible emphases on dimensions of personality arising from dimensions of cultural variation

Dimension of culture	Personality trait
Uncertainty avoidance	Low openness to experience
	Emotional stability
Masculinity	Conscientiousness
	Low agreeableness
Power distance	Agreeableness
	Conscientiousness
Individualism	Extraversion
Confucian dynamism	Emotional stability

to, and generally higher on, certain personality dimensions than are people from cultures with different emphases. Taking the Hofstede (1991) dimensions in turn, we can tentatively link each of them to the Big Five dimensions of personality, as is shown in Table 4.1. These connections are speculative and require testing.

Aggression

Another aspect of personality to have received a good deal of attention from cross-cultural researchers is aggressiveness, which we can assume to be negatively related to Costa and McCrae's agreeableness. However, it has quite often been thought of as a behaviour rather than as a more consistent personality trait, so it is appropriate to consider it separately. Faced with a great diversity of definitions, Segall *et al.* (1990) propose that we define aggression simply as 'any behaviour by a person that inflicts harm upon another'.

Murder

While a number of theorists argue that aggression is instinctually or bio-logically rooted, they must contend among other things with extremely large variations in expressed aggression among the different cultures of the world. The murder rate, for instance, is currently seven times higher in the United States than in Britain, and in South Africa it is 35 times higher. At the very least, we must argue that aggression is channelled in different ways within different cultures.

An attempt to detect the uniformities between cultures which affect murder rates is reported by Landau (1984). Landau predicted that murder rates would rise in countries where stress was increasing and social support systems were failing. He compared reported statistics for murder and other crimes for 13 countries over a decade. As a measure of stress he used the rate of inflation and as a measure of failing social support he relied upon the ratio of divorces to marriages. The predictions were supported in all countries except Japan, where he found a rising suicide rate rather than a rising murder rate. In order to test his hypothesis at this macro-scopic level, some rather substantial assumptions were required as to what would constitute valid measures. We cannot therefore be very sure that the results came out as they did for the reasons which he specified. His hypothesis was influenced by the proposition first put forward by Dollard *et al.* (1939) that frustration always leads to aggression. Their proposition was formulated about the behaviour of individuals, and we need to be very cautious about assuming that it has validity at the level of comparisons across cultures. It is equally possible that murder rates, divorce rates and inflation are linked to one another for quite other reasons.

Insults

North American experimental research has indicated that, even at the individual level, aggression does not in fact inevitably follow frustration (Berkowitz, 1989). This conclusion opens the way for investigation of a host of cultural influences upon whether and how aggression is expressed. Although murder would no doubt be included in just about everyone's definition of aggression, there is much more scope for differences across cultures in interpreting whether or not different forms of more minor harm do or do not constitute aggression. Strong criticism from one's boss, for instance, might be judged much less aggressive in a high power distance culture than in a low power distance culture. Bond, Wan *et al.* (1985) tested this idea in a study of students in Hong Kong and the United States. Students were asked to evaluate an episode in which a manager insults either a superior or a subordinate, who is either inside or outside their own department. The judgements made by the Chinese students were much more dependent upon who it was that was receiving the insult than were the American judgements. The Chinese saw the insult delivered to a subordinate within one's own department as less illegitimate, and saw less reason to dislike the superior who delivered it. The Chinese also differentiated more between insults to in-group members and out-group members. This is likely to be related to the higher collectivism of Hong Kong compared to the United States, which we shall discuss further in Chapter 7. In fact, Chinese often label in-group insults as 'scoldings', a description which accords them more legitimacy.

Expressing or suppressing aggression

A number of other studies support the view that whether or not aggression occurs has a good deal to do with social norms concerning aggression in a given cultural setting. Camino and Trocolli (reported in Leyens and Fraczek, 1984) found that in Brazil, those who believed in a just world were less likely to judge police actions to have been violent. Whether one is willing to commit aggressive acts oneself will also depend upon how much social support there is for such actions. We saw in Chapter 2 that obedience in the Milgram experiment was shown in several countries to be heavily influenced by whether others joined in the process of administering shocks or refused to do so.

Some researchers have argued that groups are always more aggressive than individuals. Jaffe and Yinon (1983) in Israel, for instance, replicated US findings that groups were more willing to administer shocks to subjects in an experiment than were individuals. However, Rabbie (1982), summarizing a series of experiments on aggression done in Holland, concludes only that groups are *more sure* of themselves, as we might expect following the discussion of group polarization in Chapter 2. Where norms favour aggression, a group will indeed be more aggressive than individuals, but where norms favour restraint, it will be less so. We thus find a broad range of evidence that both the expression of aggression and the form in which it is expressed varies with the social context, as has also been found in North America. This is consistent with the cross-cultural variation in display rules for other types of emotion, which we considered earlier in this chapter.

Pro-social behaviour

A contrast with studies of aggression is provided by studies of people's willingness to help one another in situations where some distress or difficulty has arisen. Studies have usually been conducted in public places, and involve asking for help in finding the way, asking for small change from a larger denomination coin or the staging of some minor emergency such as dropping something on the street. Studies in the USA, Canada, Australia and Turkey have all shown that help is more forthcoming in rural districts than in large cities. In Holland, however, helpfulness was equally high in all city districts and in rural areas, and Korte *et al.* (1975) attribute this to a strong norm for 'civility' in Dutch society. In Turkey, less help was given in suburban districts, whereas elsewhere it was lowest in the centre (Korte and Ayvalioglu, 1981).

Few studies have been reported which make direct comparisons of pro-social behaviours using identical procedures in different countries. Hedge and Yousif (1992) selected Britain and Sudan as contrasting countries and found that, although the previously obtained urban–rural differences again appeared in both countries, there was no overall difference in the percentages of helpful responses given between the two countries.

There is thus some evidence that responding helpfully to strangers in the street is at least widespread, if not universal. However, we have to consider more closely what we mean by 'responding helpfully'. In each of the studies of helping so far mentioned, the persons seeking help were local nationals of the country where the study was done. From these studies we know how many people received a response coded as helpful, but not what was the nature of that help nor the reasons why it was given or withheld. As Fiske (1991) points out, pro-social behaviour may be found within almost all cultures studied by anthropologists, but its meaning may vary widely. One may help another out of obligation to a group seen as similar to one's own, out of deference, out of politeness, out of a wish to impress and so forth.

Two studies which compared responses to locals and foreigners making the same requests illustrate some of this variability. Greece is one country well known to offer a welcome to foreigners, at least until the current tourist invasion. Feldman (1967) found that foreigners who asked a favour in Athens received *more* help than did Greeks who asked the same favour in the same place. The reverse was true in Paris and Boston. In a similar way, Collett and O'Shea (1976) had foreigners ask directions to two non-existent sites, as well as two that did exist. In Tehran and Isfahan (both in Iran), the foreigner was frequently given directions as to how to reach the non-existent sites. This did not occur in London. The *format* of helpfulness was thus preserved by the Iranians, although of course it is no help at all to be given fictitious directions. In some collective cultures, therefore, it appears that foreigners or outsiders are not treated in the same manner as those who are local. Instead they are treated in a manner which could imply that they are in some way more important and worthy of help.

The simple distinction between giving help and withholding it thus has its limitations. In cultures that welcome strangers, we need to look carefully to see what it is about the stranger that leads to him or her being accorded at least a semblance of help. Likely answers will include age, gender, skin colour, demeanour, presumed cultural identity and, of course, the nature of the culture's own norms about what types of behaviour are thought admirable. The format of helpfulness, like that of aggression, is culturally mediated.

Some interim conclusions

The previous chapter explored culture and related concepts. It was argued that the best hope for cross-cultural social psychology is to locate a means of classifying national cultures, in order that we can test the limits of the knowledge we already have. The most interesting candidate to emerge from the studies so far has proved to be the distinction between cultural collectivism and cultural individualism.

As a first test of the usefulness of this distinction we have now surveyed several areas in which it has been proposed that there are cultural universals. In each of these areas, we have found some evidence that it is indeed possible to formulate universal generalizations. There *are* gender differences which transcend cultures. We *can* all decode certain facial expressions. Personality traits do cluster in certain ways. Humans *are* all capable of both aggression and pro-social behaviour. It is possible that each of these generalizations has some type of biological basis. Poortinga (1990) suggests that the degree to which attributes prove to be universals will depend upon whether they are genetically transmitted or culturally acquired, as shown in Figure 4.2. Thus, universals will be most obvious for physiological and perceptual aspects of behaviour, while cultural variations are more probable in the areas of personality and social behaviour.

It is consistent with the Poortinga model that, in each of the areas of social behaviour examined, we have found that the general principles are expressed in ways which are given shape by more specific cultural referents. Furthermore, in most of these areas it has turned out that, by looking at measures of cultural individualism–collectivism, we can illuminate substantial amounts of variance in the results which had in some cases eluded the original investigators.

Some cautions

We shall therefore be making further and more systematic tests of the individualism–collectivism concept within some of the major research fields of social psychology in the remainder of this book. Before we do so, we need to insert a few cautions. We have argued already that there is a need to be clear about levels of explanation in cross-cultural social psychology. We shall speak of independence–interdependence wherever it is

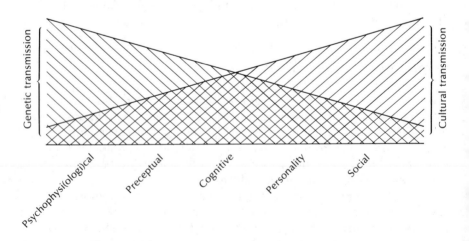

Source: Poortinga (1990).

Figure 4.2 Poortinga's model of genetic and cultural transmission

clear that researchers are referring to differences among individuals rather than differences among cultures.

However, this will not wholly protect us from the accusation that our discussion is too polarized between the concepts of individualism and collectivism. Indeed, Sinha and Tripathi (in press) argue that the propensity to make yes/no splits between exclusive pairs of concepts is itself a distinctively western way of theorizing. As Kagitcibasi (1992) points out, it is quite possible that someone could be independent and interdependent at the same time. For instance, an office worker may pursue largely independent career goals at work, but when relaxing by participating in sport or by watching sport, he or she may take on a much more interdependent set of values.

We also need to ensure that we do not stereotype particular cultures or groups of cultures. Numerous national cultures are heterogeneous. Countries such as Australia, the United States and Brazil are very ethnically heterogeneous, but most other national cultures contain substantial diversity by race, social class and region. It is the purpose of science, however, to test out the value of simplifications, and so we shall for the time being stay with our chosen concepts, in order to assess their strengths and limitations. We shall return in the final chapter to the question of whether they also have value for looking at subcultural variation.

We run yet one further risk of seeming to bracket together cultures which scored relatively similarly on the Hofstede measures. It is patently obvious that although, for instance, Chinese societies, India and Brazil are all classified as relatively high on collectivism, these countries all differ in many other respects, some of which are reflected in their scores on the other Hofstede dimensions of uncertainty avoidance, masculinity–femininity and so forth. The Schwartz studies suggest that we shall ultimately need to take into account still further dimensions of cultural variation.

Even within the domain of collectivism, there are differences. Japan is often cited as a collectivist society, but Hofstede found it only moderately high, and the collectivism there is much more focused upon the work group than in many other cultures (Nakane, 1970). In Chinese societies, collectivism is more strongly integrated with the family (Bond and Hwang, 1986). In Latin America, the Hispanic concept of *sympatia* between peers expresses the values of collectivism (Triandis *et al.*, 1984), but power distance is frequently also high. However, Marin and Marin (1982) caution against assumptions that Hispanic communities are culturally all similar. Hofstede noted in particular that in Costa Rica power distance was much lower than elsewhere in Latin America. In India, whether one behaves individualistically or collectivistically is said to depend on the context, since Indians are reported to be more tolerant of contradictions than are members of other national cultures (Sinha, 1992).

In concluding this chapter, it remains only for us to address a little further the issue of methodology. The debate about methodology often reduces to a polarization between those who favour etic approaches and those who favour emic approaches. Etic researchers look for general principles, and by the way we have chosen to write this book we show some sympathy with them. Emic researchers seek to build indigenous psychologies. This also has importance, but may take time before it bears substantial fruit, as we shall see when we explore this approach more fully in the next chapter. The debate between the two positions is like an imaginary debate which we sometimes ponder on: one faction points out that almost everyone in the world wears clothes; the other investigates the types of clothing worn at particular places or times. One faction has a not very useful generalization. The other has a mass of descriptive data. What is needed is a way of linking the two approaches – an emic way of being etic! For this to be possible, a theory is required which predicts why variation occurs from one culture to another. In the case of clothing, the theory would no doubt be based on climatic variation. In the more general case of social behaviour, individualism–collectivism appears at present to be the front-running candidate from among the various contenders. However, the concepts of individualism and collectivism, no less than other psychological concepts, have arisen from within western psychology. We must consider further how compatible they may be with emic concepts which have found favour in other parts of the world.

FIVE

Going back to one's roots: the search for indigenous psychologies

Oh, East is East and West is West and never the twain shall meet,
Till Earth and Sky stand at God's Great Judgment Seat;
But there is neither East nor West, Border nor Breed, nor Birth,
When two Strong men stand face to face, though they come from the
  ends of the Earth!

(Rudyard Kipling, *The Ballad of East and West*)

In this chapter we take a more detailed look at attempts to develop indigenous psychologies in various parts of the world. By this is meant a series of psychologies each of which reflects the preoccupations, historical antecedents and practices of a particular national culture, or even of smaller subcultures. Such an approach need not necessarily rest on either traditional Western theories or 'western' research methods, if these do not illuminate what is at issue. In effect the protagonists of this school of thought are maintaining that we might do better to borrow heavily from the approaches developed by social anthropologists and other field researchers, since these were devised in order to comprehend a far wider range of societies than were the methods of social psychologists (Heelas and Lock, 1981; Stigler, Shweder and Herdt, 1990).

The dangers of such an approach might appear to be that no generalizations about human social behaviour would then ever emerge. This is a risk which anthropologists have been willing to take on, and it has in practice proved to be the case that viable generalizations do emerge from their work. However, Needham (1981) expresses the view that anthropologists have too often focused on what is exotic and different about the societies they have studied, and have not given so much attention to whether or not basic psychological processes operate similarly or differently to those in advanced industrial societies. Shweder (1990) makes a similar point in arguing the case for a 'cultural psychology' which would be free of what

75

he sees as the limiting assumptions of earlier work both in cross-cultural psychology and in anthropology.

We should note initially that there may be some value in considering all psychologies as indigenous psychologies. As we have maintained throughout this book, theories arising within North America are likely to reflect the preoccupations of researchers who reside there, at least as much as is the case anywhere else in the world. The studies undertaken and the theories propounded in any country will be influenced by such local factors as how one becomes a social psychologist, how one's career advancement is determined, how much one is paid, how long-established is the discipline, what is the relation between governments and universities, and so forth. In contemporary North America, several of these factors have provided rather strong incentives towards studies which may be completed quickly, using readily accessible subjects.

However, the term 'indigenous psychology' is most frequently used to denote approaches which have developed more strongly outside of North America. The indigenous psychology movement has thus far put down noticeable but rather different roots in the developing countries than are found in Europe, and these two formulations will be examined in this chapter. The European approach also has adherents in North America, but we prefer nonetheless to call it European, since that is where the thrust of these ideas has been most strongly felt.

European indigenous psychologies

The essence of any indigenous psychology lies in the proposition that if we are to understand a culture, we must examine the shared meanings which are given to events. European protagonists of this approach have mostly emphasized the way in which meanings are socially constructed and have started to explore how this comes about. General models of the process have been available on both sides of the Atlantic for some time. For instance, the teachings of Mead (1934) in Chicago and of the German sociologists Berger and Luckman (1966) both emphasize the manner in which one's conception of self and of one's environment is socially con-structed. They mean by this assertion that an unending cycle of action and reaction between oneself and others creates the meanings which we give to events. More recently, several ways of gaining a more precise under-standing of this process have become popular in western Europe. These tend to stress the importance of analyzing the way in which we talk to one another, since imbedded in most talk, implicitly or explicitly, are accounts of how we understand what is going on around us. By detailed analysis of discourse we can gain a sophisticated understanding of attempts to change or create meaning (Harré and Secord, 1972; Potter and Wetherell,

1987). The essence of this approach is thus a series of methodological innovations which, it is claimed, will help us to understand more fully how socially rooted is our experience, even in the more individualist countries of the world. This line of thinking has spawned two separate lines of theorizing, both of them deriving primarily from western Europe.

Social identity theory

The Swiss psychologist Doise (1986) has explored the question of how many different levels of explanation are required for a valid social psychology. Most probably, all would agree that social psychology should be able to offer explanations both of individual and of small group behaviour. The more European flavour to Doise's formulation is provided by his inclusion of explanations at the level of intergroup relations and of society as a whole. It is through an emphasis upon these more macroscopic levels of explanation that recent European work has become distinctive.

In this and the next sections of this chapter we shall look at theories of social behaviour whose formulation reflects this particularly European emphasis. Although the first of them does not directly contradict predominant North American approaches, it is worth noting the differences because they may well reflect subtle variations in the culturally based assumptions made by some at least of the researchers on opposite sides of the Atlantic.

The analysis of social cognition which we shall present in Chapter 6 portrays the individual for the most part as an isolated processor of social information, without reference to the individual's prior history. Attributions about oneself and others are seen as dependent upon where we direct our attention and how we process the information we extract from our immediate social environment. In 1972 Israel and Tajfel edited a volume in which a number of European social psychologists argued that social psychology should become more 'social' than this. In other words, they preferred that we attend more fully to *the manner in which social information in the environment is created and maintained over time*, rather than focusing exclusively on how that information may subsequently be processed by individuals. What they meant by this will become clearer as we explore the theories which they later presented.

Tajfel's (1981) social identity theory proposes that the social part of our identity derives from the groups to which we belong. By favourably comparing attributes of our own groups with those of out-groups, he suggests that we acquire both a positive sense of who we are and a clear understanding of how we should act towards in-group and out-group members. While this biased categorizing might seem to be axiomatic in a collectivist culture, Tajfel's proposition was intended to apply equally to individualist cultural groups.

The minimal group paradigm

Tajfel devised an experimental procedure known as the minimal group paradigm which was designed to test rigorously whether the simple fact of belonging to a group was enough to affect one's behaviour. Tajfel, Billig, Bundy and Flament (1971) assigned English schoolboys randomly to two groups. Each boy was told that he had been assigned either to a group called Klee or a group called Kandinsky, on the basis of a test which supposedly measured their artistic preferences. The seating positions of group members were intermingled, and no boy knew which others had been assigned to the same group as himself. They were then asked to allot rewards to one member of their own group and one member of the other group, choosing pairs of rewards from a series of possibilities like the ones in Table 5.1. These pairings had been constructed in such a way as to make it possible to choose between various hypotheses as to why particular choices were made. The four possibilities examined were that the rewards chosen would be:

> A. Those which maximized the rewards assigned to one's own group,
> or B. Those which maximized the total rewards allocated overall,
> or C. Those which maximized the difference between the two groups,
> or D. Those which treated both groups equally.

As Table 5.1 shows, the average allocations of rewards made clustered towards the centre of the scales. This makes clear that subjects were not seeking to maximize their own group's rewards, nor were they seeking to maximize the overall rewards paid out by the experimenter. These goals could have been much better accomplished by using the ends of the scales. The closest match with the data was provided by hypothesis C, that subjects were trying to maximize the difference between their group's rewards and the other group's rewards.

When we consider the arbitrary and artificial way in which these groups were constructed, this is a remarkable finding. Simply being told that one belongs to a particular category causes one to discriminate in favour of that category. Tajfel would argue that this is because the differentiation between the group one is in and the group one is not in serves to define one's social identity in that situation. In such an oversimplified experimental situation there are few other ways in which one could mark out a distinctive identity. In more typical, everyday settings, he sees one's relevant longer-term group memberships as defining one's situational

Table 5.1 Sample reward allocation matrices used by Tajfel *et al.* (1971)

Matrix 1													
Member 74 in													
Klee group	25	23	21	19	17	15	13	<u>11</u>	9	7	5	3	1
Member 44 in													
Kandinsky group	19	18	17	16	15	14	13	<u>12</u>	11	10	9	8	7
Matrix 2													
Member 74 in													
Klee group	11	12	13	14	15	16	17	18	<u>19</u>	20	21	22	23
Member 44 in													
Kandinsky group	5	7	9	11	13	15	17	19	<u>21</u>	23	25	27	29

Note: Within each matrix, the subject must choose one of the *pairs* of numbers which are above/below one another. The underlined numbers show the choices most typically made by members of the Kandinsky group.

identity, and therefore as shaping the way in which one will think and act in that situation.

The results of studies using the minimal group paradigm have been quite frequently replicated in Britain, and in certain other individualist countries: for instance, by Doise *et al.* (1972) using German soldiers, by Simon *et al.* (1990) using Dutch students, and by Hogg and Sunderland (1991) using Australian students as subjects. In a further British study, Turner (1975) showed that his schoolboy subjects were even more willing to reward themselves rather than to reward the in-group to which they had been assigned, when the experimental design was modified to make this possible. This result indicates that the values which motivate the behaviour found in the British studies are self-serving first, group-serving second.

The wider applicability of Tajfel's theory

Minimal group effects in cultural groups likely to have more inter-dependent values have been successfully replicated by Kakimoto (1992) from Japan. Wetherell (1982) reported rather more complex results from New Zealand. Her first study compared eight-year-old children from low socioeconomic backgrounds of European and of Polynesian origin. Both groups were found to favour maximizing differences between the in-group and the out-group, but the effect was significantly stronger for the European children. The Polynesian responses also reflected some wish to maximize joint rewards. In a second study, Wetherell examined this effect more fully. By increasing her sample she was able to compare children of European, Maori and Samoan origin. She now found that the Europeans once again sought to maximize the in-group/out-group difference. The Samoans' choices favoured maximizing joint rewards, while the Maoris' responses were intermediate between the Europeans and the Samoans.

The results for the Samoan children are of particular interest, since they derive from a cultural group which has traditionally been strongly collectivist. On the surface, the results contradict Tajfel's theory and suggest that its validity may be restricted to more individualist cultural groups. However, the use of Tajfel's research procedures in a rather different setting from that in which they were first developed provides us with little information as to how the Samoan children perceived the situation. One possibility which Wetherell considers is that they were relatively unaffected by her telling them which group they had been assigned to. Their interdependent values would more likely tell them that the salient groups in the study were the overall group of Samoans on the one hand and the Pakeha (white European) experimenter on the other (Bochner and Perks, 1971). On this line of analysis, they were maximizing in-group rewards. A second possibility also discussed by Wetherell is that within traditional Polynesian culture the giving of gifts to others is highly esteemed. Thus by rewarding the out-group a Polynesian child could in fact be assuring his or her positive social identity. This interpretation would be consistent with the 'modesty bias' found in other studies from east Asia to be discussed in Chapter 6. The difficulty in choosing between these interpretations underlines the importance of using indigenous experimenters in studies comparing different cultural groups.

Intergroup relations

The value of Tajfel's theory does not rest solely upon the outcome of studies using the minimal group paradigm. Of more importance is the question of how adequately it can account for the ways in which members of existing social groups perceive one another. Numerous studies have shown the way in which members of different ethnic groups often maintain stereotyped systems of beliefs about the positive qualities of their own group and the negative qualities of other groups. Some of these studies illustrate the manner in which the mere fact of group membership can completely reverse the pattern of attributions made about an individual's behaviour.

For instance, Taylor and Jaggi (1974) asked 30 Hindu clerks in India to evaluate a series of desirable and undesirable events: for example, a shop-keeper who either cheated customers or was generous. The actions presented to subjects were said to have been performed either by a fellow

Hindu or by an out-group Muslim. It was found that the positive behaviours performed by members of one's own group were believed to arise from internal dispositions, while their negative behaviours were seen as the result of external forces. However, evaluations of these *same* behaviours when performed by a Muslim were strikingly different. In this case the desirable behaviours were seen as externally caused, and some of the undesirable ones as internally caused! Taylor and Jaggi's results are thus consistent with Tajfel's theory: the Hindu clerks would have been able to sustain a positive social identity, since they perceived the causes of behaviours by in-group and out-group members in ways that favoured their group over the other.

Tajfel's theory acknowledges that under certain circumstances it may be impossible for members of a group to find a positive basis upon which to compare one's group with other groups. This might occur, for instance, in groups which had low status in society. Under these circumstances, he envisaged that group members would do one of three things. First, they might seek new bases for comparison which would give a more favourable outcome, such as emphasizing the beauty of traditional clothing or the liveliness of the group's language, an option which he termed 'social creativity'. Second, they might leave the group and join another with more positive qualities, an option which he termed 'social mobility'. Individualistic cultures with their emphasis on equal opportunity and freedom may provide more social support for such an option. Third, they might seek to change the attributes of their group so that it would be more favourably evaluated in future, an option which he termed 'social change'.

The social mobility option is also likely to be somewhat more practicable in individualist cultural groups than in collectivist groups, although even in individualist cultures categories such as skin colour and gender do not permit such a strategy to be used. We shall explore some of the consequences of restrictions on social mobility for group behaviour in Chapters 7 and 8. The social change option is likely to be a slow and difficult process everywhere, since changes in the attributes of one whole social group may well threaten the position of other groups and take time to mobilize.

The implications of this discussion are that we might expect to find some examples of groups whose members *do not* rate their own group higher than others. They should be most frequent within collectivist societies. Indeed, Hofstede's finding that collectivist societies tend also to be high power distance societies fits in well with this proposition. In a high power distance society it would be expected that disadvantaged groups would be more inclined to accept as legitimate the idea that higher-status groups were more deserving of their higher rewards.

In-group derogation

Hewstone and Ward (1985) modified the design used by Taylor and Jaggi and used it to obtain attributions from Chinese and Malay subjects located in Malaysia. The Chinese form a substantial ethnic minority in Malaysia, and are restricted from entering certain occupations. It was found that the dominant group, the Malays, made ethnocentric attributions similar to those found by Taylor and Jaggi in India. Malays saw positive acts by other Malays as more internally caused than if the same act had been carried out by a Chinese. Likewise they saw negative acts by a Malay as more situationally caused than if they were done by a Chinese. Hewstone and Ward then repeated their study in Singapore, where the political power relations between the two ethnic communities are substantially reversed. In this changed social context, they found much less evidence of ethnocentric attributions by the Malays.

The results obtained by Hewstone and Ward in Singapore therefore provide an example of the type we might expect within a collectivist society. We find a disadvantaged group which to some degree accepts the negative image accorded to it by the dominant group. However, we cannot explain this acceptance simply in terms of the cultural values which may predominate among Malays and Chinese, because the results switch when we move from Singapore to Malaysia. A differing result is obtained among members of the same two ethnic groups from a neighbouring country which has a differing social climate.

Several European studies have illustrated the way in which disadvantaged groups use social creativity in choosing alternative criteria upon which to evaluate themselves. For example, van Knippenberg and van Oers (1984) compared the perceptions of two different categories of nurses in Holland. The more highly trained group saw themselves as superior in theoretical insight, while the less trained group saw themselves as more friendly. Mummendey and Schreiber (1984) found that members of different political parties in Germany each evaluated their party more positively on those attributes which they considered to be more important.

Linking values and intergroup relations

A series of tests of Tajfel's theory which link it to the theme of this book has been made in England by Brown and his colleagues. Hinkle and Brown (1990) reason that the central tenet of Tajfel's theory is that one will discriminate against an out-group if one identifies with the in-group. As they point out, this prediction is much more likely to be supported in the case of people endorsing interdependent values than in the case of those holding independent values. Field studies in hospitals, factories, a paper-mill and a bakery, however, have indicated that there is in fact a *highly variable* relationship between identification with the group and favouring one's in-group.

Hinkle and Brown conclude that this variation must be due to the fact that comparing one's group with other groups is not *always* important to one's identity. In some groups, such as sports teams, their very reason for existence is to compare their success with that of others. In others, such as juries or close-knit families, there is much less reason to engage in intergroup comparisons. Hinkle and Brown's reconceptualization of social identity theory is shown in Figure 5.1. An empirical study by Hinkle, Brown and Ely (1990) obtained measures of interdependence and comparative orientation. As their model predicts, they found that identification with the in-group and discrimination against the out-group were highly correlated *only* where both interdependence and comparative orientation were high.

Implications for collectivist cultures

As we pointed out earlier, social identity theory was formulated by Europeans who were concerned to make social psychology more 'social'. There is a certain irony about this intention, in so far as most commentators would agree that its hypotheses are more likely to be supported in collectivist cultures. Field tests of the theory, mostly in Europe, have yielded rather mixed results, and it may be that Hinkle and Brown's explanation will enable us to understand why. However, we have no information at present as to whether a comparative/non-comparative orientation would also prove to be important within collectivist cultures. It might be the case

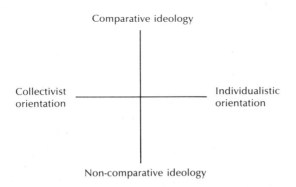

Source: Hinkle and Brown (1990).

Figure 5.1 Hinkle and Brown's reformulation of social identity theory

that in individualist cultures people make a distinction between groups that they do and do not wish to compare themselves with. In collectivist cultures, on the other hand, greater awareness of the contextual embeddedness of all behaviour might mean that a comparative orientation was part and parcel of the values of interdependence. A study by Bond, Hewstone, Wan and Chiu (1985) illustrates this possibility. They compared the effects of having an audience present or absent on explanations given for typical gender behaviours. In the United States, the presence or absence of an audience had no effect on the explanations provided. However, in Hong Kong, if a same-sex audience was absent, the explanations given became more biased towards the out-group. In other words, in the more collectivist setting of Hong Kong, a comparative orientation is suppressed by the simple presence of one's peers, whereas in the more individualist setting of America, there is less responsiveness to contextual social factors.

Perhaps the most interesting aspect of the studies by Hinkle and Brown is that the European studies have shown sufficient variability in the endorsement of interdependent values and of comparative/non-comparative orientation to enable intracultural tests of their hypothesis. Thus, variables which arose from comparative studies made *across* cultures have also proved to have some validity in understanding variations in behaviour *within* western cultures. This point applies with equal force to the other theoretical viewpoint which has arisen from distinctively European origins, to which we now turn.

The theory of social representation

A more radical perspective on how we might best understand social behaviour has been taken by those who argue that we must first decipher the ways in which the meanings of that behaviour are understood. According to this view, everyday events do not have any particular inherent social meaning. What happens to each of us as we are socialized is that we gradually learn that particular events or situations are understood in certain ways within our culture. As we come to understand things in these ways, we become better able to co-ordinate with the social activities of our cultural group members, and as we do so, we share in transmitting these meanings to those who join us. The meanings of events are thus not constructed by the individual, but are culturally shared social representations.

Some examples may help to make this viewpoint clearer. There exists in most societies in the world a social representation of the concept of 'work'. In many national cultures, work would be seen as something that one is, or should be, paid to do. However, there exist wide variations in the definition of what activities constitute work, rather than, say, helping a friend. Child-minding, assisting a tourist, or teaching someone English may or may not be considered work depending upon who does it and where it is done. The obligations of those who work also vary greatly. In Japan, the personal significance of work has been found to be greater than in many other countries (Meaning of Working International Team, 1987). One's work obligations in Japan may include going drinking after hours and sharing in other recreational activities with one's work colleagues, whereas in other cultures this could be more a matter of choice, and would most usually be thought of as something more separate from work.

Social representations of what it is appropriate to eat and when to do so also vary greatly. In many western industrial countries, the eating of cows, pigs and chickens is widely approved, while the eating of horses and dogs is not. The Chinese eat not only dogs, but also monkeys, pangolins, owls and snakes. In Hindu cultural groups, cows may not be eaten, while Jews may not eat pigs. Numerous other variations may be found and have been the object of much study by anthropologists.

Moscovici's formulation

Such variations in beliefs and values have most often been analyzed by social psychologists as variations in attitudes towards various objects. However, the protagonists of the theory of social representations, the foremost of whom is Moscovici (1981), would argue that this categorization misses the point. An attitude is a property of an individual. Social representations are collectively created and collectively maintained. Because many of the most fundamental representations exist in our cultural group long before we are born, there is a very slim chance that any one individual will create substantial change in the social representations prevalent within a cultural group. One could argue that major historical figures such as Hitler, Stalin, Gandhi or Martin Luther King did create such major changes. But even in such exceptional cases there remains room for debate as to whether or not these figures achieved prominence precisely because they spoke for a situation which was already moving their way. Other social representations may be much more volatile and fluid. Sperber (1985), for instance, distinguishes three types of social representation, which he refers to as 'culture', 'tradition' and 'fashion'. Cultural representations would be the most lasting, traditional representations would last through some generations, while fashions encompass the type of rapidly changing representations which have become highly characteristic of contemporary societies dominated by the mass-media.

The way in which a traditional social representation may over a period of time become progressively removed from its social origins is nicely illustrated by the work of Giorgi and Marsh (1990). Drawing upon the results of an earlier opinion survey with over 12,000 respondents in nine western European countries, they investigated the incidence of the Protestant work ethic. It was the hypothesis of the nineteenth-century German sociologist Weber that the rise of capitalism in western Europe was associated with a set of attitudes and beliefs found particularly among Protestant cultural groups. Giorgi and Marsh found that endorsement of work as a positive value was indeed still higher in the countries with a higher proportion of Protestants. However, they go on to report that it is no longer the Protestants who represent work in this way. The highest scorers were those who described themselves as atheists in the predominantly Protestant countries. Thus the social representation of hard work as a virtue has not shown much movement within Europe geographically, but it has become detached from its origins in a particular religious belief.

Moscovici's earliest work on social representations was focused upon the question of how the explanations of behaviour advanced by psychoanalysts were passing into everyday explanations of behaviour used by the lay public in France. He found that 45 per cent of students in his sample reported trying to understand their colleagues through the use of explanations such as 'having a complex'. In more recent work, the focus has broadened to encompass the whole range of ways in which 'commonsense' meanings are attributed to persons, groups and events in a cultural group. Moscovici points out that the nineteenth-century French sociologist Durkheim (1898) already proposed a social psychology based upon what he called 'collective representations', and work within this tradition was active in the early part of the century.

Representations of the individual

Ichheiser (1943) in Austria focused upon the social representation of the individual. He pointed out that the central concept in the social representation of the individual in western countries has been that individuals are accountable for their own actions. The representation of the individual as accountable is particularly explicit in the legal systems of many western countries. This type of analysis has evident links with Hofstede's distinction between collectivist cultures and individualist cultures, even though Ichheiser starts from an entirely different point.

If the concepts which have become widely used within social psychology are examined, it is clear that they too rest upon a representation of the individual as accountable, as Farr (1989) makes clear. This is particularly evident in the case of the processes of attribution or of the formation of an individual's self-concept as an autonomous, situation-free, independent agent.

Most of the content of the present book uses existing, implicitly individualistic, social psychological conventions to examine the way in which cultural group members most characteristically represent themselves and attribute qualities to others outside of their group. For this reason, one might argue that some at least of the studies carried through in less individualistic national cultures are of the imposed-etic type. In the next chapter we shall touch, for example, on such matters as Indians' reluctance to specify a context-free self-concept, and doubts among respondents in Niger as to what exactly is a personal possession.

So how could the social representations approach add to what these types of study have already told us about attitudes, prejudice, stereotyping and so forth? Since social representations are collectively defined and collectively transmitted, it follows that we can best study them by looking at instances of communication among members of a cultural group. The criticism has been advanced that the theory does not specify in advance how one should select the members of a group to be one's sample. Moscovici specifies only that the group *is* the people who hold a shared social representation. This definition need not be problematic if one is studying widely shared social representations, but can become more difficult where smaller groups and more transient representations are concerned.

Data on communications among group members can be collected through questionnaires and interviews, administered by members of the same cultural group, but better still may be examples of more spontaneous speech. If we can find clear themes from analyzing suitable samples, we should be better able to understand the representations which underlie them. This type of discourse analysis has become popular in several countries of western Europe recently (Potter and Wetherell, 1987), but it has rarely been used for cross-cultural studies. Indeed, the technical requirements for the making of valid comparisons between discourse in different languages constitute a formidable obstacle.

Cross-cultural studies using interviews and questionnaires have examined representations of, for example, wealth, poverty and illness. If individuals are held accountable for their actions, then one would expect that those who experience poverty or misfortune will be represented by others as deserving their fate. Indeed, Lerner (1980) developed a 'Just World' hypothesis in Canada along these lines, and his hypothesis has received extensive empirical support. Studies by Feagin (1972) in America and Townsend (1979) in Britain showed that respondents in these countries more often explained poverty in individualistic terms than in situational terms. In contrast, Pandey, Sinha, Prakash and Tripathi (1982) found situational explanations more frequently used in India.

Health and illness

Wide differences have been found in the ways in which health and illness are represented in different cultures. A detailed study by Herzlich (1973) in France found evidence of three representations of illness: illness as destructive of one's customary activities, illness as a liberation from obligations, and illness as an 'occupation' or pastime. A more general picture of representations about what constitutes illness requiring treatment can be gained from the types of symptom which are reported to doctors in different parts of the world. Patients in individualist cultures rather frequently consult doctors on account of their feelings, most frequently because they feel anxious or depressed. In collectivist cultures this is much more infrequent. Presenting problems are much more often somatic, focusing upon specific aches and pains or other physical symptoms (Draguns, 1990). Such a contrast between individualist cultures and collectivist cultures is, of course, a matter of proportions rather than an absolute difference. Draguns suggests that, in order to present one's feelings as a problem or illness, one needs to have a unified and detached self-concept, such as a person with independent values would be likely to possess. On the other hand, aches and pains could be attributed by a person with interdependent values to any number of environmental causes, be they other people, germs, poverty, climate, witchcraft, diet or God's will. Indeed, the distinction between internal and external causes as well as cures tends to be blurred by respondents from collectivist cultural systems such as the Chinese (Luk and Bond, in press).

Social representations and the future of cross-cultural psychology

Investigations by researchers into social representations to date are helping to extend the range of phenomena to be studied cross-culturally. However, their contribution has so far been mostly at the level of underlining the difficulties which still stand in the path of a truly culture-inclusive social psychology. Globally valid explanations for social behaviour may be possible only to the extent that shared social representations of what it is to be a person do exist or can be created. Whether there is any likelihood of such an increasing convergence occurring depends upon whether indigenous psychologies derived from the various parts of the world prove to have sufficient in common with one another.

Indigenous psychologies in developing countries

The type of indigenous psychology espoused in developing countries has had a rather different emphasis from European models, although they too may have a strong emphasis on the importance of language. Most frequently, indigenous concepts have only gradually been adopted, as researchers struggled to find an idiom which better captured local concerns. For instance, D. Sinha (1989) reports how, in his studies of remote communities in India, he only slowly came to realize that when he greeted a respondent by saying 'How are you?', he was imposing an individualist construction on the interchange. In the local language, greetings were expressed in the more collectivist manner, 'How are ourselves?' Enriquez (1988) has similarly reported detailed studies of nuances of meaning in the Tagalog language concerning social relations in the Philippines. He argues that psychology can be of value in that country only when it is expressed in terms of those meanings rather than by using imported concepts. J.B.P. Sinha (1992) reports a growing trend towards the indigenization of social psychology in India. For instance, models have been developed and tested concerning leader–follower relations and therapist–patient relations which take account of the high power distance characterizing social relationships in Indian society. Summarizing developments such as these, D. Sinha (1989) argues that a valid indigenous psychology should not develop entirely in isolation from concepts developed elsewhere, but should rest upon the testing of the applicability of each concept to the local setting, wherever that concept originates.

Moghaddam (1990) suggests that Third World indigenous psychology is moving towards what he calls a 'generative' focus rather than the 'modulative' emphasis of mainstream social psychology. What he means by these terms is that mainstream social psychology is mostly concerned with understanding the nature of social relationships *as they currently exist*. In contrast, generative approaches are those which seek to understand how existing social relationships can be changed and improved. Generative approaches focus upon issues such as poverty, injustice, literacy, ideology, torture and development, depending upon their local salience. The emphasis is less on dispassionate understanding and more on the type of understanding which can underpin a programme of social action. Such emphases do, of course, overlap the preoccupations of some social psychologists in the richer countries of the world, who also feel the need to work towards various types of social change.

We can take the growth of community social psychology in South America as an instance of a generative approach (Marin, 1983; Wilpert, 1991). In many of the countries of South America, social psychologists have become involved in community action projects. The theoretical models upon which their work has been based have been varied since, until recently, researchers in different countries in Latin America had little contact with one another. However, much of the work has been based upon the notion that perceptions of one's circumstances are socially constructed (as European theorists have stressed), and that the creation of change must start from a change in those perceptions. For instance, Serrano-Garcia and Lopez-Sanchez (1991) draw upon Freire's (1970) concept of 'problematization'. In other words, they encourage community groups to think of some aspect of poverty, for instance, not as inevitable, but as a problem requiring action.

In essence, the professional activities of many of these projects involve working with local populations to encourage them in the task of collecting information about some aspect of their continuing deprivation. This information is then forcefully presented to relevant authorities in an attempt to improve conditions. In principle, the method is no different from that used in some community action projects in deprived areas of the USA or Europe. Our focus upon aspects of individualism and collectivism would, however, lead us to expect cultural differences in how well such approaches worked out. Indeed, we might be able to predict which approaches had a better chance of success in which cultural settings. By reviewing case studies of projects of this kind in different parts of the world, we might therefore find ways in which such emic studies could also contribute to derived-etic generalizations about the best ways of promoting social change in various cultural settings.

Conclusion

In most of this chapter we have explored recent European theories which seek to provide an alternative, but not necessarily contradictory, explanation of social cognition to that espoused by most North American theorists. The theories of Tajfel and of Moscovici present the processes of social cognition as deriving from existing social structures. In their view we derive our identities, and our scripts for acting in any situation, from our lasting affiliations with groups and from the continuing social representations by those groups of their life-events. Both the groups we join and their characteristic ways of representing events often exist long before we join them, so that our role in creating change within them is seen as relatively modest but nonetheless possible.

To debate whether theories such as these, which are pitched at the level of intergroup relations, are better or worse than those which seek individual-level explanations is unlikely to be fruitful. They are taking different but equally valid approaches to the same phenomena. The preoccupations of Third World indigenous psychologists are much more directly focused on the creation of change, and this emphasis may well prove more compatible with theories of social representation than with theories of individual cognition. Having now explored some of the current range of indigenous psychologies, it is time to return to the major theme of this book: an examination of how successfully the currently dominant theories can explain cultural variations in social behaviour.

SIX

Social cognition

O wad some power the giftie gie us
to see oursels as ithers see us.

(Robert Burns, 'To a Louse')

In Chapter 4, we concluded that the contrast between collectivist and individualist cultures provided a promising framework within which to analyze variations in the outcomes of social psychological research around the world. In making use of this framework, we need first to test how fundamental might be the contrast between the psychological processes found in different cultural groups. Consider, for instance, the results of cross-cultural tests of 'field dependence'. This is a psychological test in which subjects are provided with a series of complex visual patterns, and asked to discern smaller figures embedded within the overall pattern (Witkin *et al.*, 1962). Two examples are shown in Figure 6.1. Although substantial variation in results has often been found within cultures, subjects from individualist countries on average score higher on field independence: that is to say, they are better able to separate out the embedded figures from their background (Witkin and Berry, 1975). In evaluating such results, we need to clarify whether we are speaking about cultural differences in the *degree* to which cognitive processes underlying these results occur, or whether we must postulate that *fundamentally different* processes occur in different cultures.

The self in its social context

To answer such questions we need to move to the level of analysis which psychologists feel they are best equipped to handle – the study of individuals, rather than of whole cultures. Our question now becomes one

93

Simple figure   Complex figure in which it is embedded

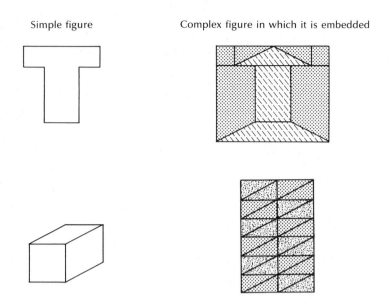

Note: The shadings in the complex figures represent different colours used by Witkin.
Source: From H. A. Witkin, 'Individual differences in the case of perception of embedded figures', *Journal of Personality*, vol. 19. © 1950 Duke University Press. Reprinted with permission of the publisher.

Figure 6.1 Examples taken from Witkin *et al.*'s Embedded Figures Test

of comparing individuals having independent values with those having interdependent values. Markus and Kitayama (1991) introduced these terms to differentiate those who consider themselves independent agents, as often found in western countries, from those who consider themselves interdependent with others, as often found in more collectivist countries. They propose that being oneself in these differing ways has profound consequences for the processes of social cognition.

The independent self

The perception of oneself as an independent agent has been a major emphasis in the life of western industrial nations in recent times. Values such as freedom and self-determination are highly esteemed, and many members of these nations will, if asked, characterize themselves as possessing traits and abilities, such as intelligence, friendliness, modesty or what you will. It is by no means certain that this was always so. In medieval times, the word 'individual' had a decidedly different meaning in the English language. It was used to refer to each of the members of the

Trinity: that is to say, God-the-Father, God-the-Son and the Holy Spirit (Williams, 1961). In other words, in the religious imagery which was predominant at the time, an individual was not a separate entity, but was indissolubly linked to others, whose identity was collectively defined.

More recent western conceptions of the individual as being in some way autonomous or separate from the social context parallel the type of analytic thinking which has been highly valued in western countries since the time of Descartes. This way of thinking often polarizes pairs of concepts as a basis for construing the world. Frequently used concept pairs in social psychology would include: self/others, individual/group, leader/follower, environment/heredity and, of course, individualism/collectivism. An instance of the way in which this type of thinking finds a ready home within western psychology is provided by the widespread use of versions of the semantic differential questionnaire, in which subjects are asked to evaluate themselves or others on a series of bipolar rating scales.

This oppositional way of construing individuals and their environments is certainly not the only possible approach to adopt. As Geertz (1974) emphatically puts it:

> The Western conception of the person as a bounded, unique, more or less integrated motivational and cognitive universe, a dynamic centre of awareness, emotion, judgment and action organised into a distinctive whole and set contrastively both against other such wholes and against its social and natural background is, however incorrigible it may seem to us, a rather peculiar idea within the context of the world's cultures. (p. 225)

The interdependent self

Thinking about oneself as interdependent is consistent with a more holistic, less analytic way of thinking. Within this approach, the inter-relatedness of concepts is more salient. In discussing western and Chinese science in historical times, Needham (1978) writes:

> We are driven to the conclusion that there are two ways of advancing from primitive truth. One way was the way taken by some of the Greeks: to refine the ideas of causation in such a way that one finished up with a mechanical explanation of the universe, just as Democritus did with his atoms. The other way is to systematise the universe of things and events into a structural pattern which conditioned all the mutual influences of its different parts. (p. 166)

Anthropologists have documented a variety of 'eastern' cultures in which the self is defined in this more contextual, multiply shaped manner (Marsella, De Vos and Hsu, 1985). This type of interdependent conception of self in contemporary societies has only recently been studied empirically by psychologists. Markus and Kitayama (1991) propose that an individual with interdependent values regards the preservation of harmonious relations with the other key people in his or her life as the primary goal. It follows from this that an interdependent person will not necessarily maintain a consistent core of actions towards other people in general. It may well be necessary to behave in different ways at different times in order to accommodate others. One's actions towards a shopkeeper, one's boss, one's maternal uncle, a neighbour's child or a fellow passenger on a bus will all be bounded by the obligations defining that particular type of relationship with that particular person.

Some western theorists have also pointed out that situations affect how individuals behave (Mischel, 1968; Argyle, Furnham and Graham, 1981). However, after a good deal of debate, most western theorists now envisage a process of person–situation interaction (Epstein and O'Brien, 1985). That is to say, while everyone may be less friendly when standing in a queue than when attending a party, certain people will be more friendly than others in both settings. However, ways of being friendly while in a queue and while at a party may also differ subtly, so recent theorists speak of the *coherence* of behaviour across situations rather than a more precisely defined consistency.

For a person with interdependent values, maintaining a coherent core of, for instance, friendliness would be less important. What would count more strongly is the immediate requirements of each specific situation and the people who make up that situation. Hence, if persons with interdependent values are asked to describe themselves, they may well find it difficult to do so, if the context for their actions is not specified.

Describing oneself

This rationale is supported by the findings of Markus and Kitayama's own studies (in press). Japanese respondents were found to make distinctions between emotions based upon how engaged or disengaged they were with the person towards whom the emotion was relevant. One might expect similar findings from other relatively collectivist societies, since degree of engagement could be crucial to the experience of emotion in such settings, whereas in individualist societies, degree of engagement would be less decisive, and one's emotions would be seen as more autonomous. A study by Stipek, Weiner and Li (1989) also supports this view. Chinese and Americans were asked to describe situations in which they had become angry. The Americans were found to be more likely to describe events which had happened to them personally. The Chinese, on the other hand, referred to a higher proportion of events which had happened to other people.

Bond and Cheung (1983) asked Japanese, Hong Kong Chinese and American students to describe themselves. They used a familiar procedure in western studies, known as the Twenty Statements Test. This simply asks respondents to provide 20 answers to the question 'Who am I?' As expected, they found that Americans used many more trait descriptions than the Japanese. However, the results for the Hong Kong students were rather more similar to those from the USA. They concluded that the Hong Kong students were more westernized, having been educated in English with more western curricula. Another possibility is that the coding system they employed to analyze references to social roles was too global to detect differences between US and Hong Kong descriptions of one's relations with others. In the scheme which they used, both an independent self-statement, 'I am a student', and an interdependent self-statement, 'I am a member of the second-year psychology class', would have been coded as a reference to role. Triandis, McCusker and Hui (1990) also used the Twenty Statements Test, comparing student responses from mainland USA, Hawaii, Greece, Hong Kong and China. They found that references to oneself as a member of a social category were much higher for the Chinese responses than for those from elsewhere. This study too may have found more differences if it had used more exactly specified categories for coding of responses.

A more precise test of differences in self-conception was reported by Cousins (1989), who asked Japanese and American students to describe themselves. Initially he used the familiar version of the Twenty Statements Test. As expected, he found that the Americans came up with many more generalized trait labels in describing themselves, while the Japanese were more likely to qualify their characterizations, by specifying the context within which they behaved in a given way. For instance, one respondent's self-description was 'one who plays Mah Jongg on Friday nights'. Cousins then modified the Twenty Statements Test so that respondents were asked to describe how they were in a series of specific settings: for example, at home, with their friends, and so forth Under these conditions, the pattern was reversed. Japanese students were now able to use more trait labels about themselves. American students, on the other hand, used fewer traits and were more inclined to add qualifications. For instance, one respondent wrote: 'I am often lazy at home.' Cousins concludes that the Americans' need to preserve an independent, context-free self-concept led them to assert that, although they might behave in a certain way in a particular setting, this would not necessarily reflect their 'real' self. The American respondent quoted above implies that he or she is not *really* lazy, just often lazy at home, thereby preserving the image of independence from the context. The Japanese respondents, on the other hand, show that they are best able to characterize themselves when the nature of their interdependence is specified.

Self-monitoring

The above studies provide some support for the distinction between independent and interdependent self-concepts, though none of them included a measure of what values the subjects actually endorsed. Further evidence comes from a series of studies by Gudykunst, which focused upon the concept of self-monitoring. This concept was first defined by Snyder (1979), who devised a test of the degree to which his US subjects monitored their own behaviour. Gudykunst *et al.* (1990, 1992) propose that Snyder's scale measures only the type of self-monitoring to be expected in individualist cultures. After conducting interviews with Japanese and Chinese respondents, Gudykunst *et al.* created a new self-monitoring scale, which they claimed had derived-etic properties. They were able to show that American and British respondents score high on items measuring monitoring of one's own behaviour, whereas Japanese and Chinese respondents score high on items measuring monitoring of others' behaviour, in order to determine socially appropriate behaviour. Furthermore, they showed that these differences were stronger for those who endorsed interdependent values than for those who endorsed independent values.

The Gudykunst studies bridge the gap in the other studies between culture-level interpretations of the data and the actual values endorsed by their respondents. This linkage gives us added confidence in our interpretation of the differences we have reported in self-concept. If we imagine that a researcher managed to intercept Mrs Robertson and Mr Chan, we can note in Box 6.1 some similar contrasts which we might find in their responses to a test of self-concept. Mrs Robertson uses traits and generalized roles to describe herself. Mr Chan specifies the settings in which he is engaged, and indicates how he behaves in some of them.

Box 6.1   *Who am I? Some answers from Mrs Robertson and Mr Chan*

Mrs Robertson	*Mr Chan*
A teacher	A student at Hong Kong University
Divorced	I come from the Chan family
Scottish	I try to work hard at my lessons
A long way from home	I join the Pokfulam basketball team
I do not suffer fools gladly	I care for my sister
Active	I visit my mother in the hospital every day
Lonely	

Clothing the self

Jahoda (1982) provides related material from another part of the world. He contrasts the wearing of the *chadoor*, or full-length veil, by women in certain Islamic countries with Zimbardo's (1970) experiments in the USA. Zimbardo showed that, when subjects in his experiments were asked to wear a full-length robe, their behaviour became 'deindividuated': that is to say, they were more likely to act in aggressive or socially irresponsible ways. Zimbardo postulates that, since they were no longer individually identifiable, they no longer felt so responsible for their actions. In contrast, Jahoda points out that in countries where it is the norm for women to be veiled, rather than setting free one's individual impulses, the veil (a garment of rather similar dimensions to Zimbardo's robes) very precisely specifies one's social obligations. In a similar way, we saw in Chapter 2 that being an identified member of a group in collectivist cultures inhibited social loafing rather than enhancing it.

Interestingly enough, the role of clothing in defining one's group identity also proved crucial in an attempt by Zimbardo to replicate his findings in Belgium. While he had used student subjects in his US studies, in Belgium he used soldiers. When the soldiers donned Zimbardo's robes, they proved less aggressive than when in regular uniform, which was the reverse of Zimbardo's prediction. It appears that, rather than deindividuating the soldiers, the robes made them feel more identifiable, whereas in regular uniform they felt less so.

If Zimbardo had used soldiers in the USA, we might expect that he would have obtained results similar to the Belgian ones. Armies, even in predominantly individualist countries, encourage an interdependent value system, within which one's obligations are publicly spelled out through the wearing of uniforms. To step out of uniform is to become an independent actor, just as it would be for an Islamic woman in an Arab country to renounce the veil.

This section began by posing the question of how fundamental might be the divergence between independence and interdependence. We have touched upon some evidence that people from different cultural groups think about themselves in different ways. However, we shall need to leave the question unresolved until later in this chapter, while we survey a broader range of evidence.

The self in its physical context

The substantial element of choice about whom we associate with in individualist cultures is likely to find expression in how we manage the spatial relationships between ourselves and others. One might expect that in individualist cultures, people would prefer to emphasize their independence by keeping others at a greater physical distance, or by protecting distinctive areas of personal space. In collectivist cultures, people might on average prefer to be closer to other members of the group with whom they will share their future and to share space with them. On the other hand, members of collectivist cultures might prefer to keep a greater distance from those with whom they are not linked. Furthermore, other matters such as relative status and gender are also very important in determining preferred spatial relations, so that we should not expect an oversimple picture.

Proximity

An early study by Little (1968) asked people in five countries to indicate how close two persons should be when having conversations on 18 different types of topic. He found some cultural differences which held up across all topics. Those who favoured greatest proximity were Greeks, followed by Italians, Americans, Swedes and Scots, in that order. However, Little's study combined together conversations between friends, acquaintances and strangers.

We look now at a series of studies which specify more closely how people are acquainted. Watson and Graves (1966) had Arab and American students in America who were friends talk to each other in pairs, with each set of pairs coming from the same country. They were instructed to speak in their own language. The results for Iraqis, Saudis, Kuwaitis and Egyptians were all closely similar. Compared to Americans, the Arabs all faced each other more directly, sat closer, had more eye-contact and talked louder. Watson (1970) extended his sample to include students at the University of Colorado from 31 countries, although he was able to locate no more than one pair from many of these countries. He found that those from Arab countries, India and Pakistan sat closest, followed by Latin Americans and southern Europeans, east Asians and finally northern Europeans, among whom he included Americans and Australians. Watson also had all his subjects rate how close was their friendship with each other, and it turned out that the Arabs, Indians and Pakistanis, who were the groups which had sat closest, also rated their friendships most highly. One could argue that this finding undermines the validity of his conclusions. Many studies have shown that we sit nearer to those whom we like. If different degrees of liking can account for how close the friend-pairs sat, we would not need to invoke cultural explanations for the results. However, it is just as likely that the different ratings of friendship were themselves influenced by cultural differences.

As we discussed in Chapter 3, comparing mean scores on questionnaires completed by different cultural groups is a perilous enterprise, since the members of some cultures are much more prone to use the extremes on rating scales than are others. Watson could have resolved this doubt by looking at the relationship between proximity and liking *within* each cultural group, but he did not take this important step. In a somewhat similar study, also in America, Sussman and Rosenfeld (1982) reported that in conversation previously unacquainted Japanese sat further apart than Americans, while Venezuelans sat closer still, an outcome pattern which is consistent with Watson's findings. Graham (1985) found that Brazilian negotiators looked at one another more and touched one another more than did Americans or Japanese. Shuter (1977) observed pairs of people talking to one another on the street in Venice, Heidelberg and Milwaukee. All-male pairs stood closest in Italy and furthest apart in the USA. Mixed sex pairs were also most distant in the USA, but did not differ between Germany and Italy.

There are also a number of studies focusing upon positioning by strangers in situations where there is no requirement that they speak to one another. Noesjirwan (1977) found that in doctors' waiting rooms, Indonesians were likely to choose a seat near to a stranger of the same sex, while Australians chose seats which separated them maximally from others. The Indonesians also more often started a conversation with the person whom they sat beside. Presumably shared gender was a sufficient reason for the Indonesians to treat one another as related. Sanders, McKim and McKim (1988) found that students from Botswana in southern Africa preferred to keep a greater distance from strangers than did American students. Mazur (1977) compared the distance apart of unacquainted men sitting on park benches in San Francisco, Seville in Spain and Tangier in the Arab country of Morocco. He found no differences, despite the fact that Arabs are widely reported to favour close proximity and frequent eye-contact. Sanders, Hakky and Brizzolara (1985) found differences in distance *preferences* between Egyptian and American students only among women. Preferences were determined by asking subjects to position markers on a chart representing an imaginary room. The Egyptian female students required both male friends and male strangers to keep rather distant, while according to this data collection method, the Egyptian men showed a pattern similar to that for both American men and women.

These results indicate that the generalizations advanced by Hall (1966) and others about the existence of overall cultural differences in preferred spatial positioning are well supported for those who are well acquainted. Among strangers the findings are less clear and it is also evident that factors such as gender substantially affect preferences. The significance of physical proximity presumably lies in what behaviours proximity permits. Watson's (1970) study showed that those who sat closer also touched one another. Similarly, Shuter (1976) found that Latin Americans show frequent touching as well as close proximity. Comparison of Costa Ricans, Panamanians and Colombians revealed that proximity, touching and holding all decrease as one travels further south. Close proximity also makes it easier to maintain eye-contact and to judge whether one's partner is doing so. Watson found that Arabs, Latin-Americans and southern Europeans maintained higher levels of eye-contact than east Asians, Indians, Pakistanis and northern Europeans.

These differences in preferred levels of contact are, of course, not just matters of academic interest. As soon as someone from one country visits another, they encounter the need to adapt their spatial behaviour to local preferences, if they wish to give the desired impression. Collett (1971), for instance, reports a programme in which Englishmen were trained to stand closer to Arabs, make more eye-contact, touch more and smile more. Trainees were better liked by Arabs than the untrained controls. When Chan Chi Lok approaches too close to Mrs Robertson in our example, she motions him to sit at a more 'proper' distance.

Homes and territories

Altman and Gauvain (1981) observe that in individualist cultures homes tend to be clearly demarcated. Doors, gardens, fences and gates indicate a relatively small internal 'home' area, which is furnished in a distinctive manner. In collectivist cultures, on the other hand, physical boundaries may be less clearly marked, and the 'inner' area may be centred on a court-yard or other open space. Some of these differences no doubt derive from climatic variations, and climatic differences may indeed have some effect on the social structures to be found in different parts of the world. While the boundaries of homes in collectivist cultures may thus appear more physi-cally permeable, Gudykunst, Ting-Toomey and Chua (1988) point out that the boundaries are nonetheless there and that they are based on rules about who has access to what space. Altman and Chemers (1980) review a series of studies showing that, even in conditions of considerable poverty and consequent crowding, rules are found that provide some degree of privacy.

One way of studying the nature of such rules is to see what happens when they are violated. Gudykunst *et al.* (1988) propose that, in indi-vidualist cultures, violation leads to an active, aggressive response, whereas in collectivist cultures there is more likely to be some kind of passive withdrawal. Bond and Shiraishi (1974), for instance, showed that where an interviewer encroached on Japanese interviewees' personal space, their response was detectable only through non-verbal cues. Viola-tion of cultural rules about appropriate positioning by visitors from other cultures is likely to be an extremely frequent event. However, it is only easy to detect a violation in the types of situation where rule violation precipitates an active response.

The meaning of spatial positioning

At present our knowledge of the relation between spatial positioning and culture is rather incomplete. One reason for this is that many of the studies so far done have used rather crude and simple measures, such as verbal preferences about one's distance from others, whereas the processes operating are likely to be much more subtle. A second difficulty is that, because physical proximity is readily measurable, it has been easy to fall prey to the assumption that it is given the same meaning in all cultures. It could be the case, for example, that in some of the highly collectivist Arab and Latin-American cultures proximity signals intimacy, whereas in some of the higher power distance cultures in east Asia proximity could signal a lack of deference. Interviews by Watson (1970) with his subjects support this view. High eye-contact was reported to have positive connotations by Arabs, Latin-Americans, Indians and Pakistanis. But Africans and east Asians described high eye-contact as conveying insubordination or anger. We shall explore additional aspects of the ways in which our non-verbal behaviour conveys messages to others in Chapter 8.

Possessions

A further, much-neglected part of the physical aspect of self has to do with possessions. We might expect that in individualist cultures ownership would be clearly delineated and that a person's material possessions would be seen as an expression of his or her identity. Conversely, in a collectivist culture, possessions would more likely be shared among the group and be seen as indicative of the group's identity. Wallendorf and Arnould (1988) compared attitudes toward possessions of adults in Arizona and in the Niger republic, an Islamic Hausa society to the north of Nigeria. The comparison was between urban Americans and rural inhabitants of Niger, so that we are looking at differences which might also be found between town and country within a single culture. Overall, the Americans rated themselves as more attached to their possessions than did respondents in Niger. One respondent in Niger reflected local values by pointing out that, if one had too many possessions, they might be lost through divine intervention, thereby indicating that for him possessions were related to religious beliefs.

The favourite possessions most frequently reported by the Americans were functional items, sources of entertainment, personal nicknacks, pieces of art and photographs. Asked why they valued these objects, 60 per cent responded that they reflected attachments based on personal memories – for instance, of friends or family members. The American responses thus emphasized one's individualized life history. In Niger, some difficulty was found in conveying the interviewer's understanding of what a possession was. Disallowed responses included 'my children', 'my fields' and 'my Koranic studies'. Once these difficulties were overcome, the women's favourite possessions proved to be almost all related to marriage or domestic goods. The men listed religious and magical objects as well as livestock and tools. The reasons given for valuing possessions did not emphasize the owner's distinctive personal history, but rather more the requirement for maintaining one's own and one's family's position within society. This contrast in the meaning attached to one's possessions suggests that they allow one to make more real the themes important in one's cultural group.

Perceiving others

If divergences between how independent and interdependent people describe themselves and their physical environment are rooted in the processes of social cognition, we should expect to find similar differences when we examine the process by which they perceive others. Shweder and Bourne (1982) compared free descriptions of their peers by 70 Indian and 17 American adults. Of the American statements about their peers, 72 per cent were context-free personality trait attributions, whereas only 50 per cent of the Indian statements fell into this category. As we might expect, a larger proportion of the Indian statements were those which specified the social context of the characteristic described. A typical American statement could thus be 'he is selfish', while an equivalent Indian statement might be 'he is hesitant to give money away to his family'. In another early study, Korten (1974) compared perceptions of others by American and Ethiopian students. The Americans characterized others in terms of abilities, knowledge and emotional style. The Ethiopians made much more use of descriptions of the person's interactions with others ('he likes to talk with his room-mates'), and of their opinions and beliefs ('he is against this country's form of government'), both of which are more context-related descriptors.

More recently, Miller (1984) also compared Indian and American free descriptions of others, and found an even stronger divergence between the two countries in the use of context-free and context-specific descriptions. Her American sample used three times as many trait attributions, while the

Box 6.2 *Why did the motorcyclist act as he did? (1)*

The episode below was contributed by one of Miller's (1984) subjects. Miller asked both her Indian and her American subjects why they thought the motorcycle driver acted as he did.

This concerns a motorcycle accident. The back wheel burst on the motorcycle. The passenger sitting on the rear jumped. The moment the passenger fell, he struck his head on the pavement. The driver of the motorcycle – who is an attorney – as he was on his way to court for some work, just took the passenger to a local hospital and went on and attended to his court work. The driver left the passenger there without consulting the doctor about the seriousness of the injury – the gravity of the situation – whether the passenger should be shifted immediately – and he went on to court. So ultimately the passenger died.

Miller cites three reasons provided by Americans and three provided by Indians as typical of the responses she found. Consider your own explanations before you look at Box 6.3.

Source: Miller (1984).

Indians used twice as many context-bound traits. She also presented her subjects with a series of one-paragraph incidents and asked them to explain why they thought the key person in the incident acted as he or she had done. An example appears in Boxes 6.2 and 6.3. Once again, the Americans gave significantly more dispositional explanations, while the Indians gave more contextual ones.

In yet another Indian–American comparison, L'Armand, Pepitone and Shanmugam (1981) asked matched samples to make ratings of who was to blame in a case history of a rape incident which was put before them. Although most respondents in both countries blamed the man, twice as many Americans as Indians assigned blame to the woman – a person attribution. On the other hand, the Indians were five times more influenced than the Americans by information about the prior sexual history of the woman. Whether she was previously chaste or not was seen as crucial – a contextual factor concerning relations with others, which would have a major effect upon her perceived responsibility and upon her future marriage prospects.

It is noticeable that, while each of these studies shows significant differences between the Indian and the American samples, the differences are simply differences in the *frequency* of using trait attributions and context-specific attributions. In other words, some Americans did provide situational explanations of behaviour and some Indians did use personality traits as explanations. We could not consequently argue plausibly that the

Box 6.3 *Why did the motorcyclist act as he did? (2)*

American responses
1. He was obviously irresponsible.
2. He must have been in a state of shock.
3. He was aggressive in pursuing his career success.

Indian responses
1. It was his duty to be in court for the client he was representing.
2. He might have become nervous or confused.
3. The injured man might not have looked as seriously injured as he
   was.

Source: Miller (1984).

processes of social cognition were fundamentally different in the samples
from the two countries. A more probable explanation would be that people
in the two cultural groups tend to direct their attention differentially.
According to this view, those with independent values would focus
primarily on the actions of themselves and of others. Those with interdependent values would give more attention to the context of actions and
to how different actions mesh together.

A further illustration of this phenomenon is provided by Miller, Bersoff
and Harwood (1990), who asked Indian and American students and
children on what basis they would decide whether to intervene in various
emergencies. They found that Indians reported much more frequently that
it would be a matter of the moral obligations inherent in their social role
to respond, whereas the Americans saw most situations as a matter for
personal choice. Only in life-threatening emergencies did the US
responses come close to the Indian pattern. The differences found were
less sharp among younger children. These results led Miller *et al.* to infer
that the different response patterns are acquired as one is gradually socialized to prevailing cultural patterns. Markus and Kitayama (1991) see this
socialization process as deriving from the gradual internalization of different rules which lay out the priorities as to what one should attend to in any
situation.

Selecting what we attend to

If the manner in which we learn to direct our attention does underlie
cultural differences in social cognition, then it is interesting to examine
what happens if we are asked to redirect our attention for a while.

Table 6.1 Responses to the Twenty Statements Test after different attention-focusing instructions

| | Statements about oneself which were: | | | |
| | Independent | | Interdependent | |
Respondents:	US	Chinese	US	Chinese
Think about what makes you different from family and friends	86	70	5	13
Think about what you have in common with family and friends	73	68	20	25

Source: Adapted from data reported by Trafimow, Triandis and Goto (1991).

Trafimow, Triandis and Goto (1991) asked Caucasian and Chinese students attending the University of Illinois to focus their attention in one of two ways for two minutes and then to complete the Twenty Statements Test. In one experimental condition they were asked to think of all the things which linked them with their family. In the other condition they were asked to think about all the things which separated them from their family. These experimental manipulations did have a substantial effect on how subjects subsequently chose to describe themselves, as shown in Table 6.1. Thinking about oneself as separate caused the Chinese to use more trait attributions, and thinking about one's family caused the Caucasians to use more role attributions.

Differences in where people direct their attention by those with independent and interdependent values may help to explain some limitations on what Ross (1977) termed the 'fundamental attribution error'. By this phrase he meant the tendency found in many studies for people to explain the behaviour of others in terms of traits and abilities rather than in terms of the context which may evoke it. The studies reviewed in this chapter so far indicate that it is an error which is absent or at least reduced in collectivist cultures. It is, then, hardly fundamental.

Some choice language

Differences in where people focus their attention are unlikely to provide the sole basis for independent and interdependent value orientations. An extensive line of research derives from the propositions put forward by Whorf (1956) to the effect that the way in which culture members think would be bounded by the structure and nature of the language they use. There is some debate as to whether the language of a culture determines or reflects the behaviour patterns within it. The aspect of interest here is whether the type of language use which is current in individualist and collectivist cultures can be shown to reflect these differences in values.

Semin and Rubini (1990) examined cultural variations in the language employed in describing people in Italy, using rather different methods than those employed in the studies so far described. They compared the types of insult available in northern and southern Italy. Southern Italians are said more often to endorse interdependent values, while in northern Italy independent values are more favoured. Their hypothesis that students from Sicily would report a larger proportion of 'relational' insults than those from Bologna and Trieste in the north was upheld. Swearwords and certain types of individualistic insult were reported more from the north. Some of the less graphic examples of these insult-types are given in Box 6.4. The importance of choosing the culturally appropriate type of insult for maximal effect is underlined by the work of Bond and Cheung (1991). They found that in Hong Kong their subjects responded more strongly to insults addressed to their group than to insults addressed to them as individuals.

Emphasizing attributes which are culturally relevant

Most of the studies reviewed thus far in this chapter started with emically valid procedures, using free responses from the subjects, thereby making it equally easy for both trait attributions and context attributions to be detected. Substantial numbers of other cross-cultural studies of person perception have used imposed-etic methods, within which theories first developed in North America are tested elsewhere. In the next three

Box 6.4 *A choice of culturally rooted insults*

Individualist insults (distinctive to northern Italy)
You are stupid.
You are a cretin.
Swear-words referring to religious figures.
Swear-words referring to sexual nouns.

Collectivist insults (distinctive to southern Italy)
I wish a cancer on you and all your relatives.
Your sister is a cow.
You are queer and so is your father.
You are a Communist.
Insults relating to incest.

Source: Semin and Rubini (1990).

sections we shall be looking at some of them. These studies can also yield valuable information, but in interpreting them, we need to bear in mind that subjects in some countries are being asked to respond to stimuli presented to them in a way which they may find difficult to comprehend.

McArthur and Baron (1983) formulated an 'ecological' theory of person perception. This proposes that the qualities of a person vary in their 'affordances' to us: that is to say, how useful they are in guiding our own future actions to achieve desired outcomes. The qualities having the most desirable affordances may well vary from one cultural group to another, depending upon what are the more crucial outcomes within one's culture. Bond and Forgas (1984) tested one aspect of the theory by comparing Australians and Hong Kong Chinese. They reasoned that, since Hong Kong has a more collectivist culture than Australia, Chinese subjects would be more affected by receiving information about the agreeableness and conscientiousness of another person. The information received would give them guidance as to whether they could relate harmoniously to the other person, whereas the Australians would see this as less essential information. As predicted, the Chinese responded by being more willing to associate with the agreeable person and more willing to trust their resources to a conscientious person than were the Australians.

Research in the Soviet Union by Andreeva (1982) is also relevant to this theme. She reasoned that the way in which we choose to describe others will be a function of what she calls the 'level of common activity'. By this she means the degree to which a group has developed an interdependent social structure. Members of more interdependent groups were found to attribute more traits to one another, and these traits were more focused upon collaborative behaviours.

The impact of physical appearances

Comparative studies between Korea and the USA have shown that information concerning *physical* qualities of stimulus persons may convey similar affordances in both cultures (McArthur and Berry, 1987; Montepare and Zebrowitz McArthur, 1987). In both countries, very similar reactions were found to various qualities of relatively baby-shaped adult faces: for example, large eyes, smooth skin and round head. Similarly, in both countries, a babyish voice was rated as weak, incompetent and warm.

Keating (1985) asked judges in 11 countries to say which of a series of paired photographs was the more dominant. There was good consensus that the more dominant persons had broad chins, thin lips and receding hairlines. These studies have something in common with Ekman's cross-cultural studies of emotional expression, discussed in Chapter 3, except that there is some degree of choice about whether or not we express emotion, whereas the affordances provided by physique are less voluntary. McArthur and Baron's theory has thus been well supported in non-American studies.

Attributing success and failure

In addition to studying perceptions of oneself and of others, cognitive social psychologists have also been very interested in the explanations we put forward when we do better or worse than others on some task. Nisbett and Ross (1980) identified a 'self-serving bias' whereby subjects in experiments are often found to attribute successes to their own skills and abilities, but are more inclined to explain failures in terms of contextual factors. The studies we have discussed in earlier sections of this chapter strongly suggest that we need to consider whether these effects will be found only in individualist cultural groups.

In evaluating the 'self-serving bias' hypothesis, we must bear in mind the findings of cross-cultural studies on the self-concept. As Cousins (1989) reported, the Japanese describe themselves dispositionally only when the situation is clearly specified, while Americans do so when it is not. Since respondents in other collectivist cultures frequently also refer to social context in describing themselves, it is likely that if Cousins' study were to be repeated there, a similar effect would be found. How then might we expect interdependent subjects to account for their successes and failures? The research design typically employed in this type of study presents subjects with a series of *specific* tasks upon which they do well or do not do well. This would lead us to expect that interdependent subjects would account for their successes and failures in terms of personal attributes at least as much as do independent subjects.

In search of the self-serving bias

Kashima and Triandis (1986) compared explanations given by Japanese and American students, all of them studying in America, for their successes and failures. A free-response format was first employed, to ensure that types of explanation not found among western samples were not overlooked. It was found that the free-response categories elicited were in fact readily classifiiable into the four categories originally distinguished by Heider (1958): namely, ability, effort, task difficulty and luck. Kashima and Triandis' experimental task required subjects to remember details of slides they were shown of scenes in unfamiliar countries. The task was a difficult one, and subjects from both countries tended to explain successes in terms of situational factors such as luck or familiarity, and failures in

Source: Reproduced with permission from Feign (1986).

Figure 6.2 A becoming modesty?

terms of task difficulty. As the self-serving hypothesis would predict, the American subjects explained their successes more in terms of ability than they did their failures. However, the Japanese subjects showed the reverse pattern – they attributed their failures to lack of ability, a 'self-effacement bias'. Overall, there was no difference in the frequency with which ability constructs were used to explain performance, but they were clearly used in a very different way.

These studies illustrate the need for us to distinguish between two issues. First, we need to look at how often interdependent subjects use dispositional trait terms to explain their performance. Second, we need to look at whether they use dispositional traits in the same manner as the self-serving bias hypothesis proposes. There is rather general evidence that terms classifiable as effort and ability are widely used by subjects to account for success and failure. For instance, Munro (1979) compared white Zimbabweans, black Zimbabweans and black Zambians. For all three groups the most frequently endorsed explanations were 'actions', 'personal' and 'chance', which are presumably similar to effort, ability and luck, respectively. Separate means are not presented for success and failure.

Boski (1983) compared responses of students belonging to the three main tribal groups in Nigeria, Igbo, Yoruba and Hausa. He found effort and abil ity frequently used to explain success and contextual factors more endorsed as reasons for failure. Within these overall effects, he predicted that each cultural group would show a different pattern, based upon prevailing cultural values within that group. In particular, Igbos are believed more frequently to endorse independent values, whereas the Islamic and more traditional Hausa are thought to hold more inter-dependent values. Boski did indeed find that his Hausa subjects explained their success significantly less than did Ibos in terms of ability and more in terms of contextual factors such as the nature of the task and luck. Few differences were found in explanations for failures. Similarly, Fry and Ghosh (1980) compared the attributions for success and failure of matched samples of white Canadian and Asian Indian Canadian children aged between eight and ten. The white children showed the usual pattern of self-serving attributions, rating effort and ability higher for success, and contextual factors such as luck and an unfair experimenter higher for failure. In contrast, the Indian Asian children saw luck as more important in their successes and ability as more important in their failures.

Limitations of the modesty bias

Each of the four studies reviewed above included samples likely to score relatively high on interdependence, and each found that, after working on an experimental task, there was little evidence of self-serving attributional bias among interdependent subjects. This conclusion appears to be con tradicted by the results of one further study, that by Chandler, Shama, Wolf and Planchard (1981), who asked students in the USA, Japan, India, South Africa and Yugoslavia to complete a structured questionnaire asking questions about the reasons for academic successes and failures. They found that in all countries except Japan subjects did rate themselves as more personally responsible for their successes than for their failures, although the effect was stronger in some countries than others.

In order to reconcile the findings of Chandler *et al.* with the other cross-cultural studies of success and failure, we can consider the different procedures which they employed. Chandler *et al.* used a questionnaire containing items which are relatively context-free. An example from the scale they used is: 'I feel that my good grades reflect directly on my academic ability'. In the other studies, experimenters contrived that their subjects did in fact succeed (or fail) on a specific task immediately before they filled out their ratings. As we saw earlier in the chapter, members of collectivist cultures often find it difficult to describe themselves or others unless they are able to specify the context. It is clear that the experimental studies do provide a specific setting and a particular person (the experimenter) who is asking for explanations of behaviour. The expla-nations given are more likely to be emically valid representations of how subjects wished to account for their behaviour to the experimenter. The Chandler *et al.* measure, on the other hand, is an imposed-etic measure, which at least in the more collectivist countries sampled is likely to have evoked what might have been thought to be an ideal student's self-perception and self-presentation. Even despite these limitations, it is notable that Chandler *et al.* found no self-serving bias in Japan. Another study using imposed-etic measures, Watkins and Regmi (1990), also found no self-serving bias among Nepalese students, when they were asked to make ratings accounting for the actual grades they had obtained.

Several studies with Chinese subjects support the view that valid tests for self-serving bias are those which specify the context. Wan and Bond (1982) found that the attributions for success and failure made by Hong Kong Chinese varied, depending upon the circumstances under which they were asked to provide their explanations. Where explanations were made to a specific, known experimenter, a reversal of the self-serving bias was again found. Where the explanations were provided in a more context-free anonymous questionnaire, the effect disappeared. Consistent with this pattern of attribution, the students who gave modest or self-effacing rather than self-serving attributions proved to be those who were better liked by their peers (Bond, Leung and Wan, 1982b). Not surprisingly, then, Stipek, Weiner and Li (1989) found that their Chinese subjects were much less likely to express pride in success than were American subjects.

It should come again as no surprise to us that the attributions provided by those with interdependent values depend upon whom they are addressing. It is, of course, central to interdependent values that someone who endorses those values will adjust their words and actions to what is appropriate in relation to specific others. A recent study by Mizokawa and Ryckman (1990) illustrates another aspect of the ways in which such adaptations may be made. They administered a questionnaire to Asian American children in the United States, comparing those from varying ethnic origins. The 40-item questionnaire asked for ratings of success and failure in specific academic subjects. They too found evidence for modesty effects as well as self-serving biases, but the effects varied between one cultural group and another. South-east Asians, for instance, showed a modesty effect for ability ratings, but a self-serving bias for effort ratings, whereas the Japanese American children showed the reverse pattern.

Thus we should not assume that a modesty bias will obtain uniformly across all the domains within which members of collectivist groups account for their actions. Indeed, it is probably also the case that the manner in which 'effort' and 'ability' are conceptualized itself varies by culture. A series of studies in India has shown that, where Indians are asked to predict the performance of someone of known ability and motivation, their predictions are arrived at *additively* (Singh, 1981). That is to say, they expect performance to depend simply on the level of ability and on the amount of effort. This contrasts with the predictions originally formulated by

Heider (1958) and supported by studies in the USA, which see performance as a function of ability *multiplied* by effort. The Heider model implies that a good level of both motivation and effort are required if performance is to be high. The Indian results indicate that at least in Singh's (1981) samples, which were extensive, it was believed that sufficient effort can compensate for lack of ability. One could speculate that this belief is more likely to be true in collectivist cultural groups, since if one member contributes ability and another effort, group performance could be high. Displays of effort are also important strategies for conveying group loyalty and commitment to one's group in collectivist cultures. A 'cult of effort' is often found in such settings.

Comparing oneself and others

The way in which we compare our attitudes and behaviours with those of other people has long been given a central role in social psychology. However, the reasons for comparing oneself with others may differ, depending upon whether one endorses independent or interdependent values. In an individualist cultural group, social comparison could provide feedback as to one's personal qualities and abilities, and hence reinforce or undermine one's sense of self. In a collectivist cultural group, social comparison can take on different meanings depending on the target of one's comparisons. In relation to other members of one's own group, social comparison will provide guidelines enabling the group member to sense what is the group consensus and to detect possible dangers of future disagreement. In relation to strangers or members of other known groups, social comparison is likely either to emphasize differences, enhancing one's group prestige or else not to occur at all.

Takata (1987) asked Japanese students to solve anagram problems. They were then asked to compare their performance with that of another subject, supposedly picked at random, who had done better or worse. Where they had done worse than others, the Japanese expressed more confidence that the estimate of their ability was accurate, whereas when they had done better they were more doubtful. A 'self-effacing' bias was thus again found. Takata then asked subjects whether they would like to seek further information. Those who had received low estimates of their abilities were less interested in obtaining more information, presumably because they were content with the evaluation they had received.

These findings contrast with the positive value placed on assertiveness and self-confidence in more individualist cultures. Markus and Kitayama (in press) made a direct comparison between Japanese and American students. Subjects were asked to estimate what proportion of students in their university would score higher than them on various traits and abilities, such as athletic ability, sympathy, intellectual ability, memory and so forth. On average, the Americans estimated that only 30 per cent would be above them, whereas the Japanese estimates were close to the (presumably correct) 50 per cent mark.

Reasons for valuing achievement

The achievement motive has often been thought of as a fundamental human need (McClelland, 1961). While it may well be the case that both those with independent and interdependent values do compare their achievements with those of others, their motives for doing so are not likely to be identical. Church and Katigbak (1992) asked college students in the USA and the Philippines to make ratings as to their motivations for doing well in their academic work. The American students ranked achievement and getting good grades higher than the Filipinos did. The Filipinos endorsed interdependent goals more often, particularly preparing to get a good job, and gaining the approval of others. In a similar way, Yang (1986) proposes that in order to understand the Chinese orientation towards achievement we must distinguish between achievement defined in an independent and an interdependent manner.

The studies examined in this brief section all concern east Asian orientations towards achievement. Although numerous other studies of achievement motivation have been conducted from other parts of the world, these studies used an imposed-etic format, which does not permit an analysis of why members of particular cultures do or do not favour achievement. The findings of the studies which we have examined are relatively clear, but we must be careful not to draw conclusions about collectivist cultures in general from such a restricted range of examples. Further studies from additional cultural groups are required before it would be wise to assert that the modesty found in these studies is part and parcel of collectivist cultures in general. We shall discuss in the next chapter some examples from the Arab world and elsewhere of communication styles in which exaggeration rather than modesty is positively valued.

Progress review

In this chapter we have commenced the task laid out at the end of Chapter 4. In reviewing studies in the area of social cognition we have focused upon some of the research fields currently attracting greatest interest in social psychology. Our task has been to see how far the individualism/ collectivism concept helps us to tease out a clear strand among results obtained from different parts of the world. Since most studies of social cognition are based upon studies of individuals rather than whole cultures, we have for the most part used the concepts of independence and interdependence to analyze the findings.

We have found substantial evidence that studies undertaken in more collectivist cultures do yield rather different results. Subjects in these parts of the world perceive themselves and others in more situational terms, demarcate themselves from others less sharply, and less often make self-serving attributions for success and failure. However, in hardly any of the studies which we have cited was any measure of the subject's independent or interdependent values actually taken. Con sequently, explanations of why these differences are found can only be speculative.

The theories of social cognition which are most strongly supported in current work in the United States rest upon models of the individual's information processing (Markus and Zajonc, 1985; Sampson, 1985). It would be consistent with such models to propose that the differences surveyed in this chapter could be explained by postulating that those with independent and interdependent values are socialized to *direct their attention in somewhat different ways.* An independent person would seek to identify the active element in any situation and to discern its effect on other elements, in something like the manner clearly laid out in Kelley's (1967, 1973) formulations of attribution theory. Rather than do this, an inter dependent person would attend to the configuration of elements in any situation, and infer causation by looking at what most often goes with what. The British philosopher John Stuart Mill (1872/1973) already identified these two alternative procedures for determining causation, which he termed the 'method of difference' and the 'method of asso ciation'. Most likely all of us can and do infer causation in both ways on occasion. All that is required to explain the differences found between cultural groups is to postulate that each of us does it more often one way than the other.

This type of explanation for the differences found has considerable plausibility. It could readily explain, for instance, why Singh found in India that subjects' estimate of performance was based upon ability *plus* effort, whereas American results show performance as based on ability *times* effort. It could also explain the differing results obtained in Witkin *et al.*'s (1962) Embedded Figures Test, which we considered at the start of this chapter.

However, reducing cultural differences in social cognition to an analysis of differences in where individuals direct their attention would be a serious oversimplification. As we saw in Chapter 3, a culture is a system of *shared* meanings. This implies that any differences there may be in how we as individuals direct our attention, or behave in other distinctive ways, are not just a matter of something which we as individuals happen to do. They occur because we grow up in particular groups, which teach us how to construe the world.

A model of social cognition which sees the optimal level of analysis as being at the level of individual choices about the direction of attention and the processing of information is likely to command more interest in individualist cultures than elsewhere and to be of greatest value in studying the behaviour of individuals. In the next two chapters we return to the key question of the individual's relation to other group members.

SEVEN

The individual and the group: pathways to harmony

One drop of indigo spoils the bucket of milk.
(Malay proverb)

If a nail sticks up, hammer it down.
(Japanese proverb)

One bad fish spoils the whole basket.
(Thai proverb)

If one finger is sore, the whole hand will hurt.
(Chinese proverb)

In Chapters 5 and 6 we have seen that there is substantial evidence that an individual's sense of identity is rooted in the groups to which he or she belongs. Furthermore, one's group membership will profoundly affect not only the different types of cognition which we have already considered in the preceding chapter, but also how one behaves towards others. In order to gain a clear picture of how these effects will occur we need to think again about the nature of group membership in individualist and collectivist cultures.

The nature of group membership

As we learned in Chapter 3, in individualist societies many of one's group memberships are a matter of personal choice. Where one works, whether one is religious, whether one is involved in political groups and so forth are all based upon overt decision, and in many cases the decision is potentially reversible. Even in the case of that group over which there is no choice at all – one's family of origin – there are wide variations in

119

individualist cultures in the degree to which family members retain contact with one another.

In collectivist societies, on the other hand, one's group memberships are much less negotiable. In many cultures, the single fact of what is one's family of origin will be sufficient to specify many of the roles one will be required to take in life. Mr Chan's obligations to his family were one of many things which stood in the way of his meeting Mrs Robertson's requirements as a satisfactory student. In other collectivist cultures – for instance, Japan – one's work organization will be the crucial group membership, at least in the case of men. The status of the firm which is willing to hire a Japanese man will be determined by the status of the university from which he graduates, and this in turn will be determined by success in examinations at high school and in turn primary school. The scope for changing one's direction in life once that direction has been set is rather narrow.

Social mobility and social change

Group membership in collectivist societies is thus more fixed. In terms of Tajfel's (1981) theory of intergroup relations, which we reviewed in Chapter 5, the options open to members of a group who are not satisfied with their lot are either social creativity, social mobility or social change. Social mobility, as defined by Tajfel, is an individualist solution, whereby the individual leaves the unsatisfactory group and goes to another. More collectivist solutions are social creativity, whereby group members collectively re-evaluate the group in their own view, and social change, where they succeed in getting out-group members also to evaluate them more highly.

An example of the contrast between social mobility and social change would be provided by the case of an industrial manager whose firm was facing hard times. In an individualist culture, such as the USA, he or she might choose the social mobility option by seeking out attractive offers to go and work for another organization. In a more collectivist culture, such as Japan, the manager would be much more likely to struggle with others to rescue the fortunes of the company. However, we must take care to avoid the assumption that individualist solutions are always chosen in individualist societies. For example, blacks in the United States have achieved some social change in the status of blacks in that country through collective actions. In a similar way, social mobility in a collectivist society is not totally ruled out, if an individual can find ways of escaping from existing group affiliations, perhaps through migration, illness or some other form of social discontinuity.

This simple difference between whether or not it is easy to leave a group can have profound effects on all aspects of group behaviour. Members of a group who know that they are indissolubly linked have a strong interest in preserving harmony within their group, as the proverbs at the head of this chapter suggested. In this chapter we shall review studies which show how interdependent persons go about achieving this state. We shall find that in collectivist societies interpersonal conflict is regulated in different ways to that found in individualist societies. This regulation finds expression in more equal allocations of resources among peers, more overt co-operation, a different perspective on intimate relationships, and a preference for non-adversarial negotiation procedures within the in-group. Where members of collectivist groups are dealing with out-groups, the search for harmony is a good deal less evident. We shall look at each of these areas in turn.

Distributive justice

In this section we are concerned with what is regarded as a fair distribution of scarce resources within particular cultural groups. We considered already in Chapter 5 the studies which show how an individual's self-concept may be linked to the manner in which one distributes resources between oneself or one's own group and others in out-groups. Here we focus instead on how a reward is distributed among one's own group members or to those outside it.

The equity theory developed by Adams (1965) in the USA proposes that we will favour an allocation of rewards which reflects the 'inputs' and 'outputs' of different group members. In other words, the theory has a clear individualist emphasis in that it implies that rewards will be differentially allocated among different group members on the basis of their distinguishable inputs. While there has been substantial debate about the validity of equity theory as formulated by Adams, it continues to command substantial support within US studies. It appears that, while Americans do favour reward allocation on the basis of equity, there are a variety of circumstances under which they would see an allocation based on equality as being fairer. For example, Elliott and Meeker (1984) studied supervisors in the USA, who were asked to allocate rewards among five members of an imaginary work team who were likely to continue working together. Under these circumstances, more than 60 per cent of allocations were based on exact equality rather than equity.

The emphasis upon harmony within collectivist cultural groups would lead one to expect that fairness would more frequently be judged on the basis of equality. However, we also have to remember that, within collectivist cultures, members are more permanently committed to their membership groups. It is therefore important to maintain the distinction between how those with interdependent values would distribute rewards within their membership groups and how they would distribute them to strangers or outsiders.

In-group preferences

In order to study reward allocation within one's group, Leung and Bond (1982) asked students in Hong Kong and the United States to consider how grades should be assigned in hypothetical groups of students taking a course. Although students in both countries favoured a group member who had made competent task contributions, the Chinese distributed their grades around the group more equally than the Americans did. In a further study, Bond, Leung and Wan (1982a) found the same effect both for task contributions and for contributions towards maintaining group harmony. Kim, Park and Suzuki (1990) replicated this study, using students in the USA, Japan and Korea. They found that equity was important in all three countries, but less so in Korea, the more collectivist country.

These three studies leave it unclear whether or not subjects perceived the group within which they were distributing grades as their own group or not. In a third study, Leung and Bond (1984) used two scenarios, in one of which it was made clear that it was one's own group and in the other that it was another group. They found that with the in-group the Chinese shared the rewards more equally through the group, but with the out-group the Chinese adhered to the equity norm more closely than did the Americans. In collectivist cultures, crossing group boundaries appears to switch the allocation rule in force.

Two studies have examined the in-group allocation of bonuses or pay cuts in India and the USA (Murphy-Berman, Berman, Singh, Pachauri and Kumar, 1984; Berman, Murphy-Berman and Singh, 1985). In this case three criteria for allocation were compared: equity, equality and need. We might expect that, as with equality, allocation within the in-group according to need would be used more in collectivist settings, in order to promote the welfare of in-group members. Presumably need as a criterion could be expected to outweigh equality, the greater the inequalities existing within the group. In both studies the Indians were found to be more likely to allocate higher bonuses and lower pay cuts to those most in need than were the Americans. The effect was stronger for the allocation of bonuses. Thus the findings show that in both countries the effects of need may to some extent outweigh a preference for equity or equality, but that the effect is stronger in the more collectivist country.

Leung and Park (1986) consider the possibility that what one considers fair will depend upon one's goals in belonging to a group. If one's prime motive is to get on with the task, then equity would seem to provide the fairest basis for reward. If the preservation of group harmony is more important, then equality becomes a more attractive criterion. Comparing Korean and American subjects, they found that allocations were indeed influenced by goal orientation in both countries. Nonetheless, overall the Koreans favoured equality more than did the Americans. Kashima *et al.* (1988) reported a stronger preference for equality than equity among Japanese than among Australians who were asked to evaluate the fairness of bonus payments at work.

In a study of 12-year-old Japanese and Australian schoolchildren, Mann, Radford and Kanagawa (1985) examined preferences as to who should do the allocating of rewards in the group. As we might expect, the Japanese favoured sharing the task around equally, whereas the Australians preferred giving the power to allocate differential rewards to a subgroup.

The impressive consistency of these studies is balanced by Marin (1985), who failed to find any difference in allocation preferences between Indonesian students in America and Americans. However, the Indonesians had been in the USA for nearly two years. More surprisingly, Leung and Iwawaki (1988) failed to find any differences in in-group allocations among Japanese, Korean and American students. In this case the authors had also collected data on the preference for independent or interdependent values of the Japanese and American students within their sample. They were surprised to find that their Japanese sample scored no higher than the Americans on interdependence, and suggest that this may account for the failure to find national differences in allocation preference. Consistent with the argument about collectivism, however, they did find that in these countries, the students who favoured interdependent values were those whose allocation preferences were more towards equality. A further test of the link between interdependent values and preference for equality is provided by Hui, Triandis and Yee (1991). They found that Hong Kong students shared rewards for work done more equally than did American students, and that this difference was accounted for by the levels of interdependent values which they had endorsed on an individualism–collectivism questionnaire.

The comparisons between Asian countries and the USA thus make it clear that equality is relied upon more frequently in more collectivist countries in the case of in-group reward allocation. As one might expect, the differences are not so marked in comparisons between the USA and western European countries, many of which also score quite highly on individualism. In a complex study, Pepitone *et al.* (1967) studied reward distribution by American, French and Italian students playing an experimental game. The US and French students allocated rewards on the basis of equity, taking more for themselves when they were led to believe that their ability was high. The behaviour of the Italians was less clear, possibly because there is said to be much higher collectivism in southern Italy than in the north. A further study by Pepitone *et al.* (1970) showed that the Italians did favour equality to a greater extent, reducing their allocations to themselves when they had already been given a monetary reward before the experiment started. In these studies and in others comparing the Americans with Austrians (Mikula, 1974) and Germans (Kahn, Lamm and Nelson, 1977), it appears that situational factors may have been more important than cultural factors in determining preferences for equity or equality.

Out-group preferences

If we turn now to the fair allocation of rewards to those outside of one's own group, we find a series of studies supporting the view that collectivists do not extend the same principles to them. Aral and Sunar (1977) found that Turkish students favoured the equity norm more than Americans in dividing rewards between two architects. Mahler, Greenberg and Hayashi (1981) asked students in Japan and America how rewards should be divided in a set of stories describing two workers. They found no difference where the story presented implied that the two workers were not strongly connected, but in one of the stories where the two workers did the same work the Japanese favoured equality more strongly. Marin (1981) compared Colombians and Americans and found that the Colombians favoured equity more strongly in allocating rewards to subjects in a psychological experiment. We have mentioned already the study by Leung and Bond (1984), which found that, when dealing with an out-group, Hong Kong Chinese were closer to the equity norm than were Americans.

The studies of distributive justice do thus yield a rather clear picture. In more collectivist countries there is greater reliance on the criteria of equality and need *within* the in-group, but greater use of the equity criterion *outside* the group. This conclusion rests on the assumption that most people within a country labelled as 'collectivist' will themselves hold more interdependent values. In one of the two studies so far reported in which measures of subjects' values were obtained this proved not to be the case, but in both of these studies subjects' values did actually accord with their behaviour. This variability of values within countries should help us to understand why occasional studies have been reported in which differences between countries do not fit the overall pattern. We shall return to the question of relations between groups later, but for the moment we must look further at the dynamics occurring within groups.

Co-operation and competition

In a sense, the whole of this chapter thus far has been concerned with whether or not groups in collective cultures have more co-operative relationships with one another. In this section we shall examine a series of cross-cultural studies which have adopted a particular operational definition of co-operation which is embedded within various tightly structured experimental games. Each of these games provides the subject with a finite series of options, which the experimenter labels as 'co-operative' or 'competitive'. In the light of what was said earlier (in Chapter 3), we need to scrutinize these studies closely to see whether the way the experimenter defines what is going on is also the way that the experimental subject perceives the situation. The danger is one of imposed-etic research: that is to say, research which takes a concept or procedure from one culture and uses it in other cultures without allowing any possibility of examining it to see what meaning it is actually being given within those other cultures. This is, of course, a danger with many of the studies discussed in this book, but it is particularly acute with the studies now to be reviewed, because they are so tightly structured, and because many of them involve subjects in playing games within which they neither speak to one another nor provide the experimenter with any direct explanation of how they experience what is happening.

Of the experimental games which became popular in the study of cooperation and competition in the United States, the most widely used was certainly the Prisoner's Dilemma game. This involves two players making one or more simultaneous choices. Depending upon how the players' choices are co-ordinated, both may benefit, one may prosper at the expense of the other, or both may lose out. A typical payoff matrix is shown in Table 7.1. Each player has the choice to co-operate (C) or to defect (D). The

Table 7.1 Typical gaming matrices

		Game 1 Prisoner's dilemma matrix		Game 2 Maximizing differences matrix	
		Player 2		Player 2	
		Choice C	Choice D	Choice C	Choice D
Player 1	Choice C	3\3	1\4	3\3	1\3
	Choice D	4\1	2\2	3\1	1\1

Note: The first figure in each cell gives Player 1's payoff and the second figure gives Player 2's payoff.

numbers in the table represent the money or other rewards which each party will receive when decisions have been made. Thus if both players choose C, both receive a reward of 3. But if Player 1 chooses C while Player 2 chooses D, then Player 1 receives only 1 and Player 2 gets 4. Each party can therefore prosper at the expense of the other if they can induce the other to make 'co-operative' choices while they themselves defect. Of course, if both players defect then both do less well than if they had both co-operated. The closely related Maximizing Differences game, which makes it easier to see whether it appears that a subject is trying to maximize winnings or to outdistance the other player, is also illustrated in the table.

McClintock and McNeel (1966) and McNeel, McClintock and Nuttin (1972) compared the performance of American and Flemish Belgian students on the Maximizing Differences game. They reported that the Belgians were much more competitive. However, Faucheux (1976), who is French, published an extensive critique of what he saw as the pro-American bias of the data analysis. He pointed out that the Belgians had behaved more competitively only when they were losing, whereas the Americans had been competitive when they were winning. His interpretation of the data was thus that the Americans were more truly competitive, whereas the Belgians were trying to utilize the structure of the game in a manner which preserved the equality of the participants.

A same type of ambiguity in interpretation emerged from a series of studies by Marwell and his colleagues. Marwell and Schmitt (1972) found Norwegians much more competitive than Americans when they were faced by a risk of exploitation. However, Marwell, Schmitt and Boyesen (1973) found that, where the risk of exploitation was eliminated, the Norwegians became much more co-operative than the Americans. Through these studies we are introduced to the notion that a supposedly objective record of co-operative and competitive behaviour by this or that cultural group is in fact open to alternative interpretations upon closer inspection.

A similar study by Carment (1974) found 35 per cent competitive responses among Canadian students as against 55 per cent among Indian students. The implication that Indians are more competitive than Canadians was contradicted by Alcock (1974), who found Canadians more competitive than Indians when time pressure was introduced into a different game. In a further study, Alcock (1975) found that where Indians felt that they were in a strong position they became more competitive, whereas under these conditions Canadians became less competitive. These studies suggest that, rather than labelling this or that nation as more or less competitive, it is better to look at what situations evoke competitive behaviour from each national sample.

A final study in this series, by Carment and Alcock (1984) strengthens this viewpoint. In a Maximizing Differences game, Indians were again found more competitive than Canadians. However, when the gaming matrix was modified to make much higher winnings available to one player than to the other, a complex series of effects was found. Canadians became more competitive: that is to say, the player who could receive the extra winnings was inclined to take them, while the disadvantaged player sought to prevent this outcome. Among the Indians, the reverse pattern appeared: the advantaged player was likely to avoid the extra winnings, while the disadvantaged player tried to make sure that the advantaged player did receive the bonus. One way of interpreting this would be to say that the Canadians perceived the situation as becoming more competitive, whereas the Indians acted as they might in a hierarchical situation, with subordinates showing deference and superiors showing magnanimity.

In another study also involving Indians, L'Armand and Pepitone (1975) found that American students were willing to reward a stranger when it cost them little, but not when it reduced their own rewards. For Indian students this made little difference: they were not willing to give much reward in either condition. Some clarification as to why this may have been so is provided by the study by Pandey (1979), which showed that the willingness of Indians to give to others is heavily dependent upon the status of the groups to which both the donor and the recipient belong. In L'Armand and Pepitone's experiment, the stranger to receive the rewards was visible to subjects but they could not speak to him. However, they would have been able to see that he was a high-status Brahmin. Further analyses by L'Armand and Pepitone showed that those among the Indian subjects who were also Brahmins were more willing to reward the stranger than were the non-Brahmin subjects.

The last two studies reviewed show how experiments which have a relatively clear structure in an individualist culture such as the USA or Canada yield puzzling findings when they fail to take account of the collectivist basis upon which Indians might decide how to allocate rewards in the experimental procedure.

Putting competitiveness into context

The experiments reviewed so far in this section have all involved comparisons of the co-operativeness or competitiveness of North Americans with others. Table 7.2 summarizes some consistencies in what was found. In each case the investigators, who were all North Americans, found the 'foreign' group to be more competitive. In five of the six studies they then went on to amend the circumstances of the experiment in some way, and found that, while the competitiveness of the foreign group declined, that of the North American group rose. This way of looking at the results fits in well with the proposition that the experimental subjects from outside of

Table 7.2 Gaming studies comparing North Americans and others

Study	Overall effect	Effect of changed context
McClintock and McNeel (1966)	Belgians compete more	Belgians compete less[*] Americans compete more[*]
Carment (1974)	Indians compete more	———
Alcock (1974, 1975)	Equal	Indians compete less Canadians compete more
Carment and Alcock (1984)	Indians compete more	Indians redefine situation as superior–subordinate? Canadians compete more
Marwell et al. (1972, 1973)	Norwegians compete more	Norwegians compete least Americans compete less
Rapoport et al. (1971)	Danes compete more	Danes compete less Americans compete more

[*] In this case the experimenters did not make a change, but they provided subjects with feedback which enabled them to see how they were faring as the experiment proceeded, thus enabling subjects to adapt to the changing context.

North America are more 'context-sensitive' than the North Americans. Of course, the North Americans did respond to the changed circumstances as well, but usually to a lesser degree. We should expect subjects from more collectivist cultures to be more context-sensitive, but it is notable that three of these five studies were comparing Europeans with North Americans. Belgium, Denmark and Norway were ranked eighth, ninth and thirteenth on individualism by Hofstede (1980) compared to the USA and Canada at first and fourth. We might therefore expect larger differences in results from cultures which fall further towards the collectivist end of the spectrum, so long as we bear in mind that whether a member of a collectivist culture chooses to compete or co-operate will depend very much on who is the other party to the transaction.

This analysis provides a hypothesis with which we can now examine further studies from other parts of the world. Bethlehem (1975) proposed that westernization would increase competitiveness. He compared traditional and westernized members of the Tonga tribe in Zambia, as well as Asian students also resident in Zambia. As expected, he found that the traditional Tongans played a modified version of the Prisoner's Dilemma game in a much more co-operative manner than did the more westernized groups.

In another study conducted in Africa, Foley Meeker (1970) compared westernized and traditional members of the Kpelle tribe in Liberia. It is likely that the westernized Kpelle would have a more independent value orientation than the traditional Kpelle. When using a version of the Prisoner's Dilemma game, it was again found that the traditional players were much more co-operative. However, in this case Foley Meeker also used an adaptation of the Maximizing Differences game, and the results for this showed traditional and non-traditional players to be equally and highly competitive. Once again we find that, as a way of measuring cultural competitiveness, experimental games give confusing results. We do not know why Foley Meeker's subjects responded to the two games in a different manner. She suggests that in the Maximizing Differences game each subject receives a clear message from the other as to whether they are seeking to compete or co-operate, and both groups reciprocate competition with competition. However, in the Prisoner's Dilemma it is less easy to get a clear picture of what the other party is doing. In these circumstances, Foley Meeker suggests that westernized game players tend to compete, whereas traditional players decide to trust the other party.

An interestingly similar pattern of results was found in a study concerning ethnic groups within the United States by Cox, Lobel and McLeod (1991). Using a Prisoner's Dilemma design and student subjects, they found Anglo students more competitive than Hispanic, Black and Asian Americans. Furthermore, when given feedback that the other party was making co-operative choices, the Anglos became still more competitive, while the Hispanic, Black and Asian Americans became more co-operative.

Co-operation among children

A slightly different approach to the cross-cultural study of co-operation has been used by Madsen and his colleagues in their studies of children around the world. Madsen devised pieces of experimental apparatus upon each of which groups of two to four children work. They are required to steer a ball, guide a marble or open a box collaboratively by pulling on strings. If they co-ordinate their efforts the tasks are fairly simple, but if they compete they rapidly become impossible. The world-wide series of studies by Madsen and others using his experimental methods have shown that, in many countries where group rewards are offered, co-operation becomes established. However, when individual rewards are offered, the children find it much less easy to co-operate. Table 7.3 summarizes what has been found to occur under these circumstances. It is clear from the table that rural children are more co-operative than urban children. However, the only differences between countries apparent from direct comparisons in this series of studies – those between Mexico and the USA – could equally well be explained as due to urban–rural differences, since Madsen's studies compared children from Los Angeles with those from a small town in Baja California.

A study by Kagan, Knight and Martinez Romero (1982) also found rural Mexican children more co-operative than Americans or Mexican

Table 7.3 Results of studies using the Madsen apparatus

Study	Location	Results
Sommerlad and Bellingham (1972)	Australia	Aboriginals more co-operative
Thomas (1975)	New Zealand	Polynesians and rural Maoris more co-operative than urban Maoris or whites
Munroe and Munroe (1977)	USA, Kenya	Kikuyus more co-operative
Miller and Thomas (1972)	Canada	Blackfoot Indians more co-operative than whites
Shapira (1976)	Israel	Kibbutz more co-operative than urban
Shapira and Madsen (1969)	USA, Israel	Urban children, no difference
Shapira and Lomranz (1972)	Israel	Arabs less co-operative than Jewish kibbutz, more than Jewish urban
Madsen and Yi (1975)	Korea	Rural more than urban
Madsen (1971)	USA, Mexico	Mexicans more co-operative
Madsen (1967)	Mexico	Rural more co-operative than urban
Madsen and Shapira (1970)	USA, Mexico	Mexicans more co-operative
Kagan and Madsen (1972)	USA, Mexico	Mexicans more co-operative
Madsen and Lancy (1981)	Papua New Guinea	Rural more co-operative
Marin et al. (1975)	Colombia	Rural more co-operative
Hullos (1980)	Hungary	Rural more co-operative

Americans. However, in this case an interview method was used, with children being asked what they would do if a toy were taken from them, or if they were hit by another child. The study therefore confirms the previous finding by showing that the same differences in level of co-operativeness can be obtained by a quite different research method.

Strube (1981) subjected all available studies of children's competitiveness to the statistical technique of meta-analysis, in order to determine how uniform were any gender differences that had been reported. He concludes that boys are more competitive in Anglo-American and Indian cultures, while there is a trend in the opposite direction in Israel. As we found in Chapter 4, gender differences may well vary by culture.

The differences found between boys and girls and between urban and rural populations leave us with the question of whether this series of studies has also detected any differences between samples which could be confidently attributed to the effects of different cultures. Table 7.4 shows the results of four studies, which all used the marble-pull apparatus with urban children aged between 9 and 11, before they had been given any explicit coaching on ways of using the apparatus to co-operate. It is evident that the American children were rather more unco-operative than those in

Table 7.4 Co-operative behaviour in the Madsen marble-pull apparatus

Study	Country	Average number of co-operative trials
Madsen (1971)	USA	0.20
Shapira (1976)	Israel	1.67
Madsen and Yi (1975)	Korea	1.44
Madsen and Lancy (1982)	Papua New Guinea	2.20

Note: All studies used 10 trials, except Shapira who used 12. The Israeli mean has been reduced to make it comparable with the others.

the other three countries, presumably because of their more independent orientation.

Co-operation and the identity of the partner

More recent research into aspects of co-operation and competition has taken greater account of the likelihood that your behaviour in experimental games will be a function not just of your values or cultural background, but also of your perception of your partner. Van Lange and Liebrand (1991) compared the willingness to contribute to a group bonus of students who were characterized as individualistic–competitive or as pro-social–altruistic. They found, both in Holland and in the USA, that when subjects were led to believe that the other player was intelligent, pro-social players became more co-operative, whereas individualists did not. Thus, even in two of the national cultures which Hofstede (1980) characterized as most individualist, we find some subjects whose behaviour assumes the inter-dependent pattern once they know they are relating to a co-operative partner.

A similar issue was addressed by Yamagishi and Sato (1986). They found that the willingness of Japanese students to make individual contributions to a group bonus depended both on whether the five-person experimental groups were composed of friends or strangers and on what were the rules as to how the bonus would be calculated. If the bonus was to be at the level of the lowest individual contribution or else at the level of the average contribution, friends contributed more than did strangers. If the bonus was to be at the level of the highest individual contribution, the behaviour of friends and strangers did not differ. Thus even in a collectivist culture, knowing that the other players were friends only enhanced co-operative behaviour when the rules of the game also enhanced interdependence.

These recent studies of co-operative behaviour emphasize, just as did the series of studies on children's co-operation, that interdependence is affected by many factors within cultures as well as by differences across cultures. What we now need are more studies which examine factors at both levels concurrently.

Negotiation

A good deal of the difficulty in understanding the findings of cross-cultural experiments concerning co-operation and conflict has arisen because the partner's identity has often not been clear to the subjects in the studies. In a collectivist society it is crucial to know this information if one is to behave in the appropriate manner. With studies of negotiation the situation is clearer. Negotiation is usually defined as a specific type of interaction which an individual or group has with groups known to be other than one's own, or with representatives of those groups. A further advantage is that, in studies of negotiation, the parties typically meet each other face to face. This means that their behaviour is more likely to be representative of everyday behaviour than that found where people can communicate only by the restricted means available in games such as the Prisoner's Dilemma.

Kelley *et al.* (1970) undertook an extensive study, comparing performance on a negotiating task in Holland, Belgium, France and five different sites in the USA. Few differences emerged in rates of agreement, but some more systematic measures were also included in this study as to how the game players perceived co-operative behaviour. It emerged that at Leuven (Belgium), Paris and Hanover, NH (USA), co-operative behaviour was rated high on an 'evaluative' dimension: that is, it was seen as good. At other sites in the USA, co-operative behaviour was perceived more in terms of 'dynamism': that is, as strong and active. In Holland, co-operative behaviour did not score high on either dimension. In a related study using similar measures in India, Misra and Kalro (1979) found that co-operative choices were rated high on the evaluative dimension.

One can only speculate as to how these findings might be interpretable in terms of the concepts which have become popular more recently. It is possible that, at those sites where negotiators saw co-operation as good, they were aiming towards a resolution based on equality, and that at those sites where co-operation was seen as dynamic, negotiators were thinking in a more assertive or even Machiavellian way about the tactical advantages of appearing to be co-operative.

Setting the goals of negotiation

More systematic attempts to understand negotiation in different cultures require that we refer once more to the concepts of individualism and collectivism. One would expect that, within individualist cultures, negotiators would see as the main priority that agreements are reached on the basis of the logical requirements of the tasks to be accomplished at the present time. In contrast, we could expect that, within collectivist cultures, negotiators would be particularly concerned about the continuing harmony of their relations with other parties. This would not necessarily mean that members of collectivist cultures would be any more generous to those with whom they are negotiating. We have seen already that those with interdependent values are just as likely as those with independent values to be competitive towards out-group members. However, we should expect interdependent subjects to prefer methods of negotiation which preserve the harmony of the relationship. For instance, they are likely to prefer mediation and indirect communications rather than overt argument or other adversarial procedures. Of course, negotiators in both types of culture would have some regard for both task criteria and the maintenance of the relationship: the difference would be a matter of relative emphasis.

Negotiating styles

Glenn *et al.* (1977) studied styles of international negotiation by analyzing transcripts of meetings of the Security Council of the United Nations. They propose that the excerpt shown in Box 7.1 illustrates the difference between what they call the 'factual' and the 'intuitive' styles of discourse. The factual style, used by the United States representatives, concentrates on what they perceive as the key issue and plays down the context of the alleged incident. The intuitive style, used by the Syrian representatives, addresses the broad context of US–Arab relations and resists US attempts to focus on specific detail. The difference in styles is consistent with what we might predict from the fact that interdependent values are likely to be more strongly espoused in Arab societies than in western societies. The exchange is a rather heated one, which is explained by the fact that it occurred at the time of the 1967 Arab–Israeli war. Similar differences of style are apparent during much more recent interchanges between representatives of Arab and western countries. Private negotiations may, of course, prove more fruitful than those conducted in the full glare of publicity, but even in private the differences of style are likely to persist.

Porat (1970) compared simulated union–management bargaining in five European countries. Both the management role and the union role were in fact played by managers who were attending training courses. Table 7.5 shows that the more adversarial targets were set by those from countries which Hofstede characterized as more individualist. However, all five countries represented score relatively high on individualism. Harnett and

Box 7.1   *Negotiating cross-culturally as a representative*

US ambassador: 'The representative of Syria made a statement in reference to a remark of mine. I will recall the circumstances of this remark. The remark was made in the context of a malicious and false accusation that United States aircraft from carriers had participated in the attack. And I said, with respect to that remark, that people ought to put up evidence that such an accusation was true. There has been no evidence offered. There can be no evidence offered of that, because there is no basis for that accusation. That accusation was a false and malicious and scandalous one. That is the remark I made, and I was impelled to make, because of the dangers of indicating to anybody involvement on the part of the United States, which has never been the case in this particular situation.'

Syrian ambassador: 'I would not reply to the distinguished representative of the United States were it not for some of the very words he used in reference to my statement, when he said, referring to a previous statement, that it was a false, malicious and scandalous accusation. I confirm categorically that the United States has helped Israel in its invasion of the United Arab Republic and Jordan and is to be held responsible for whatever destruction and killings have taken place in the United Arab Republic and Jordan, and are taking place right now in my own country, Syria. If anything is scandalous, it is the policy of the United States, which has been shameful for the last twenty years vis-à-vis the Arab world and vis-à-vis the Arab nations.'

US ambassador: 'Ambassador Tomeh's personal comments, which are in violation of every type of diplomatic usage, are beneath contempt, and I would not purport to dignify them with an answer. The remark to which I referred and which I said was utterly false and malicious was the remark that carrier planes from the Sixth Fleet had intervened in this conflict, and I challenge anybody, including the Ambassador, to bring evidence before the Council to this effect.'

Syrian ambassador: 'I shall ignore the venomous attack made personally against me by the representative of the United States. I would merely say this, that it is not enough to belong to a Great Power. The United States with one bomb can destroy the whole of Syria. But it is much greater and much stronger to belong to a great cultural and intellectual tradition. And this I am proud of.'

Reprinted with permission from Glenn *et al.*, 'Cultural styles of permission', *International Journal of International Relations*, vol. 1 © 1977 Pergamon Press Ltd.

Table 7.5 Adversarial target setting and individualism

Country	Percentage of negotiators setting adversarial goals	Hofstede ranking on individualism
United Kingdom	43.6	3
Sweden	33.3	10
Denmark	25.0	9
Switzerland	21.1	14
Spain	12.5	20

Source: Adapted from Poret (1970).

Cummings (1980) found that buyers from the USA, Finland, Spain, France and Belgium all used their bargaining power to extract maximum profit. However, buyers from more collectivist Thailand and Japan were more inclined to share the profit equally between buyer and seller, presumably because they expected that this would benefit longer-term relations with the seller.

Druckman, Benton, Ali and Bagur (1976) compared children playing a board game which involved the making of a series of bids to the other player, bids which could be accepted or rejected. Data were collected in the USA, India and Argentina. Individuals played the game, but each individual was said to be the member of a team and had to share the winnings in any way he or she chose afterwards with the non-playing member of the team. Under these conditions the Indians were found by Druckman *et al.* to be most competitive and the Americans most co-operative. The data also show that the Indians bargained longest and subsequently made the most unequal division of the spoils with their non-playing partner. These findings fit in with the view that relations with an out-group in collectivist cultures will be at least as competitive as those found in individualist societies. In some ways the most interesting aspect of this study is the uneven division of the spoils by the Indians. Since there was nothing in the structure of the game which required this inequality, one must presume that it does reflect a cultural difference from the Argentinian and American players. Druckman *et al.* also asked their subjects to complete questionnaires asking how sums of money should be distributed in various hypothetical situations. Their answers to these questions confirm that the Indians favoured more unequal distributions.

According to Hofstede, Argentine society is just as collectivist as Indian society. However, the Argentine children did show a rather different pattern of negotiation. One possible explanation for this discrepancy may lie in one of Hofstede's other dimensions of cultural variation: namely, power distance. India scores high on this dimension, whereas Argentina and the USA score a good deal lower. The Indian bargainers may have assumed that since they did all the bargaining their status was high, which

Box 7.2 *Negotiating cross-culturally on behalf of oneself*

The negotiation between Mrs Robertson and Mr Chan was clearly a failure. Mrs Robertson's negotiating position was based upon rigid adherence to an abstract principle which she considered logical: that failed exams must be retaken. Chan explored various bases for compromise, drawing on a wider range of circumstantial factors, such as his effort, his mother's illness, etc. He was also inventive in devising new means of reaching agreement, as illustrated by his proposal of a 'compassionate pass'. Each had a different idea as to the issues and as to the means by which the dispute should be resolved.

would entitle them to the lion's share of the winnings. Another contextual factor which Druckman *et al.* did not pursue was the ethnic and religious homogeneity of their different samples. Their Indian sample, from schools in Hyderabad, was 75 per cent Hindu and 25 per cent Muslim. The Argentines were 80 per cent Catholic and 20 per cent Jewish, but this may have been a less salient factor in determining whether the children, who were all from the same schools, opted to treat one another as in-group members or out-groups members. More information on mutual perceptions would help us to interpret the results of future studies.

Conflict resolution

Having considered some studies which focus primarily on the relative 'toughness' of negotiation styles, we turn now to look at the process by which agreement can be achieved. Lind *et al.* (1978) surveyed samples of students and found that adversarial ways of resolving legal conflicts are preferred in individualist countries such as France, Germany, Britain and America. Leung and Lind (1986) asked students in Hong Kong and the USA to evaluate which of several methods would be best in resolving various hypothetical conflict situations with which they were presented. The Chinese were more favourable towards an inquisitorial type of investigation: that is to say, the appointment of a senior figure such as a judge, who sifts the evidence and apportions blame. The Americans preferred the adversarial system, whereby separate accounts are put forward by prosecutors and defenders.

In a further study, Leung (1987) presented additional data designed to clarify why these different preferences were held. One needs to remember that both Hong Kong and the USA have British-style adversarial justice systems, so that in preferring the inquisitorial mode the Chinese respondents were actually rejecting the system already existing in their society. Leung found that the modes of conflict resolution favoured by his Chinese subjects were those which they thought most likely to reduce animosity. Although inquisitorial investigation was preferred over adversarial adjudication, more informal procedures such as mediation and bargaining were even more strongly preferred. These studies therefore favour the view that the preservation of harmony is a major goal in collectivist cultures such as Hong Kong. Indeed, Leung went on to show that those of his subjects who scored higher on a measure of inter-dependent values were those who saw mediation and bargaining as most likely to lead to the reduction of animosity.

A similar result was achieved by Trubisky, Ting-Toomey and Lin (1991), who compared the preferences of Taiwanese and American students as to how a conflict within a student group should be resolved. The Taiwanese students favoured the use of conflict resolution styles identified as 'obliging', 'avoiding', 'integrating' and 'compromising'. In the United States the use of these styles was lower, while preference for the style identified as 'dominating' varied, depending upon the personality of each individual American. Trubisky *et al.* point out that Hofstede identified the USA as strongly individualist and Taiwan as strongly collectivist, but found little difference between these two countries on his other three dimensions. They argue that the differences found must therefore be explained by the varying levels of collectivism of the two countries. The findings of both Leung and Trubisky *et al.* are consistent with Ting-Toomey's theory, to be discussed in Chapter 8, that in collectivist cultures the preservation of positive face is a high priority.

Extending the range of cultural explanations

Leung *et al.* (1990, 1991) took their sequence of studies one step further. They proposed that the conflict resolution procedures preferred in different national cultures will reflect not only differing levels of individualism and collectivism, but also some of the differences tapped by Hofstede's other dimensions. They therefore made a comparison between Canada and the Netherlands, since on Hofstede's measures these two countries are similar on three dimensions, but differ on cultural masculinity–femininity. They predicted and found that their student subjects believed more strongly that harmony would be best restored by mediation in the more 'feminine' culture (the Netherlands) than in Canada. The result is an interesting demonstration that behaviours in cultures identified as individualist do differ in ways which can be predicted by attending to other dimensions. The reason why more differences of this kind have not so far been detected by researchers could be that it has only recently become possible to use

Source: Reproduced with permission from Feign (1987).

Figure 7.1 Differing approaches to conflict resolution

theory in the way that Leung *et al.* did to suggest where to look for the differences.

Another recent study also found differences between Dutch and North American data which are broadly consistent with Leung *et al.*'s conclusions. Wubbels and Levy (1991) found that American teachers laid more emphasis on strictness, whereas Dutch teachers favoured greater student responsibility and freedom. We shall encounter a third study detecting differences between Holland and North America in the next section.

Intimate relationships

Theories about conflict and co-operation are tested nowhere more validly than in the field of intimate relationships. Marriages are, of course, contracted in numerous different ways in different cultures, and in many countries there is currently a decline in the occurrence of arranged marriages and an increase in 'love' marriages. If this change implies an increasing element of choice, then we could presume that the change might be related to the emergence of increasingly independent values. Cross-cultural studies in this field have not yet achieved a high level of sophistication, and have mostly relied upon simple comparisons of mean scores obtained by people in different countries.

Is romantic love a culture-bound concept?

The most frequently used measure has been the Love Attitude Scale of Munro and Adams (1978). This provides a measure of how strongly respondents endorse three dimensions identified as 'romantic power', 'romantic idealism' and 'conjugal love'. The romantic power items portray love as a powerful force affecting one's life and causing obstacles to fall away. The romantic idealism items assert that loving is the essence of life. The conjugal love items state that love should have a calming and sobering effect, which demands careful thought. The scale was developed in Canada, where the three dimensions were found to be reliably separable. High school and college students have completed the scale in the Caribbean (Payne and Vandewiele, 1987), Senegal (Vandewiele and Philbrick, 1983), Uganda (Philbrick and Opolot, 1980), the USA (Philbrick, 1987) and in numerous populations of blacks and whites in South Africa (Stones and Philbrick, 1991). No checks were made upon the validity of the scale outside North America, so we are dealing here with an imposed-etic measure.

It is not appropriate to compare means between country samples, since they may be biased by cultural differences in predisposition to use extreme points in responding to the various items. However, we can overcome this problem by comparing which dimension is more strongly endorsed within each sample. After correcting for the fact that one dimension has fewer items, we do find some differences of emphasis. The conjugal love scale was favoured most by the Ugandans, the Senegalese and the US engineering students. The romantic idealism scale was favoured by the Caribbeans. The romantic power scale was strongly favoured by all of the South African samples, both black and white. The Canadian sample included a wider age range, but among the younger respondents romantic idealism scored highest.

A somewhat similar approach was followed by Simmons, von Kolke and Shimizu (1986) and Simmons, Wehner and Kay (1989), except that they used different measures to assess romantic love. They found that on the Hobart (1958) scale of romantic love, French and German students scored highest with Japanese somewhat lower. One sample of Americans scored above the Japanese and another sample was below them. However, analyses of responses to individual items on the scale indicate that romantic love is given a somewhat different meaning in each country. For instance, the statement 'lovers should freely confess everything of personal significance to each other' was accepted by 75 per cent of Germans, 53 per cent of Americans and 25 percent of Japanese.

The pattern of results indicated by these studies does suggest that romantic conceptions of love may be somewhat more frequent in the more individualistic countries sampled. However, the scores for the US engineering students do not fit this pattern. Munro and Adams' Canadian results also indicated that attitudes moved towards endorsement of conjugal love as one grew older, so there are evidently a number of other relevant factors which would need to be taken into account before a clear picture could be obtained.

Existing relationships

Cross-cultural studies of existing intimate relationships are scarce indeed. Ting-Toomey (1991) asked large samples of students in the USA, France and Japan to make ratings about their current relationship with a close friend of the opposite sex. The Americans reported more 'love commitment' and more open disclosure, but also more ambivalence about whether to continue the relationship, as one might expect in an individualist culture. The French reported a lower level of conflict than either the Americans or the Japanese. Ting-Toomey attributes this to high uncertainty avoidance among the French, but this explanation is unconvincing, since Japan scores even higher on this dimension. It is quite likely that one could not fully understand the differing results for conflict level without examining also whether there are differences between the three countries in how important other peer relationships are at the same time. It might be the case, for instance, that conflict is not so much surprisingly low in France, but surprisingly high in Japan. This could be because many male Japanese will have strong commitments to same-sex work-related peer groups, which may generate conflict with their opposite-sex relationships. Consistent with this speculation, Ting-Toomey found that Japanese women respondents reported more conflict than did Japanese males, an effect not found in the other two countries.

VanYperen and Buunk (1991) also made a valuable contribution to our understanding of intimate relationships, by comparing Dutch and American couples. A number of US theorists have applied adaptations of Adams' (1965) equity theory, which we discussed in an earlier section of this chapter, to this field. VanYperen and Buunk examined whether equity theory could explain couples' satisfaction with their relationship in the way that has been demonstrated in US studies. They found that among their US subjects those who were most satisfied with their relationship were those who felt that they and their partners were putting an equal amount into the relationship. However, in the Netherlands the most satisfied were those who were 'overbenefited': in other words, those who felt that their partner was putting more into the relationship than they were themselves.

These results are particularly interesting from our point of view because VanYperen and Buunk also asked their subjects to complete a measure of what they called 'communal orientation', which may well tap interdependent values. The US sample in the study was drawn from Pennsylvania and from Hawaii, where more than half the respondents were Asians. VanYperen and Buunk show that in the sample as a whole it was the subjects who were high on communal orientation whose responses departed from equity theory predictions. Thus they lead us away from a stereotyped conclusion that relationships in the Netherlands differ from those in the USA. The alternative explanation is that relationships differ between those who endorse interdependent values and those who do not. In fact they found that the link between endorsement of communal orientation and departure from equity theory predictions was stronger in their US results, probably because their US sample was more diverse.

This diversity would be caused not only by ethnic diversity but also by gender differences. Like Leung *et al.* in the preceding section, VanYperen and Buunk paid some attention to Hofstede's characterization of the Netherlands as 'feminine'. Hofstede's labelling of this dimension leaves something to be desired, since it encourages us to confuse the character- izations of cultures and individuals. However, his characterization of a feminine culture is one in which communal values predominate, whereas masculine cultures are those in which achievement (usually by men) is more highly prized. Hofstede found the Netherlands and the Scandinavian countries to be the most 'feminine' by this definition. In line with this, VanYperen and Buunk found no difference between the evaluations of relationship contribution by Dutch men and women, whereas there were significant gender differences in the US sample. In both countries the women were more communally oriented. The most likely overall explana- tion of the findings is therefore that the Dutch mostly scored moderate to high on communal orientation, whereas the American scores varied much more widely, on account of both gender and ethnic background.

So why should the responses of couples with interdependent values not adhere to equity theory? We noted in the earlier section concerning distributive justice that in collectivist cultures resource allocation was more often guided by equality and by need rather than by equity. Within an intimate relationship, we might expect that interdependent values would lead partners to see the relationship as a unit rather than calculating individual contributions. Indeed, recent US research suggests that, even in individualist cultures, the degree to which partners start to keep count of whom they see as the cause of difficulties can predict relationship break- down (Bradbury and Fincham, 1990).

Conclusion

This chapter has yielded a relatively clear picture. In collectivist cultures there are discernible differences in the management of potential conflicts within groups from those found in more individualist cultures. These differences may well stem from the different basis upon which group membership rests in each setting. The differences found are not absolute ones so much as differences in the degree to which different principles obtain. Members of collectivist groups favour other members of their group more strongly and treat them more equally. Such a pattern cannot be said to be either better or worse than a more individualist life-style without our becoming engulfed in a welter of competing value-systems. In the next chapter we shall examine further consequences of this high level of in-group solidarity, particularly in regard to the ways in which group members exert influence on one another.

EIGHT

Social influence processes

'When I use a word,' Humpty Dumpty said, in a rather scornful tone, 'it means just what I choose it to mean – neither more nor less.'

'The question is,' said Alice, 'whether you can make words mean so many different things.'

'The question is,' said Humpty Dumpty, 'which is to be master – that's all.'

(Lewis Carroll, *Through the Looking Glass*)

The collectivist search for harmony which we explored in Chapter 7 implies that influence processes will be both more indirect and more potent than those found in individualist societies. In this chapter we will examine differences in the styles of communication which occur, and in related attitudes towards time. We shall then be in a position to examine the different types of social influence which have been studied in groups with differing cultures.

Communication style

The variety of ways in which English is spoken in everyday life can make it difficult for a native English speaker to accept the idea that there is something unified about the communication patterns found within, for instance, white Anglo cultural groups. There is, of course, a rich variety of forms of spoken English within any one of countries such as the USA, Britain, Australia or Canada. Such variations often serve to demarcate subcultural groups in terms of class, ethnicity or regional location. For instance, the manner in which Mrs Robertson spoke to Mr Chan marks her out as a lowland Scot. Several of the phrases which she used would make it particularly difficult for Chan to understand her. When she said, 'I doubt you are 20 minutes late', she meant that she was sure that he was 20

143

minutes late. However, she had failed to think through the fact that, although her meaning would be clear enough in Edinburgh or Glasgow, particularly if delivered with an appropriate accent, it would confuse most English speakers from outside Scotland.

Regional dialects pose difficulties in Chinese or any other language just as much as they do in English. However, in the present context, the emphasis is more upon the issue of whether there are distinctive aspects of communication *style* which can be related to individualist or collectivist cultures in general. In order to address this level of generality, we need to consider those aspects of communication which transcend the specific language being spoken.

High- and low-context cultures

Hall (1976) has proposed that language usage in different cultures can be classified as high context or low context. For Hall, a low-context culture is one in which speech is explicit and the message intended is largely conveyed by the words spoken. In contrast, a high-context culture is one in which a good deal of the message is implicit and the words spoken will convey only a small part of the message. The remaining part of the message is to be inferred by the listener on the basis of past knowledge of the speaker, the setting of the particular conversation, and any other contextual cues available. Hall classifies numerous countries around the world as falling into one or the other category, on the basis of his observations.

Gudykunst, Ting-Toomey and Chua (1988) point out that there is a close match between Hall's classification and where different national cultures were located by Hofstede (1980) along his empirically derived scale of individualism–collectivism. Neither Hall nor Gudykunst *et al.* would expect that any country would fall at the extreme ends of the high/low-context spectrum. They do, however, see sufficient variation between different countries for it to be worthwhile to order them in this way. Gudykunst *et al.* go on to investigate how high- and low-context communication may serve to sustain individualist and collectivist cultures.

They propose that discourse in individualist countries can be characterized as direct, succinct, personal and instrumental. This contrasts with the indirect, elaborate, contextual and affective emphases of communication in collectivist societies. From this general proposition one may derive predictions such as that in individualist cultural groups, speech will be more focused and briefer, and will involve more reference to 'I' and to specific goals. In collectivist societies, speech will be more discursive and will include more qualifiers such as 'maybe', 'perhaps' and 'probably'. It will also be adapted to reflect the status of the persons addressed and will involve the speaker in a good deal of scanning of the listeners for affective cues as to how they are responding to the message they are receiving.

Empirical testing of such propositions would be a massive project. What are already available are piecemeal comparisons of communicative styles in specific pairs or groups of cultures. Katriel (1986), for example, compares communicative styles of Jews and Arabs in Israel. She contrasts the relatively individualistic Jewish Sabra preference for 'straight talk', with the collectivist preference in Arab languages for *musayra*, which is translated as 'going with the other, ... humouring, ... accommodating oneself to the position or situation of the other (Katriel, 1986, p. 111)'. The contrast she describes is in agreement with the predictions of Gudykunst *et al.* (1988).

Self-disclosure

Disclosure of personal information about oneself can be thought of as one type of direct communication. Won-Doornink (1985) compared self-disclosure in the USA and Korea and found as she expected that it was higher in the USA. After reviewing other studies, she concludes that the difference she found is typical of differences between eastern (collectivist) and western (individualist) cultures. Mutual self-disclosure is of greater value in individualist cultures since it enables the taking of choices as to whether one wishes to get to know another person further. In a collectivist culture, it is less crucial to know a person's history or current feelings, and more important to be clear about the other person's affiliations and status, and the rules governing the immediate context. Disclosure is something which has greater value within already established in-group relationships.

Derlega and Stepien (1977) compared attitudes toward self-disclosure in Poland and the USA. The somewhat more collectivist Poles made a stronger distinction between disclosure to a friend and to a stranger than did the Americans. Taking this line of analysis further, Gudykunst *et al.* (1992a) compared how sharply distinctions were drawn between in-group relationships and out-group relationships by students in the USA, Japan, Hong Kong and Taiwan. They found that in the three more collectivist countries there was more self-disclosure and more questioning of the other within in-group relationships than in out-group relationships. In the USA, on the other hand, there was no significant differentiation between in-group and out-group on these measures.

The preservation of face

A more general account of the functions of the differing styles of communication in individualist and collectivist cultures is provided by Ting-Toomey's

(1988) theory of face. She argues that in all cultures we seek to save face, but the concept has different referents in individualist and collectivist cultures. In all cultural settings we are concerned with both 'positive face' and 'negative face'. In an individualist culture the focus of face is primarily the 'I', who is concerned that his or her positive qualities be seen and his or her negative qualities be hidden or excused. The work of Goffman (1959), for instance, emphasizes procedures for 'facework', or the avoidance of the loss of negative face in western countries.

In collectivist cultural groups, says Ting-Toomey, the preservation of harmony is the major goal and positive face is sustained where this result is accomplished. Where there is a danger of conflict, the danger is not that 'I' specifically would be embarrassed, but that 'We' need to ward off that danger by reading the indirect communication cues sufficiently early that the untoward situation may be averted. In a comparison of informal rules about how one should relate to others, Argyle *et al.* (1986) found greater endorsement of rules for restraining emotional expression, preserving harmony and avoiding loss of face in Japan and Hong Kong than in Italy and Britain. These rules would cover a much broader range of conversational topics than simple self-disclosure.

Of course, even in individualist cultures we may seek to avoid embarrassing others, but in terms of Ting-Toomey's model, this would be for somewhat different reasons than in a collectivist setting. Choi and Choi (1992) present an analysis of the Korean concepts of *noon-chi* and *che-myun*, which they translate respectively as 'tact' and 'face-saving'. They point out that tact in English has overtones of diplomacy or manipulation, whereas in Korean the meaning is more collective and focused on the avoidance of conflict. They quote an example of *noon-chi*, where A wishes B to leave his office. A therefore asks B what is the time. Being used to indirect communication, B correctly infers that A would like him to leave and does so, leaving the harmony of their relationship intact. The Japanese have a related distinction between *tatemae*, which translates as 'public' or what is supposed to happen, and *honne*, which translates as 'private' or what does in fact happen. So long as the parties to a transaction preserve the shared understanding that *tatemae* has been upheld, actual events can deviate from them substantially.

Despite our best efforts, situations do arise from time to time where we lose face. Ting-Toomey's theory predicts that, in individualist cultures, someone who is insulted is more likely to seek to repair face by rebutting the insult, particularly if others have witnessed the insult. Bond and Cheung (1991) examined what happened when Hong Kong students were insulted by an experimental stooge who was role-playing as their teacher in an experimental task. If the insult was addressed to them personally, the Chinese subjects resisted the insult *less* when there was an audience present than when they were alone. Bond and Cheung interpret this as

Box 8.1 *Direct and indirect communication*

Some of the general principles of Ting-Toomey's theory are illustrated by the interchange between Mrs Robertson and Mr Chan. Mrs Robertson's talk was focused upon the point at issue: Chan's having failed the exam. Chan raises a series of points concerning the context of his performance, including his career prospects, his commitment to his family, the difficulties faced by his fellow students and the vagaries of the bus service.

showing that subjects were more concerned to avoid open conflict, thereby bringing shame upon their group, than to save personal face. In a separate experimental condition, the insult was directed not just to them but to their group. In this condition subjects showed more direct response, but they were also noted to glance much more frequently at the other member of their group who was present, perhaps in the hope that they could learn how their colleague was responding to the insult.

Ting-Toomey's theory summarizes a wealth of ethnographic description and examples of facework, but has yet to be tested in a more explicit manner. Indeed, the diversity of language usage both within and between specific countries must mean that it provides only an overall framework, rather than specific predictions about how members of particular cultures will communicate.

The plausibility of Ting-Toomey's theory may also be examined by looking at the varying preferences for conflict resolution in different cultures which we reviewed in Chapter 7. However, the purpose of different communication styles does not reside solely in the need to avert embarrassment. Consider, for instance, the role of silence in different cultures.

Is silence golden?

Giles, Coupland and Wiemann (1992) compared the beliefs of Chinese and Americans about talking. The Americans described talking as pleasant and important, and as a way of controlling what goes on. The Chinese were more tolerant of silence and saw quietness as a way of controlling what goes on. Studies of negotiation have shown that the Japanese also tolerate silence and frequently use it to control how negotiation proceeds (Graham, 1985). Even among more individualist countries the meaning of silence and of talk may vary. In Finland, for instance, it is said that silence often conveys attentiveness and encouragement to the speaker to continue, whereas in some other countries the speaker is more likely to continue only where there is active verbal or non-verbal acknowledgement that the message is being heard. Scherer (1979) found that in both Germany and the USA dominance may be expressed through talking, but that the dominant person's manner of speaking differs between the two countries. Dominant Americans spoke more loudly and with a greater range of expressiveness; dominant Germans showed a lesser range of expressiveness but high verbal fluency.

The varieties of truthfulness

A further aspect of communication style has to do with what is considered to be 'true' and what is deceitful communication in different cultures. Christie and Geis (1970) reported a series of studies of what they termed 'Machiavellianism' in the USA. Machiavellians are those who seek to manipulate others through a variety of deceitful strategies. Studies of Machiavellianism and ingratiation have been reported from various countries, some of them using Christie and Geis's questionnaire measures. Tripathi (1981) showed that the Machiavellianism scale had some validity in India, since those who scored high on it proved to be those candidates who told lies while attempting to obtain university scholarships. Oksenberg (1971) found that westernized Hong Kong students scored higher on Machiavellianism than did non-westernized students. This supports the view that the questionnaire items refer mostly to the types of strategy which would obtain in individualistic settings.

Pandey (1981, 1986) made a series of studies of ingratiation, also in India. He found that ingratiation tactics were most frequently used towards one's boss, in which circumstance they were expected rather than thought of as deviant. He surveyed the range of tactics employed and found several not reported by US researchers. These included self-degradation, emphasizing one's dependence upon the superior, name-dropping and changing one's opinions to gain favour.

Almaney and Ahwan (1982) discuss the practice of *mubalaqha*, translated as 'exaggeration', in Arab language countries. They argue that, if an Arab does not make statements in a form which westerners would call exaggerated, other Arabs will not believe that they mean what they are saying, and might even infer that they mean the opposite. The kinds of cross-cultural misunderstanding which this belief about sincerity may generate between Arabs and westerners were all too vividly illustrated during the 1990–1 Gulf Crisis. These examples illustrate the principle expounded in Chapter 3, that while there may well be etic principles with transcultural validity, the emic means by which they are expressed will vary from culture to culture. In the present case, it may well be true that in all cultures people wish to impress certain others; but the means of doing so will be culturally specific.

Time perspective

It follows rather directly from the notion that in collectivist cultures one will have less choice over one's group affiliations that members will have a different perspective on time. If I know that within all or most of my life-time I shall be a member of a particular group, my thinking about that group will extend further – both into the future and into the past – than if there is a possibility of my moving to another group next week or next year. It will also be less important that I keep track of time, since what is not taken care of today could be handled another time. Unfortunately, very little attention has been given to these issues by social psychologists, although anthropologists have been much more interested in this important issue than social psychologists.

Monochronic time and polychronic time

Hall (1983) distinguishes cultures which view time monochronically from cultures which view time polychronically. A monochronic view of time sees it as a scarce resource which must be rationed and controlled through the use of schedules and appointments, and through aiming to do only one thing at any one time. In monochronic cultures people sometimes see spare time or time spent waiting as something which needs to be 'killed'. We should expect to find a conception of time as monochronic in many individualist cultures. A polychronic view of time sees the maintenance of harmonious relationships as the important thing, so that use of time needs to be flexible in order that we do right by the various people to whom we have obligations. We should expect this to be characteristic of many collec-tivist cultures. While there is a good deal of plausibility to Hall's model, there are other attributes of cultures which are also likely to be important in relation to time. For instance, Hofstede's dimension of uncertainty avoidance is most probably linked to the degree to which we plan our time usage carefully in advance. The dimension of Confucian work dynamism identified by the Chinese Culture Connection researchers (1987) is also strongly linked with time. As Hofstede (1991) stresses, Confucian values stress perseverance and thrift in obtaining long-term goals.

An intriguing series of studies by Levine, West and Reis (1980) and Levine and Bartlett (1984) compared various aspects of time management in seven countries. They found substantial correlations between the accuracy of clocks in public places, the speed at which people walked down the street and the speed at which a post office clerk completed the sale of a small-denomination postage stamp. By these criteria, the speedy countries were the USA and Japan, and the slower ones were Indonesia, Brazil and Italy. In further comparisons between Brazil and the USA, they found that in Brazil someone who always arrived late for appointments was rated as more likeable, happy and successful than someone who did not, whereas in the USA someone who always arrived early was more likely to be seen in this way.

The characterization of the USA as 'speedy' is consistent with the expectation that individualist cultures will have a monochronic view of time. However, Japan was found to score even higher on Levine *et al.*'s criteria, so this outcome cannot be explained in the same way. Hofstede found Japan to be high on uncertainty avoidance, and this suggests that the Japanese orientation towards time is based more on a need for precision than on a view of time as a scarce commodity.

Looking ahead

Hofstede (1991) proposes that the essence of the value-cluster identified in the Chinese Culture Connection (1987) study as Confucian work dynamism is a focus on the future rather than on the short-term present. We should expect this to show up in comparisons between Americans on the one hand and Chinese or Japanese on the other. Doktor (1983) made observational studies of Japanese managers at work. He found that, within his sample of observations, 41 per cent of Japanese managers undertook tasks which lasted more than one hour, compared to only 10 per cent of US managers. In a similar way, 49 per cent of US managers did tasks which lasted less than nine minutes compared to only 18 per cent of the Japanese managers. This implies that the Japanese managers had longer time perspectives, but does not provide a direct measure.

A study of the duration of activities was also made by Wheeler, Reis and Bond (1989), who asked students in the USA and Hong Kong to keep diaries of their activities over a period of two weeks. The Chinese spent more time in groups and less with one other person. They spent longer on their activities and did them with a narrower range of other people. The result for the Chinese is consistent with the polychronic emphasis on people rather than activities, but again does not directly measure orientation towards the future.

Two studies did obtain direct measures, but unfortunately these studies have data only from countries which vary in their level of collectivism but which all score low on Confucian dynamism. Sundberg, Poole and Tyler (1983) surveyed 15-year-old adolescents in small towns in India, Australia and the United States. They were asked to list seven future events to be chosen by themselves. The average time into the future of these seven events was significantly longer for the boys from the more collectivist India than for the boys from the more individualist Australia and USA. However, the Indian girls had the shortest time perspective of all. Only in India was there a significant difference in the perspectives of the boys and the girls. The prediction of longer time perspectives in collectivist cultures is thus upheld for boys but not for girls. Such findings underline for us the hazards of generalizing about national cultures as a whole. In countries such as India where gender roles are rather more sharply differentiated than in the USA or Australia, the study highlights the importance of subcultural variations. Sundberg *et al.* point out that entry into the Indian school studied was more selective for girls than for boys. These girls may therefore have been more independent in orientation than females elsewhere in India.

Meade (1972) also compared time perspectives between Americans and various Indian samples. His subjects, who were all male, were asked to write short stories, starting with single sentences provided by him. One of these was: 'L.B. is beginning his new job ...'. The stories were analyzed to determine whether the major theme referred to the future or to the past. No separate coding was provided for references to the present. He found that, while 62 per cent of American stories were set in the future, future reference in his Indian samples varied from 8 per cent among Brahmins and 16 per cent among Muslims to 56 per cent among Parsees and 58 per cent among Kshatriya Hindus. Before we could know whether these substantial differences are related to variations in interdependence or other cultural values, we should need separate measures of values from each of the cultural groups sampled. The results again underline the heterogeneity of Indian culture, and the dangers of hasty generalizations.

Many more studies will be required before it is clear how closely differing time perspectives are correlated with differences in cultural values. The evidence thus far is inconclusive.

Conformity revisited

If members of collectivist groups spend more time with one another and seek in-group harmony, then we should expect that social influence processes would lead them towards greater levels of conformity than those reported from groups in individualist cultures. In Chapter 2, we touched upon the various replications of the Asch (1951) studies of conformity in making judgements about the lengths of lines. These studies are not ideal for our present purpose, since we cannot be sure that judgements about physical stimuli of this kind respond to social pressure in the same way as do social stimuli such as attitudes or social representations. However, researchers have attempted precise replications of the Asch experiment in a much wider range of countries than is available for any other social psychological study, so that they provide us with the firmest data available. Table 8.1 summarizes the results, subdividing between countries thought to be predominantly individualist and countries thought to be collectivist.

The comparison of errors recorded in the different studies should not be considered as very precise, because not all studies used exactly the same procedures. Some studies used the Asch (1951) procedure, whereby subjects have face-to-face contact with one another. Others used the Crutchfield (1955) technique, in which subjects communicate electronically. However, two trends are fairly clear from the table. First, the percentage of errors made is more consistently high in the studies done in collectivist societies. Second, more errors are recorded for subjects who were not students.

In interpreting what these results mean, we need to think more about who the subjects were in these studies. The original Asch studies were

Table 8.1 Asch conformity studies by national culture

Study	Subjects	% errors
'Individualist' countries		
The original Asch studies (1951, 1956)	Students	37
Eight later US studies (averaged)	Students	25
Four British studies (averaged)	Students	17
Vlaander and van Rooijen (1985)	Dutch students	24
Perrin and Spencer (1981)	British probation clients	22
Perrin and Spencer (1981)	British unemployed blacks	39
Hatcher (1982)	Belgian students	24
Doms (1983)	Belgian students	14
'Collectivist' countries		
Whittaker and Meade (1967)	Brazilian students	34
Whittaker and Meade (1967)	Hong Kong students	32
Whittaker and Meade (1967)	Lebanese students	31
Whittaker and Meade (1967)	Zimbabwean Bantu students	51
Claeys (1967)	Zairean students	36
Frager (1970)	Japanese students	25
Chandra (1973)	Fijian teachers	36
Chandra (1973)	Indian teachers in Fiji	58
Rodrigues (1982)	Brazilians	35
Amir (1984)	Kuwaiti students	29
Williams and Sogon (1984)	Japanese sports club members	51
Williams and Sogon (1984)	Japanese students not known to each other	27

Note: American studies which were averaged: Deutsch and Gerard (1955); Whittaker et al. (1957); Levy (1960); Gerard et al. (1968); Larsen (1974); Larsen et al. (1979); ; Lamb and Alsifaki (1980); Nicholson et al. (1985). British studies: Seaborne (1962); Perrin and Spencer (1981); Nicholson et al. (1985); Abrams et al. (1990).

made with students who were mostly strangers to one another. While most of the studies reported following the same procedures as Asch, hardly any of them specify whether subjects were or were not strangers to one another. This is crucial information, since we would expect a member of a cultural group with interdependent values to conform if the pressure came from in-group members, but not if it came from strangers. The studies from Japan are particularly interesting in this connection. Frager (1970) used students who were strangers to one another and to his considerable surprise found a low level of conformity. Indeed, he also recorded high levels of anti-conformity, which is movement *away* from the majority opinion. This may have been related to the high level of student unrest and rebellion at the time in Keio University, where the study was undertaken. The more recent Japanese study by Williams and Sogon (1984) showed a much higher error rate for intact groups, and a lower rate for unacquainted students. This result supports the view that conformity rates

Box 8.2 *Fitting in with the group*

Mr Nakagawa Takehiro was very honoured to have obtained admission to a prestigious graduate school in the United States. He was not familiar with the work of the professor he was to be working with, but had been advised that the university he was going to had the highest status of those which had made him offers, and he had chosen to go there on that basis. He had never been outside Japan before, and he was naturally apprehensive about his first meeting with his professor and keen to give the right impression.

Soon after settling in, Mr Nakagawa located the professor's office and, finding her at her desk, presented his card. She shook his hand warmly and glanced briefly at his card.

'Oh, my goodness,' she said, 'we're going to have a hard time with your name. How would it be if we call you Taki?'

She went on to explain that she was holding open house the following Sunday, and that would give him a chance to meet colleagues and other students. After instructing him on how to reach the house, she said that he should come whenever he would like. Mr Nakagawa wondered whether this was to be a formal occasion, but his professor reassured him that he should wear whatever he found most comfortable.

Mr Nakagawa quickly told his professor that he would be coming and left her office. As he walked away he reflected that it was going to be very difficult to find out how to do the right thing. He thought that perhaps his imperfect English had caused him to miss his professor's guidance as to when he should come and what he should wear.

for interdependent subjects are strongly influenced by their relationship to the other judges in the experiment.

Looking at the table more carefully, we can discover that some of the other high error rates are also recorded where the subjects may have had some strong reason to hold interdependent values linking them with other members of their group. For instance, conformity was particularly high among unemployed blacks in Britain and among members of the minority Indian population in Fiji. This way of looking at the findings encourages us to think not so much about levels of conformity in different national cultures, but about conformity as a consequence of interdependent values, whether those values characterize a whole culture or particular subcultures within a larger society. Indeed, interdependence need not necessarily stem from some long-lasting set of values, but may arise from the manner in which the experiment is set up. The recent British study by Abrams *et al.* (1990) found much greater conformity when subjects were led to believe that the other judges were fellow students of psychology than when they were told that they were students of ancient history.

We thus have a range of experimental results ranging from the ecological studies of conformity in agricultural and hunting societies by Berry (1967) and Berry and Annis (1974), which were discussed in Chapter 2, to laboratory studies in individualist and collectivist cultures, which all support a similar conclusion. The more one's fate is interdependent with that of others, the greater is the likelihood of conformity occurring.

Minority influence

The Asch experiments have been taken by most researchers as an opportunity to look at the way that the majority could induce a minority to conform. In recent years, an alternative field of research has developed which examines the circumstances under which a minority might influence the majority to change its views. Originally proposed in France (Moscovici and Faucheux, 1972; Moscovici, 1976), this approach has taken root much more firmly in Europe than in North America. Moscovici sees minority influence as more 'indirect' than majority influence. By this he means that a minority may *gradually* induce changes in a majority by maintaining their deviant position with a high level of consistency. The change created in this way will most likely not show up on direct measures of influence, but may be detected only by looking for changes in related attitudes. Moscovici also asserts that the effects of minority influence will persist longer than will those achieved by majority influence.

In one of their more striking experiments, Moscovici and Personnaz (1980) showed that the minority were able to influence the judgements of the majority when evaluating the colour of a series of blue-green slides, by consistently stating them to be green. This experiment had two stages. First, majority and minority members made their colour judgements together. Subsequently, the group members were asked to report privately the colours of the after-images they saw after viewing each slide. The after-image is the colour which appears if one looks at a white screen after looking at a bright colour for a while. In this stage of the experiment, majority members never heard the judgements of after-image colour made by the minority, but they nonetheless reported that they were seeing red-purple, which is the after-image of green. The effect persisted even on further trials after the consistent minority was no longer present. The process of minority influence is thus not actually at all indirect – it is based on the consistent statement of dissent – but its effects may be detected only indirectly.

Positive results of this type have been repeatedly obtained by Moscovici and his colleagues in Paris, and by Doms and van Avermaet (1980) in Belgium. However, Sorrentino, King and Leo (1980) could not reproduce the effect in Canada. Numerous other studies in Europe have succeeded in detecting various types of minority influence (Moscovici, Mugny and van Avermaet, 1985), but results in North America have been more mixed (Maass and Clark, 1984). US researchers mostly prefer the view that majority and minority influence are both explained by the same influence process. They see minority influence just as happening more rarely than majority influence, because there are fewer people arguing for the minority view. In a further development, Mugny and Papastomou (1980), working in Switzerland, have shown that minority effects are not always greatest when the minority is rigid in its views. By introducing a number of variations in their experimental design, they were able to show that both flexible and rigid minorities could be influential.

Where should minority influence be strongest?

Examined from a cultural perspective, Moscovici's work is interesting in two particular ways. First, there is the question of what it is about the cultures of European countries which has led to greater interest in the topic of minority influence and greater success in supporting Moscovici's hypotheses. Second, and in the long run more important, Moscovici's emphasis upon minority influence can be related to the notion that in collectivist cultures influence and indeed communication will be more indirect, in order to avoid the loss of harmony which might otherwise ensue. We might speculate that, although minority influence would be widespread in collectivist cultures, the means by which it may be accomplished would not be the type of rigidly consistent deviance which Moscovici originally found to be effective in France. By contrast, in cultures which are even more individualist than France, Belgium or Switzerland, we might expect frustrated minority members to be more likely to leave the group and join some other group where their views are more positively valued.

The only tests of Moscovici's hypotheses from outside Europe and North America have been reported from Japan. Koseki's (1989) study reported substantial minority influence in groups judging the numbers of dots projected on a screen. However, her results illustrate some of the difficulties of arriving at research procedures with equivalent meaning in different cultures. In Koseki's initial study the confederate 'always spoke first or at a very early stage, disregarding precedence and in a confident fashion'. The significance of this sequencing is that who speaks first in Japanese society is often a strong indicator of high status. We may therefore be looking here at the effects of high status rather than of minority status. In further studies, Koseki systematically varied when her confederate spoke. She found that when the confederate spoke last, minority influence was very much weaker, although still significantly present.

Yoshiyama (1988) also found minority influence, this time on a task involving the matching of line lengths. He reported that the majority perceived the minority to be less competent than themselves but more confident, particularly when the gap between majority and minority was wide. Atsumi and Sugiman (1990) used a discussion task and found that both the majority and the minority exerted some influence. Where the gap between majority and minority was small, the minority was more likely to prevail, whereas when the gap was wider, they yielded to the majority. As Moscovici's model predicts, where minority influence occurred its effects were more persistent.

All of the Japanese findings are consistent with the view that subjects may have been seeking the optimal way of maintaining group harmony. The minority appear to achieve their influence because, as in the West, consistent behavioural style is taken as a sign of confidence. However, the Japanese studies indicate that the majority will rely upon this confidence only where the majority are closer to the minority in the first place. Parallels to these experimental findings may be seen in the proceedings of the Japanese Diet. The majority Liberal Democrats rather frequently compromise with the views of the minority political parties, instead of voting them down as would occur in western legislatures. The minority parties rather often exploit this situation by threatening to withdraw if a compromise is not reached.

Hierarchy and leadership

This chapter has so far mostly discussed relations between group members

Box 8.3 *Signifying hierarchy*

Mrs Robertson and Mr Chan are both aware that their relationship is based upon hierarchy. Mrs Robertson reflects her feeling of superiority by referring to Mr Chan simply as 'Chan'. Mr Chan is unsure what is the best way to express deference to Mrs Robertson, particularly as she is a woman, and he avoids naming her, except when he calls her 'teacher', an important honorific in Chinese culture.

as though there were no status differentiation within them. However, as we saw in Chapter 3, those countries which score high on collectivism typically also score high on power distance. Western theorists, from Lewin *et al.* (1939) onwards, have long been in the habit of contrasting autocratic with democratic leadership and thinking of hierarchy as the opposite of participation. When we find that, in many parts of the world, power distance and hierarchy are part of a social structure which is also collectivist and participative, we must then begin to look carefully at the generality of the western model.

Leadership functions and leadership roles

In individualist cultures a group member's position in the group will be bounded by choice processes – the group member's choice to be there, and the group's valuation of the contribution which he or she makes to the life of the group. In a collectivist culture there will be less reason for individual members to have a clearly delineated role, since their identity is defined not by what they do in the group but by the fact that they belong to it. In a classic series of studies in the USA, Bales (1951) showed how discussion groups of students developed separate 'task' and 'socioemotional' leaders. While the task leader took on the function of organizing the task, the socioemotional leader cracked jokes or defused conflicts in a manner which enabled the group to function smoothly even when the task was unrewarding. If the above reasoning is correct, we should expect this type of fixed role differentiation to be less frequent in collective cultures.

Krichevskii (1983) found that such role differentiation did occur among sports teams and student groups in the Soviet Union. However, since no firm data on the level of collectivism of Soviet society are available, this result is equivocal. Smith (1963) using English groups of students and of managers on training courses, and Koomen (1988) using Dutch groups of students, showed that the amount of role differentiation varied depending upon how strongly members were attracted to the group. This fits the pattern of Bales' original US findings. No empirical studies are available from more collectivist societies, but it is widely reported that members of work teams in Japanese organizations do not have precisely differentiated roles: all members are responsible for fulfilling whatever functions are required at a particular time.

Leadership effectiveness

Although few researchers have addressed the matter of role differentiation directly, abundant evidence is available more indirectly, through study of the effectiveness of leadership, especially in work teams. Western theories of leadership have frequently differentiated leader styles which emphasize the task function from those which emphasize the socioemotional or group maintenance function. For example, Fiedler (1967) differentiates task- and relationship-oriented leadership, while Vroom and Yetton (1973) distinguish autocratic, consultative and group-oriented styles. Tests of these and related models in the United States have found different effects of style on productivity in different settings (Yukl, 1989; Smith and Peterson, 1988). A series of 'contingency' theories have been advanced in an attempt to explain the circumstances under which this or that style of leadership is more effective.

Studies of leadership within collectivist cultures have come up with markedly different results from those obtained in western countries. Among the most extensive are those of Misumi (1985) in Japan. Misumi's studies have included such varied organizations as coal mines, banks, shipyards, bus companies and local government offices. Over a period of more than 30 years Misumi has found that in a wide variety of Japanese groups and organizations the most effective leaders are those who are simultaneously high on *both* task *and* relationship behaviours. Although Misumi terms his two aspects of leadership style as 'performance' and 'maintenance', they have a good deal in common with the formulations of leader style developed in the USA.

Misumi's findings are echoed in other countries with collective cultures. Bond and Hwang (1986) review studies of leadership in Taiwan. Studies using translated versions of the Ohio State leadership scales developed in the USA again showed that leaders high on both task and relationship dimensions were the most effective. Sinha (1981) reports findings on effective leadership in India. The most effective style is characterized as high on both task behaviour and nurture of subordinates. Ayman and Chemers (1983) obtained a similar result in Iran, as did Farris and Butterfield (1972) in Brazil. Although all of these studies support the importance of two similar-sounding dimensions of leader behaviour, the specific questionnaire items making up the scales reflect the different cultural values which are emically important in each location.

In more individualist countries, such as those of Western Europe, studies of leadership have yielded results which are more similar to those obtained in the United States. Different types of leader style are found effective in different settings (Smith and Tayeb, 1988). Zhurvalev and Shorokhova (1984) from the Soviet Union also report findings favouring contingency theory. They reported that Lewin's distinction between autocratic, democratic and *laissez-faire* styles was insufficient to distinguish all the approaches found in Soviet enterprises. They observed also managers whose styles were intermediate between Lewin's styles, and some who combined elements of all three styles. Their findings were that all of these styles of leadership, except the passive style, could be effective in particular circumstances. They also list some of the environmental circumstances which affect leadership effectiveness.

When is leadership needed?

A leader within an individualistic culture may perhaps best be seen as an individual who provides to the group whatever task- or relationship-oriented functions are lacking. Recent US theorists (e.g. Kerr and Jermier, 1978; Manz, 1983) point out that in certain circumstances, which they attempt to specify, a group may be almost entirely self-managing. In other words, it would require virtually no input from an externally appointed leader, although of course the necessary leadership functions would be provided by the various members of the group.

In contrast, it would be most unlikely that one would find a group without a leader within a collective culture, since the principle of seniority or power distance is embedded within such cultures. An effective leader in a wide variety of collective cultures proves to be one who is seen as having all the required task and group maintenance attributes and does not have a role which differentiates separate functions of leadership.

However, we should not assume that the presence of a seniority system indicates that leadership in such groups is autocratic in the sense understood in western cultures. The manner in which leaders and their group members will relate to one another will be determined by the communication style prevailing in each cultural setting, as discussed in an earlier section. The leader will be owed deference, but in one culture this deference might be conveyed by waiting to be told what to do and in another it might be conveyed by coming up with suggestions as to what to do. By differentiating these two different ways of showing deference, we may hope to understand some of the diversity in the results of the studies of group decision in collective cultures which were touched upon in Chapter 2.

Box 8.4   *Group participation in Israel and the USA*

Erez and Earley (1987) compared the response of three groups of
students to different ways of setting goals. The students were asked to
construct as many class schedules as possible for their colleges, such
that no student would have conflicting obligations. In one experimental
condition, the student groups were *assigned* their goal by the
experimenter. In the second condition they appointed a *representative*
who negotiated a goal for the group. In the third, the group participated
in reaching a decision. By 'guiding' the groups as to what goals were
realistic, the experimenters ensured that in all three experimental
conditions similar goals were set. The students compared were from the
US Midwest, from Israeli cities and from Israeli kibbutzim. In Phase 1 of
the experiment low goals were set, while in Phase 2 there were higher
goals. The diagram below shows that the Israelis were much more
strongly affected by the goal-setting procedures, especially in Phase 2.
They reacted against assigned goals and responded positively to
participative decision making.

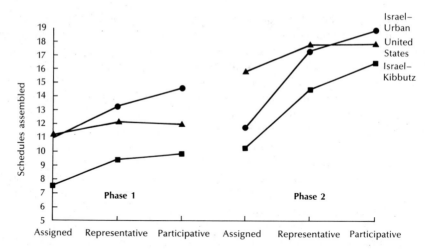

Erez and Earley propose that this difference in results is to be
explained by the difference in cultural values obtaining in the USA and
Israel. They collected measures of the students' values about
interdependence and power, and showed that higher endorsement of
interdependent values and lower endorsement of power distance by the
Israelis went along with the way they responded to the experimental
manipulations. Thus, response to different styles of group participation
at the cultural level is predicted by differences in the individual cultural
values of the subjects in the study.

As we saw there, a number of studies from Japan have shown that group decision making is highly effective in that culture. The continuing central role of group discussion in Japanese culture is confirmed by the extensive use of 'Quality Circles' and other methods of group decision making, such as the *ringi* procedure for consulting all concerned, in Japanese manufacturing firms (Smith and Misumi, 1989). Japan can be seen as an example of a culture which is hierarchical, but in which one expresses deference to one's superior by active participation and the making of numerous suggestions. Significantly, the leader often does not participate in these meetings but receives their output after the consultation is over.

In contrast, the experiments in group decision reported from Puerto Rico (Marrow, 1964; Juralewicz, 1974) were failures. In Hispanic cultures, decision making is more likely to be seen as the prerogative of the leader, and to be too active in group participation would be to challenge or doubt his or her authority.

While participation is very widely discussed, surprisingly few studies have made direct comparisons of participative management in different cultures. Box 8.4 examines a direct comparison between Israel and the USA.

Leadership is thus embedded in group structure to a greater degree in collective cultures than in individualistic cultures. The functions of effective leadership will nonetheless be exercised within each type of culture through the distinctive style of communication appropriate to that setting.

Conclusion

This chapter has amplified the material we surveyed in the previous chapter. The search for harmony found in more collectivist groups is aided by indirect communication styles and a polychronic view of time. The more long lasting time commitment involved in collectivist group membership makes likely higher levels of influence both by majority members and by minority members, as well as providing a key role for leaders.

In so far as no country has a totally homogeneous culture, the differences we have discussed are likely also to be detectable among subcultures within any particular country. For example, we might well find within a predominantly individualist country, members of different ethnic or regional minorities, social classes or groupings such as gender, who have more interdependent values. Such variations should encourage us to make fewer generalizations about national cultures and more about the social behaviour of groups with known types of value.

As was the case in Chapter 7, only a few of the studies which we have reviewed used measures checking whether the members of the individualist countries sampled did in fact have independent values, and whether interdependent values predominated in the samples from collectivist countries. The study in Box 8.4 as well as a recent study by Earley (1991) underlines how fruitful it can be to do so.

In Chapter 2, we discussed two previous studies by Earley which compared the incidence of social loafing by managers in the USA and China. Earley concluded that in the more collectivist culture of China social loafing did not occur. In his new study, Earley compared managers in Israel, the USA and China on the same simulated decision-making task he had used before. He found that both in Israel and in China no social loafing occurred when managers believed they were working with an *in-group* of others very similar to themselves, whereas there was some loafing if they believed they were working with an *out-group* of others who were dissimilar to themselves. The US managers showed equally high social loafing whether they were working with an in-group or an out-group. This pattern of findings is exactly what one would expect, given that Israel and China are characterized as collectivist cultures and the USA as an individualist culture. Earley's measures confirmed that the US managers did in fact have values which were much more independent than were those of the Israeli and Chinese managers. This study also underlines again how crucial it is in analyzing behaviour within collectivist cultures to distinguish social influences within the in-group and behaviour towards strangers.

In the next chapter we look in more detail at some of the consequences of increasing world-wide contact between individuals and groups from different cultures. This will involve us in exploring more fully the contrast between in-groups and out-groups.

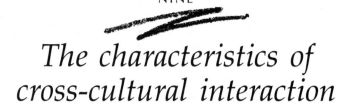

NINE

The characteristics of
cross-cultural interaction

'What kind of a bird are you,
    if you can't sing?', chirped the bird.
'What kind of a bird are you,
    if you can't swim?', retorted the duck.

(Serge Prokofiev, *Peter and the Wolf*)

The abstractions and niceties of cultural analysis become quickly focused on practical concerns when people from different cultures meet. Such encounters are becoming ever more frequent in a world where the forces of trade, migration, the media, travel and human rights are pushing people and governments to confront and accommodate ethnic diversity ever more frequently (Naisbitt and Aburdene, 1990).

Social scientists are increasingly being asked to examine interactions occurring across cultural lines. In what ways do people of different cultures behave differently? Which of these differences are important when people of different cultures live and work together? How do these differences have an impact on the communication process? In attempting to answer these sorts of question, we are fortunate to enjoy the legacy of considerable work on intergroup behaviour done *within* nations sharing a broader single culture (e.g. Worchel and Austin, 1979). Much of this work can be extended to encounters across different cultural lines.

This chapter provides a litmus test for the preceding chapters by discussing our present understanding of the challenges inherent in cross-cultural contact. We shall begin by examining the process of relationship development in its universal aspects. The encounter with anybody unknown produces anxiety and a need to develop expectations of their behaviour in order to interact effectively with them. The process of person perception is the first step in this direction. The initial identification of the other often elicits stereotypes associated with the other's group or cultural membership. We then use this set of assumptions about the other to guide our behaviour towards them and to structure our interpretation of their behaviour towards us, often negatively.

When the stranger is from a different cultural background, his or her communicative behaviour will often puzzle or irritate us because we interpret it as inappropriate. This confusion is reciprocal and may be complicated by language differences. Each party attempting to repair the situation may do so in ways that are culturally different, further compounding the difficulties. As a way of grounding our presentation of these various problems, we will conclude this chapter with an analysis of the unhappy encounter between Chan Chi Lok and Mrs Robertson.

Meeting others

Encountering the stranger

As originally described by Simmel (1950), a stranger is a person simultaneously 'within' and 'without'. Although physically present and sharing the same environment, the newcomer is not acquainted with the others present and does not know how they are likely to respond, either verbally or non-verbally. As Herman and Schield (1961) analyzed such encounters:

The immediate psychological result of being in a new situation is lack of security. Ignorance of the potentialities inherent in the situation, of the means to reach a goal, and of the probable outcomes of an intended action leads to insecurity. (p. 165)

Furthermore, the physique, dress, mannerisms and speech of the stranger may suggest to observers that he or she belongs to a different group than the observers' group. They may believe that the stranger's group follows a different life-style and is aggressively disposed towards their own group. In addition, observers often worry that their own group members may interpret interacting with an out-group stranger as disloyalty to their own group. These intergroup considerations (Stephan and Stephan, 1985) increase the anxiety already attendant upon encounters with strangers (Gudykunst and Hammer, 1988).

The probable outcome of such an encounter is avoidance, especially if the observer is introverted and anxious in personality; it is generally too effortful and dangerous to construct a bridge from the known to the unknown. Role constraints, however, may preclude this option. The stranger may be a customer, or a guest, or a teacher, or an employer. Furthermore, we may be curious and open to novel experiences as persons, find the stranger physically attractive, or come from a culture which discourages intolerance (Chinese Culture Connection, 1987). Such factors may lead us to interact, despite the uncertainty. In such cases how do people proceed?

Uncertainty reduction.   As Berger (1987) has proposed:

To interact in a relatively smooth, co-ordinated, and understandable manner, one must be able both to predict how one's interaction partner is likely to behave, and, based on these predictions, to select from one's own repertoire those responses that will optimize outcomes in the encounter. (p. 41)

In meeting a stranger, then, Berger would argue that concern for gathering useful information about the other is heightened because one knows so little about him or her.

Sharing the other's culture is extremely helpful in filling this need, of course, because people from the same culture have been socialized to share similar role expectations, situational understandings (Forgas and Bond, 1985), implicit theories of personality (Yang and Bond, 1990), and event sequences or scripts (Abelson, 1981). As Forgas (1981) has written:

It is the unique capacity of human beings for symbolic processes which allows them to build up expectations and internal representations about their daily interactions with one another. These representations, in turn, are the elementary building blocks of both socialized personalities and social systems. (p. 168)

If strangers come from the same cultural system, then their capacity to anticipate the other's responses will be greatly increased.

In addition, the context of the encounter (e.g. a political rally or a classroom) will eliminate many behaviours as possibilities and help to focus each party's anticipations on areas relevant to the situation.

Thereafter, Berger (1987) argues, we undertake a variety of 'knowledge acquisition strategies' which include passive, active and interactive techniques. Passive techniques involve unobtrusive observation with preference given for social, informal settings when a target's real personality is believed to be more apparent. Active techniques involve manipulating the social environment without directly interacting with the target, such as asking the target's social network for information. Interactive techniques involve direct, face-to-face contact and include question asking, disclosure and relaxing the target. The use of these strategies yields information about one's particular interaction partner, further reducing uncertainty.

It has been confirmed in Korea, Japan and the United States that lower levels of uncertainty about the other are associated with greater attraction across a number of different relationships – acquaintance, friendship and dating (Gudykunst, Yang and Nishida, 1985). Given the breadth of these findings, it seems reasonable to accept as universal the proposition that persons are motivated to reduce their levels of uncertainty about strangers and that increased certainty is one aspect of viable relationships with others. 'Getting to know you' is essential in un-becoming strangers to one another. The first step in this process is identifying who the stranger is.

Identifying the other

Much of our daily life is spent interacting with others in a state of mindlessness (Langer, 1989). In many contexts we relate to others in routine, automatic ways determined by social scripts. As defined by Abelson (1976), a script is a coherent sequence of events expected by the individual and involving him or her as a participant or observer. Scripts are learned throughout the individual's lifetime both by participation in event sequences and by observation of them.

By relying on shared scripts, people in various roles, such as passengers, ticket vendors, librarians and telephone operators, can process normal exchanges without paying any attention to the special qualities of those requiring their services.

When some novel exchange is initiated or when one of the parties wants to move outside the role relationship, however, the situation changes. Novel but appropriate action must be taken, so the individuals become 'mindful'. One feature of that mindfulness involves ascertaining information about one's interaction partner.

Identity cues

A number of psychologically useful cues are immediately apparent when interacting with others. Gender, age, race, physical attractiveness, body shape, baby-facedness and so forth are all visually apparent. When the other talks, volume, speed, fluency and accentedness are likewise quickly available in addition to the content of the other's speech. Other non-verbal behaviours, like distancing, posture, kinesics and patterns of gazing, can also be monitored.

Each of these characteristics in others is informative about their personality. Categorical cues, like gender, provide information about the other through the mediation of stereotypes. Individual cues, like speech volume, can be directly informative and allow us to make 'snap judgements' (McArthur and Baron, 1983; Schneider, Hastorf and Ellsworth, 1979) about the other's mood and personality. Together, this information allows us to reduce our uncertainty about people, generate expectations about how they will respond, and develop an 'unconflicted behavioral orientation' (Jones and Gerard, 1967) towards them. In short, we are better able to act. Of course, as we have discovered in previous chapters, people from different cultures may focus on different cues and interpret these cues differently in order to direct their behaviour.

Out-group identification. A key issue in initial perceptions of the other concerns whether he or she is categorized as an out-group member. There are many categories possible for distinguishing people from one another, such as gender, age, ethnicity and so forth. Which of these categories becomes salient, indeed whether such categories become salient, is an important issue for much of what follows in this chapter (see Zarate and Smith, 1990).

Procedures used in studies of social perception often simplify the stimulus conditions so as to focus respondents on the variable of interest to the researcher. So, for example, subjects may be asked to imagine a particular group of people, say Blacks, and asked to rate their characteristics (e.g. Quattrone and Jones, 1980). Such procedures sharpen experimental control, but they blunt ecological validity by begging the question of whether people would notice the other's blackness outside the laboratory. What then *is* noticed in natural settings?

A number of factors appear to influence the salience of categories in everyday person perception. First, it may be that certain categories assume universal salience. Brewer (1988), for example, has hypothesized that both gender and race constitute 'primitive' categories. As such, these categories are immediately processed in social perception and accorded priority over all other possible categories.

Second, the distinctiveness of the category in the social field is another factor (McGuire *et al.*, 1978). The lower the proportion of members within a group, the more likely they will be noticed as members of their group. Behaviour of such 'solos' will be better remembered, perceived as more influential, and interpreted in terms of their group stereotype (Taylor *et al.*, 1978).

Third, a person's 'prototypicality' (Cantor and Mischel, 1978) as a physical exemplar of a group probably influences the likelihood of categorizing that person as a group member. Atypical persons are harder to place and are less likely to be categorized into a particular group.

Fourth, it is possible that deviations from normal speech in the form of accent, syntax or grammar are salient cues for out-group membership. Speech is an important component of effective task completion, and those speaking to one another must quickly gauge each other's productive competence (Coupland *et al.*, 1988) in order to manage their discourse smoothly. The probability that one must adjust to the other's manner of speaking to co-ordinate effectively is increased when the other departs from normal speech patterns, so one's anxiety is increased. The need for uncertainty reduction is sharpened, and informative social categories, like ethnicity, then become salient (Gallois *et al.*, 1988).

The most dramatic divergence of speech occurs when the other uses a foreign language. In this case the first step is correctly to identify *which* language is being spoken, so that one can decide if the language is within one's repertoire and in what way speech norms in the situation permit one to accommodate to the other's language. Cues about the other's culture or ethnicity become prominent in guiding such a categorization.

Finally, a history of conflict between one's group and the other's group will serve to 'educate the observer's attention' (McArthur and Baron, 1983), heighten the sense of threat, and make the other's group membership salient (Giles and Johnson, 1986). Personality dispositions of the observer enter the picture here, with ethnocentric, aggressive and insecure persons being more prone to notice the other's membership of an out-group (Scott, 1965). In this situation the responses of the parties, starting with their perceptions, is shifted towards the intergroup end of the interpersonal vs intergroup continuum (Hewstone and Brown, 1986). Each person then responds to the other almost exclusively in terms of the other's group membership, behaving in a manner unguided by the other's distinctive personal characteristics.

Certainly more needs to be known about the conditions leading to a person's being categorized as an out-group member. Even more important is the need to discover when additional, non-category-based information about the other also becomes salient. This latter consideration is critical because research indicates that subjects do not always apply category-based stereotypes to a person when additional personality information is available (Pratto and Bargh, 1991), or when they are motivated to attend to individual differences (Zebrowitz, Montepare and Lee, 1991).

Beliefs about out-group members

Let us assume, then, that the result of contact between two persons of different cultures, races or ethnicities has led one or both parties to classify the other as an out-group member. What then are the probable consequences for the expectations they will hold about one another?

Stereotypes

A stereotype is a group of beliefs about persons who are members of a particular group. Gender, ethnicity, age, education, wealth and the like may form the basis for a stereotype, as indeed can any identifiable social marker. Stereotypes vary in many aspects: they may be widely shared by others, even by the stereotyped persons themselves, or they may be idio-syncratic to the individual holding them; they may involve beliefs about the traits, values, behaviours, opinions or, indeed, beliefs of typical persons from that other group; they may be simple or differentiated, positive or negative, confidently or unsurely held (Triandis *et al.*, 1982).

The early work on stereotypes was dominated by an interest in groups that typically shared a history of conflict, abuse or atrocity (Brigham, 1971). Against such a background, stereotypes about the out-group were extreme, simple, negative and symmetrical, with members of each group rating their own group members positively while denigrating members of the out-group (Schwartzwald and Yinon, 1977). The elimination of stereo-types was widely believed to be a prerequisite for intergroup harmony (Taylor, 1981). This liberal distaste for stereotyping was held by many social scientists and reinforced by the cultural emphasis on personal uniqueness (Snyder and Fromkin, 1980) characteristic of the individualist societies where most research into stereotypes is conducted (Markus and Kitayama, 1991).

Recently, however, psychologists have been developing a more balanced appreciation of stereotypes. Many have noted the 'kernel of truth' (Mackie, 1973) that stereotypes possess; others have observed that inter-acting social groups often hold positive stereotypes about one another (e.g. Berry, Kalin and Taylor, 1977). Furthermore, stereotypes of some groups may be defined across many dimensions, giving opportunity for judges to ascribe a broad, differentiated identity to their own and other group members (e.g. Bond, 1986). Taylor (1981) has argued that this last outcome of the stereotyping process may in fact be an important component in sustaining harmonious intercultural relations.

The function of stereotypes. Stereotypes consist of pre-established expec-tations about members of other groups. They allow those who hold them to reduce their uncertainty about what members of other groups are likely to want, to believe and to do. As such, they are one form of cognitive schema (Rumelhart, 1984). They reduce the need to attend to and process individual information about the other (Hamilton and Trolier, 1986), so that attention may be devoted to other aspects of the interaction. This redeployment of consciousness may be especially useful in cross-cultural encounters, where surprises are likely to abound.

Additionally, stereotypes assist individuals to maintain a positive sense of self-esteem deriving from their group memberships. As mentioned in Chapter 5, Tajfel (1978) argued that people's memberships of various groups constitute one aspect of their self-concept. They strive to establish a sense of esteem in part by differentiating their groups from other groups along dimensions that yield favourable comparisons.

In the 'minimal group' situation which Tajfel used to examine this inter-group process, the subject can only differentiate his or her group from the other using the payoff matrix provided by the experimenter. In more naturalistic settings, the possibilities widen. One may differentiate one's group from another on the basis of power, ancestry, religious propriety, language, culturedness, or what you will. Within a category like power, one can focus on political, economic, social or other aspects of one's relative strength. Members of different interacting groups can obviously derive self-esteem from their group membership in many different ways. This richness makes the study of the actual stereotypes held by interacting groups especially informative.

A key dimension identified in all ethnic or cultural stereotypes of character is the 'beneficence' dimension (Giles and Ryan, 1982), involving traits like honest, kind, loyal and trustworthy. This dimension appears to be a combination of the conscientiousness and agreeableness factors of the 'Big Five' components of personality (Digman, 1990). Generally, group members rate themselves higher on beneficence than they rate out-group members. Out-group members do the same, resulting in the 'mirror image' (Bronfenbrenner, 1961) pattern of intergroup perceptions. Such 'in-group enhancement' is probably a basic feature of all socialization in any viable cultural group (Bond, Chiu and Wan, 1984). The critical question for intergroup harmony is the *size* of the gap between the in-group and the out-group rating. A moderate difference may be socially necessary for a group to remain viable; a large difference, socially destructive.

An additional basis of comparison often appears in real-life stereotypes, a 'competence' dimension (Giles and Ryan, 1982). This dimension involves traits like intelligent, successful, wealthy, educated and so forth. Ratings on this dimension have some basis in intergroup social reality, as these groups have considerable shared history to use in anchoring their judge-ments. Not surprisingly, there is often agreement between the groups about the relative standing of their own and other group members on competence-type dimensions. For example, both British and Hong Kong Chinese in Hong Kong acknowledge the higher average status of the British (Bond and Hewstone, 1988).

Other dimensions of comparison may appear if the measurement scales provided to the respondents are sufficiently comprehensive. Neuroticism, extroversion and openness have all been isolated in stereotype research (e.g. Bond, 1986). So, simply at the level of stereotyped perceptions of character, group members have a wide array of dimensions which they may use to derive an adequate measure of self-esteem.

Stereotypes have a further important function for groups in contact, which is that they guide the behaviour of people from these different groups when they interact. Gibson (1979) has argued that 'Perception is for doing' and research has shown that perception of another's personality relates to the behaviour which one undertakes with that other person. So, for example, both Chinese and Australians are more likely to associate in various ways with someone they regard as 'beneficent' (Bond and Forgas, 1984). Conversely, they will avoid and probably criticize or attack people they regard as evil-natured. It is this view of the enemy as evil which sustains all group conflict (Becker, 1973).

Members of different groups can interact in more harmonious ways, of course. Here, perceptions of out-group members on competence dimensions will probably guide subordination behaviour. In a similar way, perceptions of neuroticism will guide formal as opposed to self-disclosing and intimate behaviour, and perceptions of extroversion will guide initiating, sociable behaviour (Bond, 1983).

So, stereotypes of the out-group can further reduce uncertainty by guiding our behavioural choices towards members of the out-group. When groups have some experience of interacting, they may come to agree on the stereotypes they hold about one another. At the Chinese University of Hong Kong, for example, both local Chinese and American exchange students believe that the Americans are more extroverted, the Chinese more introverted (Bond, 1986). This shared perception guides behaviour in a complementary fashion – typically the American initiates and the Chinese responds. It is probable that mutual, interaction-facilitating stereotypes arise among all groups which work together (e.g. Everett and Stening, 1987), thereby easing the uncertainty and anxiety of encountering a stranger from a different group.

The origin of stereotypes. The early work on stereotypes (e.g. Katz and Braly, 1933) revealed that people can hold intense stereotypes about persons from other cultural and ethnic groups, even though they have never met such persons. These polarized attitudes probably arise out of a generalized distrust of persons foreign and their reinforcement at home, by the media and in educational curricula. Stereotypes are likely to be particularly clear and consensually held if one's own group has a long history of dealings with an out-group within one's borders. In this type of situation, the anxiety surrounding intercultural encounters can be attenuated by the high predictability the stereotype affords.

Ethnocentrism

Sumner (1940) defined ethnocentrism as 'the view of things in which one's own group is the center of everything, and all others are scaled and rated with reference to it (p. 13)'. This rather neutral definition of a probably universal cognitive process has assumed more volatile connotations over time; more contemporary definitions treat ethnocentrism as favouritism of one's in-group and rejection of the out-group (LeVine and Campbell, 1972).

It is probable that ethnocentrism shows variability from country to country (Ramirez, 1967). Bond (1988b) identified significant differences among students in 22 countries along a value dimension of 'social integration' versus 'cultural inwardness'. Social integration was defined by values like tolerance of others and harmony with others, whereas cultural inwardness was defined by values like a sense of cultural superiority and respect for tradition. We believe that persons from countries where the typical individual is high in cultural inwardness will be more likely to avoid contact with outsiders and discriminate against them in various ways (see, for example, Bond, 1991a on human rights). When people from such countries do meet culturally different persons, the difficulties that arise are likely to be even greater. We now turn to such interactions.

Communicating with foreigners

The act of communicating has components and dynamics which are basic to the process anywhere. How these components are weighted and evaluated and how these dynamics are engaged, however, show important cultural differences. These differences must be accommodated in some way if cross-cultural exchanges are to remain viable. This section examines the challenges inherent in communicating across cultural lines.

Communication

Briefly, the act of communication involves transmitting messages to another person who translates those messages by giving them meaning. These messages may be sent by conscious intent or not, and include information about both the content of the message and the relationship among those communicating (Watzlawick, Beavin and Jackson, 1967). Much communication behaviour is scripted so that exchanges proceed in a routine manner and lead to desirable, expected outcomes.

Occasionally, the communication process breaks down. A partner may disrupt the routine, for example by saying, 'I have an excruciating headache' when asked, 'How are you?'; or the consequence of the exchange may not be what one or both of the parties anticipated, as when an appointment is not kept. At this point one or both parties to the communication become 'mindful' (Langer, 1989) of their communication and must decide how to respond. They may withdraw from the interaction, adopt a new routine, or process the impasse by explicitly confronting the

Source: Reproduced with permission from Feign (1987).

Figure 9.1 The cultural meanings of 'yes'

difficulty – 'meta-communicating' as Watzlawick *et al.* (1967) describe the repair process.

These forms of response themselves meet with responses from the other, and together they constitute an ongoing negotiation of the relationship. Communications are steps in this negotiation process. Accurate communication occurs when both parties to the communication agree about the meaning of the various communications exchanged. Such accuracy is tested by the outcome of events and is typically addressed only when a breakdown occurs and the parties engage in conscious 'repairs' (Schwartz, 1980). Considerable inaccuracy probably exists during most communication exchanges but is never assessed, because the outcome is either acceptable to the parties involved or else not worth confronting even though it is unacceptable.

Effective communication, then, means that the outcome of the process continues to meet the needs and wishes of the parties involved. As Wish (1979) has shown, stable relationships in the United States are perceived to vary across five dimensions:

- Co-operative to competitive.
- Intense to superficial.
- Task oriented to socioemotional.
- Hierarchical to egalitarian.
- Formal to informal.

These dimensions probably apply to relationships in all cultural systems (Adamopoulos, 1988; Lonner, 1980).

Cultural groups probably vary in their frequency of, and preference for, certain types of relationship. Such differences should not lead us as social scientists, however, to define as effective communication that which leads to the types of relationship idealized in our own cultural group. Communications between two parties can be effective *regardless* of how their relationship may be characterized, providing that each party is achieving a desired sort of relationship.

On occasion one or both parties to a communication may wish to change the nature of their relationship. So, for example, the subordinate in a hierarchical relationship may wish for more egalitarian exchanges. Such a desire may temporarily disturb the relationship, but their communications may continue to be accurately understood and may be effective in communicating the subordinate's dissatisfaction with the status quo. In short, effective communication does not entail agreement about the nature of a relationship or current satisfaction with that relationship.

As will become apparent, these issues of communication accuracy, breakdown confrontation, repair strategies and desired relationships become especially critical in exchanges across cultural lines.

The context for communication

Persons from different cultural groups come into contact with one another in a variety of contexts – a French graduate student doing field work for her thesis meets a Chinese peasant at a factory, a Zulu reports for work to his Afrikaner boss at a diamond mine in the Transvaal, a Turkish child of immigrant parents attends her first day of classes at a German primary school. The possibilities are legion, whether contacts take place between members of the same society or between members of different societies. In an attempt to organize this variety, Bochner (1982) conceptualized cross-cultural contacts within the table shown in Box 9.1.

Many of these contact variables have been widely researched in social psychology. For example, the variable of time-span has been examined by Kiesler, Kiesler and Pallak (1967). They found that, when those in contact expected no future interactions with the other, they were more extreme in their dislike of 'inappropriate' actions by those others. Similarly, Bond and Dutton (1975) found that those anticipating no future interaction with others aggressed against them more freely. These findings have obvious implications for how locals may treat tourists, a dynamic which may be exacerbated by the relative wealth of the tourists.

Likewise, each of the other contact variables in Box 9.1 will set social psychological processes into motion. They will operate whether those

Box 9.1 *Types of cross-cultural contact*

Contact variables:	Between members of the same society		Between members of different societies	
	Type	Example	Type	Example
On whose territory?	Usually joint	Black and white Americans	Home or foreign territory	Tourists Overseas students Immigrants and their respective hosts
Time-span	Long term	Black and white Americans	Short-term Medium-term Long-term	Tourists Overseas students Immigrants
Purpose	Make a life in	Black and white Americans	Make a life in Study in Make a profit Recreation	Immigrants Overseas students Workers Tourists
Type of involvement	Participate in society	Black and white Americans	Participate Exploit Contribute Observe	Immigrants Workers Experts Tourists
Frequency of high contact		Black and white Americans	High Medium Low	Immigrants Overseas students Tourists
Degree of intimacy between participants	High to low social distance (variable)	Black and white Americans	High to low social distance (variable)	Immigrants Overseas students Tourists
Relative status and power	Equal to unequal (variable)	Black and white Americans	Equal to unequal	Tourists Overseas students Immigrants
Numerical balance	Majority– minority Equal distribution	Black and white Americans Chinese Japanese and Caucasian Hawaiians	Majority– minority	Host and students Immigrants Tourists
Visible distinguishing characteristics	Race Religion Language	Black and white Americans Irish Indians Canadians	Race Religion Language	Immigrants Overseas students Tourists

Source: Bochner (1982).

interacting are members of the same or of different cultures, unless the ideology of one or both groups is engaged to resist the pattern. The work of Dutton (1973) on reverse discrimination, for example, shows that under certain conditions members of minority groups are given preferential treatment by members of the dominant majority. Each of the variables which form the context for contact helps structure background considerations for examining any particular interaction across cultural lines.

The culture of situations

All encounters between people take place in what Barker (1968) called 'behavior settings', where the participants have some type of relationship with one another. So, classmates meet in the school canteen, an employer joins his employees at a company wedding, spouses discuss their day's events while preparing dinner. An understanding of these social episodes is shared by the participants, so that their interaction may proceed according to script, with both parties focusing on the event at hand (Forgas, 1979).

If the participants in a social episode come from different cultures, however, there is a high probability that their initial understanding of that event will differ. To demonstrate this likelihood, Forgas and Bond (1985) had Australian and Chinese students evaluate a number of episodes common to both groups, such as arriving late to a tutorial. What emerged from this study was that persons from each cultural group used four criteria for evaluating this set of situations. Both Australians and Chinese evaluated the episodes in terms of whether they were involving or not, and whether they were task or social in nature. The problem was that the same situation elicited different levels of response along these two shared dimensions. For example, giving directions was more involving for Australians than for Chinese, but studying was more task-oriented for Chinese than for Australians. In terms of the remaining two dimensions of evaluation, there was no overlap of meaning at all between the Australians and the Chinese. Australians considered the episodes in terms of whether they elicited competitive responses or confident responses. In contrast, the Chinese considered whether the episodes elicited egalitarian responses or happy responses.

At the very least, this study demonstrates that the same situations can mean very different things to persons of different cultural backgrounds (see also Oatey, 1992). The behaviours evoked by these different situational representations are thus also likely to differ (Furnham, 1982), so that the participants' responses to the same behaviour setting often disconfirm one another's expectations. Co-ordinating behaviour effectively becomes difficult, and attention must be shifted towards negotiating shared meanings about the situation if the relationship is to continue.

Communication breakdown

Disconfirmed expectations and misattributions

Living across cultural lines constantly produces surprises for those involved. People are late for appointments, or early, or do not make appointments at all and simply arrive. People stand too close or too far away; talk too much, or too little, or too fast, or too slow, or about the wrong topics. They are too emotional, or too moderate, show too much or too little of a certain emotion, or show it at the wrong time, or fail to show it at the right time. The list of possible surprises is as long as the list of behavioural domains where cultural differences have been documented.

The human response to surprise is to search for explanations (Pyszczynski and Greenberg, 1981). The discovery of an explanation for the unusual behaviour of the other will reduce our uncertainty, as Berger (1987) has argued, and make the other's behaviour more predictable. The intercultural problem, of course, is that the person explaining the other's behaviour has his or her own cultural guidelines for interpreting the surprising behaviour. Often these guidelines will lead to an unfavourable personality attribution about the other. So, the American businessman who gazes intently at a prospective Malaysian partner and addresses him by his first name may well be regarded as 'disrespectful' (LaFrance and Mayo, 1976).

Such negative attributions are likely because there is a normative aspect to many of our expectations about behaviour from others (Burgoon and Walther, 1990). In the perceiver's culture, behaviour which deviates from expectation often violates social rules and is diagnostic of somebody rude, neurotic, ignorant or simply uncivilized. This last attribution is commonly employed after intercultural encounters and is actually quite fitting. As assessed against the cultural standards of the observer, the behaviour of the other is indeed 'uncivilized' (Burgoon, 1989). The other person is probably behaving, however, in ways that are situationally appropriate in his or her own culture.

The net result is a cross-cultural 'misattribution': that is, an attribution about the reason for an event given by a foreigner which differs from that typically given by a member of the host culture. The other person may intend to communicate friendliness by asking you about your family, but is instead perceived as 'nosey'; may spontaneously be communicating respect by lowering his or her eyes, but instead is regarded as 'indifferent'. The outcome of the attribution process is determined by the cultural programme used to decode the behaviour, and where these codes differ, misattributions will be rife.

Positive misattributions?   Not all misattributions are negative, of course.

For example, an Australian teacher may be delighted with the extent of the courtesy shown by the principal when he gives a guest lecture at a Japanese high school. This departure from expectation would be incorrectly explained, however, if the teacher made a situational attribution like 'The principal behaved in this way because he considers me a talented academic.' The principal would simply have been observing Japanese academic etiquette towards a visitor, and not communicating special deference to the teacher. The teacher would have misinterpreted the principal's courtesies.

If the teacher uses this self-serving attribution to guide his future behaviour towards the principal, some negative surprises may then begin arising. Should the teacher request a job, or invite the principal to dinner, or offer a further lecture, the response to these initiatives may not confirm his Australian expectations about how a talented academic is treated. At this point the frustrated teacher may begin to regard the principal as inconsistent, inscrutable or uncivilized.

With respect to violations of expectancies surrounding non-verbal behaviours, Burgoon (1989) has shown that certain forms of departure from expectation are positively evaluated, at least in the United States. For instance, where a communicator came closer, made more eye-contact or used more of some forms of touch than expected, the reactions of the other party were found to be positive. The first issue cross-culturally is to discover which types of non-verbal violation by what types of communicator are positively evaluated in other cultures. Then one needs to know if *foreigners* are allowed to violate the norm with the same positive reactions as locals. A double standard may well be applied, especially when other members of the host culture are present. Currently, social scientists know nothing about either of these two issues. It seems judicious to presume, however, that most violations of the host's non-verbal code will be negatively evaluated by locals.

In conclusion, then, until people from different cultures become more knowledgeable about the other's cultural code, the cycle of misattributions will continue (Brislin *et al.*, 1986). This cycle will eventually result in distressing experiences which set a withdrawal dynamic into motion.

The ultimate attribution error

As defined by Pettigrew (1979), this error is 'a systematic patterning of inter-group misattributions shaped in part by prejudice'. Such patterning will entail people's explaining the positive behaviours of in-group members as arising from their positive personality traits (e.g. she is generous in giving to charity), but positive behaviours from out-group members as arising from situational factors (e.g. he gave money to charity because others were watching). Conversely, negative behaviours of in-group members are explained away as due to situational forces, whereas negative behaviours from out-group members are attributed to their (negative) personality dispositions (Hewstone, 1989). This 'group-serving bias' clearly has much in common with the self-serving bias, whose generality we examined in Chapter 6.

We have argued that cross-cultural encounters lead to many negative outcomes for the parties involved. As demonstrated in a variety of studies (e.g. Stephan, 1977), the behaviours of out-group members leading to such outcomes are often explained in terms of their (negative) personality dispositions. These attributions about the personality of out-group members typically confirm the negative stereotype about them that already exists. This stereotype is highly available because the out-group categorization of the other is likely to be salient in a cross-cultural encounter. Given the confirmatory bias in event processing (e.g. Rothbart, Evans and Fulero, 1979), each party's explanatory search is likely to end at this point, with the polarization between members of different groups reinforced yet again.

As we found with the self-serving bias, however, an ethnocentric bias is not always found. Social–political factors can play a role, whereby institutional forces that favour intergroup harmony lead to moderation of such attributional outcomes (e.g. Hewstone and Ward, 1985). Cultural factors may also reduce the bias, with persons from more individualist cultures less ethnocentric in their attributions about the out-group (Al-Zahrani, 1991). Structural aspects of the intergroup situation are also important. Accepted minority group status may lead to attributions unfavourable to one's own group (e.g. Milner, 1975), whereas resented minority group status may sharpen the ultimate attribution error (Amabile and Glazebrook, 1982). Finally, personality dispositions, like world-mindedness (Sampson and Smith, 1957), probably attenuate the bias as well.

The language barrier

Language is an efficient means of transmitting symbolic information to achieve instrumental and affective goals. Cultural conventions regulate basic features of language use from microscopic issues like syntax, vocabulary, sentence structure and accent, to macroscopic considerations such as how much one speaks, about what topics and with whom. Within the same culture there are striking differences in these aspects of language use (e.g. Bernstein, 1971); across cultural groups, these differences are further compounded.

The first cross-cultural consideration is that a language casts a net of mutual intelligibility around those who use it and becomes a unifying force for group cohesion. As Fishman (1972) has argued, one's mother tongue assumes a powerful, emotional resonance, and for people of many cultural groups it is a defining characteristic of a valued national identity (Smolicz, 1979).

Speech accommodation.   A second problem arises in cross-cultural interactions and is most obvious when partners to the exchange speak different mother tongues. Who will accommodate to whom, so that they can communicate effectively? Speech accommodation involves shifting one's speech patterns towards those of one's interlocutor, so that greater similarity of language use is achieved (Thakerar, Giles and Cheshire, 1982). That accommodation may be one-way or mutual depending on the interpersonal attraction and relative power of the parties concerned (Giles and Johnson, 1981).

If the two cultural groups are antagonistic towards one another and if group membership is a salient component of the interaction, divergence of speech will probably occur (e.g. Bourhis *et al.*, 1979). Participants will refuse to speak the other party's language, effectively isolating one another behind a wall of inscrutability. Given the close perceived association between language and culture, members of one cultural group may even refuse to learn the other group's language. They may believe that including it in their educational curriculum would subtract from their own cultural heritage (Lambert, 1967), or perpetuate the dominance of a resented cultural group over their own (Giles and Byrne, 1982).

Even if relations between the two cultural groups are positive and stable, the issue of whose speech moves towards whose must still be negotiated. The roles of those who are interacting are a key consideration, as is the relative status of the ethnic groups involved and their solidarity, the ethnolinguistic vitalities (see Box 9.2) of each speech community, and the interaction goals of each party (see Gallois *et al.*, 1988, for a review). This negotiation is a socially delicate task for both participants. The effort they put into accommodation will be appreciated and reciprocated (Giles, Bourhis and Taylor, 1977), but may be interpreted negatively by their own group members who are present. Those who switch into a second language, for example, may be perceived to have political preferences more like those of the other language community (Bond, 1985), and may evoke more ethnic affirmation from members of their own speech community in response (Bond and Cheung, 1984). In addition, the users of a second language may discover their own attitudes shifting towards those of the out-group (Bond and Yang, 1982).

Clearly, language is an important medium for eliciting ethnically charged responses both for those who use it and for those who hear it. The increasing use of English as 'the language of wider communication' (Naisbitt and Aburdene, 1990) may defuse this dilemma somewhat, as the English language becomes more detached from any particular cultural

Box 9.2 *Ethnolinguistic vitality*

The 1970s ushered in a renewed interest in the study of ethnicity and intergroup relations around the world. In order to conceptualize and integrate these studies, it became necessary to analyze the features of the sociostructural context in which intergroup behaviour occurred. Language use came to be regarded as an important reflection of intergroup relations. A group's ethnolinguistic vitality was defined as, 'that which makes a group likely to behave as a distinctive and collective entity in the inter-group context (Giles, Bourhis and Taylor, 1977, p. 308).' Factors proposed to influence group vitality were as follows:

○ *Demographic:* the numbers and concentration of ethnolinguistic groups within a political unit.
○ *Institutional control:* the degree of formal and informal representation of the ethnolinguistic group within the social apparatus of government, education, business, mass media, religion and so forth.
○ *Status:* a speech community's prestige – historically, culturally and linguistically, as ascribed both locally and also internationally.

A group's ethnolinguistic vitality may be assessed both subjectively and objectively. Subjective assessments may show variable levels of consensus both within a given group and across the various groups in a society. How people perceive their group's ethnolinguistic vitality is related to their attitudes towards second-language learning and to their degree of speech accommodation in cross-linguistic encounters.

Source: Harwood, Giles and Bourhis (in press).

group. In the case of other language groups, however, the question of language choice for competent bilinguals will continue to be a charged one. This fact of intercultural life adds another layer of difficulty to cross-cultural interactions.

Linguistic ability. The language competence of the interacting parties is another important issue to consider. Regardless of other factors, they must find a common language they can both use if they are to work effectively. Across different language communities, the general outcome is that one of the two parties must use his or her second language. This requirement introduces cognitive strain on the second-language user, who may already be contending with heavy demands in dealing with the task that brought the parties together in the first place.

Additionally, second-language users face an issue of impression management, as they are likely to be rated as higher in competence and

Source: Reproduced with permission from Feign (1986).

Figure 9.2 Linguistic accommodation

benevolence the more proficient they are in that foreign tongue (Wible and Hui, 1985). This concern about appearing competent will be even more acute for a second-language speaker who is of lower status in the relationship, which is frequently the case. In fact his or her second-language ability may be one of the criteria by which performance is evaluated in the organization where he or she is working. This concern adds tension to the encounter for the second-language speaker. It may also lead to inaccurate communication if language uncertainties produced by higher-status speakers go unchallenged because the second-language user is reluctant to appear stupid.

There is some evidence that first-language speakers in a cross-language interaction are responsive to the linguistic competence of their partner (Pierson and Bond, 1982). They modify aspects of their speech, like the use of filled pauses, rate of speech, complexity of sentence structure and so forth. These 'interpretability strategies' (Coupland *et al.*, 1988) make their speech easier to understand. To effect this modification, however, they must adopt a greater 'addressee focus' (Gallois *et al.*, 1988) than is normal, so that they can monitor the intelligibility of their speech for their partner. Again, this requirement shifts attention from the task at hand to the communication process itself.

As a further concern, the first-language speaker must create an interpersonal environment where confusion signals are acceptable, even encouraged. If not, the second-language speaker may pretend that he or she understands, with negative consequences later when events reveal otherwise. Of course, the first-language speaker must be able to read these confusion signals (e.g. laughter, furrowing of the brow, slackening of the jaw, uttering 'What?', etc.). They, too, are culturally variable, so the first-language speaker must be correctly attuned to these signals (Loveday, 1982).

The net result of these various considerations is that a cross-language encounter may be equally demanding for the native-language speaker as for the second-language speaker, though for different reasons. Both must pay more attention than normal to the vehicle of communication. Misunderstanding of one another's speech and failed expectations are more likely, with the attendant danger that negative stereotypes of one another's group will be confirmed.

In addition they must each balance a host of delicate personal, social and cultural factors in deciding whether, and how, and how much they will accommodate to one another linguistically. Not surprisingly, most bilinguals follow the law of least effort and avoid second-language encounters outside the workplace. Instead, they socialize within their own linguistic communities.

Speech pragmatics. In faultless English, Mr Chan greets his teacher Mrs Robertson with 'Have you had your lunch yet?' In faultless Thai, a French engineer contributes to a planning session in Bangkok with 'Permit me to demonstrate to you several ways in which your conclusions are mistaken.' In faultless Portugese, a Dutch visitor asks his Brazilian host, 'What time should I *really* arrive for dinner?' In each of these cases the speaker has accommodated linguistically to the other's language and has used that language fluently. In each case, however, they have violated the code of language *usage* in the other's culture. In Scotland one does not ask one's teacher about her eating activities; in Thailand one does not contradict one's business associates; in Brazil one does not confront one's host with a demand for precision about time.

Speech pragmatics refers to 'the characteristic communication patterns, values and attitudes governing the use of language' (Fliegel, 1987). As was discussed in Chapter 8, each culture has a normative communication style. The way in which an argument is structured, the directness of the presentation, the amount of self-disclosure and the topics of conversation are all bound by convention from culture to culture (Blum-Kulka, House and Kasper, 1989). Violation of these conventions will set into motion the misattribution cycle described earlier.

Indeed, the negative consequences may be even more dramatic if one speaks the other's language fluently. In this case the other party will probably assume that, because you know the language, you 'should have known better'. If this reasoning occurs, the other may construe your talk as 'insulting' rather than simply 'ignorant', and counter-attack (Felson, 1978). Competence in another's language can thus become a two-edged sword if one handles it incorrectly.

Corrective feedback

So far, we have suggested that people from different cultures are likely to understand the same situation differently. In consequence they will behave towards one another in ways that violate one another's culturally based scripts for those situations. Such disconfirmations lead to surprise, eventually to frustration and often to the confirmation of negative stereotypes about the other's group. Where choice is involved, each party may well choose not to interact further.

Choice is often not available, as in a co-operative work setting. People may also be strongly motivated to forge a viable relationship with people from other cultures for personal reasons. In order to co-ordinate their behaviours more smoothly with one another, then, they must learn to confront disfluencies and engage in repairs (Schwartz, 1980). Here further cultural problems are lurking.

Embarrassment. Goffman (1956) defined 'face' as 'the positive social value a person effectively claims for himself by the line others assume he has taken during a particular contact (p. 213)'. When that line is brought into question by developments during encounters with others, we feel embarrassed. Embarrassment is an acute social pain which quickly spreads its 'dis-ease' to others present (Edelmann, 1982). It is a universal phenomenon (Ho, 1976) and highly aversive, especially for those high in self-consciousness and social anxiety (Yuen, 1991).

Cupach, Metts and Hazelton (1978) distinguish two major types of embarrassment as 'improper identity' situations and 'loss of poise' situations. The former occur when one's actions violate a social expectation associated with a role; the latter, when one's composure is undermined by events. Both abound in cross-cultural interactions.

There is some evidence that persons from certain cultural groups feel more embarrassment across a wider range of social situations than do those from other cultural groups (Yuen, 1991). As we discovered in the previous chapter, one's face is more closely tied to the behaviour of one's group members in a collectivist culture, making one more broadly vulnerable (Ting-Toomey, 1988). Additionally, in collectivist cultures the subordinate party to an interaction will feel a particular responsibility for any untoward events involving a superior (Bond and Lee, 1981).

The first consequence of these cultural differences is that collectivists will tend to avoid interactions likely to lead to embarrassment more than individualists. This avoidance applies especially to cross-cultural interactions and to interactions with superiors. Second, they will tend to mask their embarrassment more than individualists, and so 'smooth over' the situation. Both of these tendencies will reduce the probability of generating the feedback necessary for interacting parties to know that something is amiss. Without feedback, no correction will occur.

Remedial strategies. Once embarrassment has been felt and communicated, people take steps to restore face and put the interaction back 'on track' (Felson, 1978). Strategies range from apologizing, justifying and excuse-giving to ignoring the event, making a joke out of the *contretemps*, or attacking the other.

The choice of strategy is influenced by a variety of factors, including the cultural context. Sueda and Wiseman (1992), for example, found that Americans were more likely to use humour and justification, while the Japanese used more apologies. These differences were explained in terms of cultural demands, which emphasize autonomy protection in individualist cultures, and relationship protection in collectivist cultures (Ting-Toomey, 1988).

Both these remedial actions are normative within their own cultural context. The cross-cultural question is how they will be interpreted by members from the other cultural group. As the repair strategies occur at a critical juncture in the relationship, the outcome of this attribution process may well be decisive. With the groups described above, the danger is that the Japanese may interpret the American's humour as insincerity, just as the American may interpret the Japanese person's apology as acceptance of responsibility. Both would probably be wrong. A failure to understand the culturally based style of remediation could then set in motion a further set of embarrassing failures to communicate successfully.

Giving feedback. A definition of the meaning and function of feedback in communication is given by Haslett and Ogilvie (1988). Feedback refers to 'the response listeners give to others about their behavior ... Feedback from others enables us to understand how our behavior affects them, and allows us to modify our behavior to achieve our desired goals (p. 385).' No feedback, no correction.

Feedback comes in many forms, verbal or non-verbal. It also comes at different removes from the event, immediately or some time later, as subsequent events indicate to the participants that something unintended was in fact transmitted. Feedback may also be conveyed from different sources, by the person involved or by some third party. It may be communicated in person or more impersonally, perhaps by letter. However feedback arises, it is essential for effective communication. By using it, interacting parties can engage in 'a series of diminishing mistakes – a dwindling series of under- and over-corrections converging on the goal (Deutsch, 1968,

p. 390)'. The cross-cultural problem, of course, is whether people from different cultural groups notice the feedback they are being given and whether they can decode it correctly.

As noted in the last chapter, there are differing cultural conventions guiding all communication, including feedback. Particularly important is Hall's (1976) distinction between high- and low-context cultures. Persons from low-context cultures have been socialized to provide relatively precise, immediate and verbal feedback in person as part of their social contract. Those from high-context cultures are more likely to use vague, delayed, non-personal and non-verbal feedback.

When feedback is provided in a culturally different way, the potential for misunderstanding it is considerable. One may miss it entirely or translate it incorrectly. Such failures may initiate a new round of ineffective co-ordination and subsequent embarrassment. Even when a culturally different form of feedback is correctly understood, it may be resented. The other party may be regarded as 'blunt' or as 'devious' because he or she is providing feedback in a manner which deviates from the cultural conventions used by the receiver. The cultural divide widens.

Pushing for preferred relationships

As described earlier, Wish (1979) identified five dimensions of relationship variation found in the United States. We expect that these variations can be identified in all cultural groups. Furthermore, we believe that cultural systems vary in the extent to which they encourage various forms of relationship, and are characterized by such different types of relationship. Although no direct evidence exists to support this belief, Hofstede's (1991) five dimensions of cultural variation suggest some testable conjectures. We hypothesize that cultural uncertainty avoidance is related to greater formality in relationship, masculinity to greater task-orientation, power distance to greater hierarchy, individualism to greater superficiality, and Confucian dynamism to greater competitiveness.

If these conjectures are sound, then an additional difference must be confronted by those interacting across cultural lines. Even if each party has learned to translate the other's behaviour correctly, each may be pushing the relationship in different directions. The American housewife may want a less hierarchical relationship with her Sri Lankan maid, the Swedish teacher may wish a less formal relationship with her Arab student, the English businessman may want a more co-operative relationship with his Chinese supplier, a Filipino may want a more friendly relationship with his Canadian colleague, and a Brazilian husband may want a more intense relationship with his Finnish wife. Of course, all relationships must be negotiated over time. Barriers to this negotiation may arise, however, when cultural backgrounds discourage certain forms of relationship relative to others.

One more time: Mr Chan and Mrs Robertson

Having read this chapter, readers may find a review of the encounter between Chan Chi Lok and Jean Robertson in Chapter 1 revealing. Many typical areas of cross-cultural difficulty related to the themes identified in this chapter can be detected in their exchange.

Before extracting some of the key problem domains, it is worth noting that the prognosis for Mr Chan and Mrs Robertson is at present not hopeful. Both appear innocent of any awareness of the fundamental capacity of culture to influence behaviour. They are aware that the other comes from a different culture, but appear not to understand any of the conventions associated with the other group's behaviour. In consequence every act is interpreted by the other 'culturo-centrically': that is, in terms of the receiver's cultural norms. Confusion and irritation are the inevitable results. Not until they become culturally mindful is any progress possible.

Such mindfulness may develop, of course. Their separate frustrations may prompt them to search for more sophisticated attributions than merely labelling the other 'troublesome' or 'uncivilized'. They may express their grievances to a knowledgeable cultural mediator, pick up an informative book on the other's culture, see an illuminating movie, or hear a stimulating lecture on cultural differences in behaviour – there are many potential resources for cultural awakening. Certainly Mrs Robertson will need to receive some feedback on the language difficulties she creates cross-culturally or her job is in jeopardy! Given the increasing appreciation of the cultural component in second-language learning (Valdes, 1986), Mrs Robertson has a good chance of developing cultural awareness should she continue teaching English in Hong Kong. As for Mr Chan ...

Language

One can only hope that Mrs Robertson speaks more slowly and less collo-quially in class than she does in her office. Expressions like 'a wee bit slippery' and 'never bother' place extraordinary demands on second-language speakers, and the statement, 'I doubt you are 20 minutes late' is in fact a literal disclaimer of what Mrs Robertson actually believes. Peculiar questions like 'You don't get it, do you?' are a perplexing construction for learners of English with their apparently contradictory stance towards the same issue. Chan's 'yes' affirms that he does *not* understand; the English convention is to say 'no' in that case, so Mrs. Robertson is surprised by

Chan's unexpected answer. Many languages, like Chan's native Cantonese, present questions both positively and negatively, requiring responders to affirm or to deny in their answer. Ambiguities are thereby reduced.

Mr Chan also creates a few problems for his teacher. He makes many common errors in grammar and syntax, as one would expect. The connotations of English are too much to master at this stage of his English language acquisition, and his statement that Mrs Robertson 'stinks' produces a dramatic reaction. The pragmatics of his English usage are similarly undeveloped, and Chan's question about whether his teacher has yet eaten lunch is judged as impertinent by Mrs Robertson. It is a direct translation from a typical Cantonese greeting around noon-time and an appropriate conversational opener from Chan's perspective. Even when Mrs Robertson learns this Chinese convention, she may well continue to regard it as too personal a greeting, especially from students.

Proxemics

Doors are boundary markers of personal territory in individualist cultures. To knock and enter before receiving permission is to insult and challenge the occupant. Chinese, indeed collectivist, conventions about doors and territory are different. Chan knows that Mrs Robertson is expecting him, so he announces his arrival by knocking and immediately opens the door. Mrs Robertson spends much of the remaining encounter seeking to re-establish her authority, an authority Chan does not realize he has questioned.

His direct physical approach to Mrs Robertson's chair further offends her. Chan does not detect the coldness with which his teacher directs him to sit, but finds it unusual to be positioned so far from someone he is addressing. Chinese comfort zones are much closer than the Scottish, and Chan begins the process of confirming the stereotype that westerners like Mrs Robertson are *mo yan ching* (without compassion).

Time

One way people from individualist cultures protect their freedom and depersonalize control issues is to insist on careful scheduling of time. Given the power disparities in collectivist cultures, people have a more flexible attitude towards commitments generally, and about appointments in particular. By being 20 minutes late, Mr Chan has insulted Mrs Robertson and put her under time pressure, since she has a lunch appointment with her departmental chairman. This sense of pressure leads her to usher Chan out of her office before their business can be concluded, in turn insulting his face.

Attributional style

The 'cult of effort' is very important in collectivist cultures (e.g. Stevenson *et al.*, 1985), since by trying hard or appearing to do so no one challenges the existing order or shows a lack of loyalty (Bond, 1991b). In individualist cultures, greater explanatory emphasis is given to the ability factor. Variations in ability are consistent with the uniqueness theme in individualist cultures (Snyder and Fromkin, 1980) and justify individual resistance to group pressure for conformity. Consequently, Mr Chan emphasizes his effort in Mrs Robertson's class, while she stresses his lack of ability, in their negotiation about Chan's performance.

Chan also makes a group-level attribution about the task difficulty when he tells Mrs Robertson that 'We all found your test very difficult.' His teacher interprets this statement as an influence strategy. This cognition generates reactance (Brehm, 1966) and leads to the individual-focused retort that Chan should assume personal responsibility and not rely on others.

Lying. External attributions are common in collectivist cultures as strategies for saving superiors' and subordinates' faces when potential conflict arises (Ting-Toomey, 1988). Often a palpable lie will be mutually accepted by both parties in order to preserve harmony. In individualist cultures, lying violates the social contract and is condemned when it is detected. Mrs Robertson's statement that Mr Chan is 'a wee bit slippery' is in fact a mild reflection of her belief that he is speaking falsely.

Praise and compassion

In collectivist cultures, superiors have considerable authority and discretion. Subordinates attempt to soften the use of this power by allying themselves with their superior through demonstrations of loyalty, praise and other tokens of appreciation. In individualist cultures, leaders are bound by the rules which are negotiated in some detail by those involved. Objective criteria and the facts assume a legitimizing function in this process. Those led are expected to inform themselves of the rules (criteria, schedules, standards) and work accordingly.

When Mr Chan correctly detects his teacher's resistance to passing him, he begins praising Mrs Robertson. She interprets this move as a form of interpersonal bribery and focuses Chan back on to the issue of ability.

Chan responds by informing his teacher about the difficult family circumstances in which he must function. Mrs Robertson is adamant about Chan's prime duty to his 'job' and incredulous when he openly asks for a 'compassionate pass'. For Mrs Robertson to give him a pass would constitute a betrayal of her 'professionalism'.

Other issues?

The above are some of the main problem areas for Mr Chan and Mrs Robertson. There are others which readers will be able to detect as their sensitivity develops. All these differences are real, produce palpable consequences and are difficult for both parties to resolve satisfactorily. To do so would require sustained uphill effort.

Conclusion

The prognosis for effective communication across cultural lines is not good. Freedle (1979) has defined culture as 'a set of interactive schemata for habitual ways in which interacting individuals can dynamically discover what each person intends to convey given the immediate context (p. xiii)'. When cultural backgrounds differ, the interacting parties are cast adrift from these shared schemata, including language. The use of different systems for decoding meaning frequently results in mutual misattributions and consequent difficulties in co-ordinating interaction.

These misattributions will often reinforce and justify pre-existing negative stereotypes about the out-group which function to separate the parties further. Despite these centrifugal forces, they may still be motivated to commit themselves to the time, energy and embarrassment necessary for understanding one another's communications accurately and hence co-ordinating effectively. Having done so, they may discover that they do not share similar goals for the relationship. In the face of such obstacles to communication, one might wonder if relationships are ever successful across cultural borders! If so, how can this success be accomplished? We take the issue further in the next chapter.

TEN

The consequences of cross-cultural contact

The people of this world have been brought together technologically, but have not yet begun to understand what that means in a spiritual sense. We have to learn to live as brothers or we will perish as fools.

(Martin Luther King)

In the previous chapter we discussed many features of cross-cultural contact which make it a difficult challenge for all parties concerned. Despite its complexity and its dangers, people continue to live their lives inter-culturally. Indeed, multiculturalism is fast becoming a fact of life as we approach the twenty-first century. It is important for us to know what happens to people when they interact with persons from different cultural traditions.

Culture shock

The concept of culture shock was introduced by Oberg (1960) to describe the pervasive and negative responses of depression, frustration and dis-orientation experienced by people who live in a new culture. It is a global concept that has since inspired a kaleidoscope of studies. Researchers have charted its development across time in the new culture (the 'U' curve of adjustment – see Furnham, 1990), and related its magnitude to life's little hassles (Lazarus, 1981) and to major life changes (Holmes and Masuda, 1974). They have examined personality dispositions making one more or less susceptible, and examined factors in the relocation, such as the degree of choice, which moderate the impact of culture shock (see Furnham and Bochner, 1986, for a comprehensive review).

A number of points are worth making with respect to culture shock. First, 'culture shock' is a very broad concept. There are many factors which

191

produce 'acculturative stress', as Berry *et al*. (1987) prefer to call it, only one of which involves cross-cultural communication problems. Separation from previous support networks, climate differences, increased health problems, changes in material and technical resources, lack of information about daily routines (e.g. how to travel from A to B) and so forth all exact their price on the migrant. Second, these additional problems serve to distract the new arrival from the culture-learning task, and deplete the energy and motivation necessary to master the communication process. They thus have an indirect effect on the acquisition of skills for effective functioning within cultures new to oneself.

Finally, adaptation to a new cultural system can result in reverse culture shock upon return to one's culture of origin. The adaptive habits one has struggled to master in a new culture may not fit back in the old one, and readjustment will be required. Former friends and acquaintances are often indifferent to one's overseas experience and may now appear narrow and provincial in their interests. In some cultures, interpersonal support for returnees will be further undercut by a general suspicion that they have been tainted by their foreign contact (e.g. Kidder, 1991). Indeed, returnees sometimes find that their values and preferences have shifted as a result of their foreign experience, leaving them alienated from the culture of their birth. This 're-entry shock' (Adler, 1981; Black and Gregerson, 1991a) is made worse because it is typically unexpected. After all, one is returning home. However, both home and traveller have changed!

Work on culture shock was inspired in part by practical concerns about failures in cross-cultural adaptation. We now turn our attention to how best to study these outcomes.

Cross-cultural outcomes

The results of cross-cultural contact may be analyzed in many ways. One may focus on individual consequences, like personal satisfaction, or on group consequences, like genocide; one may focus on internal responses, like stereotypes, or on overt responses, like premature termination of contract; one may focus on the adjustment process across time or only upon some arbitrary end-point. Finally, one may obtain self-reports on these outcomes or ask observers to rate the adapting individual. As in all research, certain populations like exchange students are more readily accessible, so that more is known about the adjustment pattern of such groups than, say, about businessmen.

Further complicating the picture is the observation that what constitutes a 'successful' outcome may itself be shaped by the values about relationship of a particular cultural group. Individualist cultural groups are likely to emphasize the equal treatment of the groups involved and a reduction in stereotyping. Feminine as opposed to masculine cultural groups will emphasize the development of intimate relationships as opposed to effective task completion. It has been found, for instance, that students generally maintain close, intimate friendships with co-nationals when abroad; their contacts with host nationals tend to be focused on their professional or academic goals (Bochner and Orr, 1979). Whether such cross-cultural contact is deemed a success or failure would then depend on whether the outcome measures tapped social or task outcomes. The list could be extended. The point is that outcomes will be evaluated in culturally shaped ways.

Domains of intercultural effectiveness

Different observers have offered different lists of psychological attributes regarded as important in successful adaptation across cultural lines (Furnham and Bochner, 1982; Ruben, 1976). Recently, Hammer (1987) has integrated these various lists and presented his questionnaire to sojourners: that is to say, people who have lived abroad for various periods of time. He concluded that there are three basic skill domains involved in effective cross-cultural living. The first has an intrapsychic focus and involves the ability to tolerate and manage the stress which arises from relocating to a novel physical and social environment. The second skill domain involves the capacity to establish and nurture relationships with strangers from a different culture. The third involves the skills of effective communication, such as the ability to deal with miscommunications, to understand the other's point of view and so forth.

These domains are independent of one another and require psychologically distinct capabilities. They also appear to be culture-general and to apply regardless of the cultural background of the hosts or the new arrivals. Different outcome studies have often focused on just one of these areas to the exclusion of the others, producing complexity and confusion when comparing their results.

Outcome studies

The contact hypothesis (Amir, 1969) maintains that interaction between members of different groups can reduce intergroup prejudice and hostility. Subsequent research addressed to this hypothesis, however, has progressively narrowed the range of circumstances under which this is thought likely to occur (Amir, 1976; Hewstone and Brown, 1986). Neither does contact necessarily improve interpersonal outcomes (Stroebe, Lenkert and Jonas, 1988). At the intergroup level, open conflict is sometimes found;

where clashes are suppressed, resentment and hatred may be simmering beneath the surface. Even in harmonious intergroup climates, such as that in Canada, a national ethnic hierarchy exists in the stereotypes that citizens hold about the various cultural groups in the country (Berry and Kalin, 1979). Ethnocentrism is common, with all groups favouring their own group (along with key reference groups), relative to other out-groups. Negative perceptions of other groups are reciprocated in the perceptions reported by those groups. Many social scientists would regard such an attitudinal configuration as the best that could be expected in any multiethnic situation.

At the interpersonal level, a scattered selection of results is available for different types of contact. For example, Furnham and Bochner (1986) conclude that 'The evidence is overwhelming that many overseas students do not know a single host national intimately, even after many years of residence in the country being visited, and are therefore quite isolated socially from the host society (p. 16).' Triandis (in press) reports premature termination of overseas placements for executives from the United States of between 25 and 40 per cent. Concerning intercultural marriages, divorce rates tend to be higher than those for monocultural marriages (Carter and Glick, 1970). Research on helping behaviour generally shows compatriots receiving more assistance than foreigners (Bochner, 1982, pp. 21–2).

Such results appear rather piecemeal and unco-ordinated. They do, however, support the expectation that cross-cultural relationships are more difficult to manage than are monocultural relationships. However, social scientists with a pragmatic agenda have moved beyond the issue of average outcomes to ask which are the specific predictors of successful outcomes across cultural boundaries.

Cultural predictors.   One might expect that persons socialized in stable exclusive collectivities would suffer more intensely when culturally relocated than would those socialized for greater self-direction and inter-actional flexibility. The former have more to lose, and the latter more to gain from new environments.

A recent study by Carden and Feicht (1991) supports this reasoning. They examined 'homesickness' in Turkish and American females who were living in campus dormitories away from their home towns. The more collectivist Turkish women reported being much more homesick than did the American women. These reactions occurred within the women's own culture. It is probable that a similar pattern of homesickness would occur when more interdependent people travel overseas.

Additionally, we can use Hofstede's (1980) dimensions of culture to advance a more broad-brush hypothesis. Cluster analysis of his results revealed that some countries, such as Denmark and Sweden, had closely similar profiles; other pairs, such as Italy and Mexico, were much more dissimilar. A simple prediction would be that persons travelling to nations with greater cultural dissimilarity will experience more difficulties. This hypothesis could be further refined by examining each dimension of cultural difference separately. Areas of difficulty and ways of overcoming them could be derived from knowledge of each underlying dimension of difference. Triandis, Brislin and Hui (1988) used just such a strategy for guiding training 'across the individualism–collectivism divide'. Other dimensions could be similarly treated.

Demographic predictors. Results from recent work are consistent with those found earlier in relation to the personality dimension of authoritarianism:

In all cases higher status respondents held more positive attitudes [towards other cultural groups] than did those of lower socio-economic status. These differences were particularly evident for educational level, but the same pattern was generally exhibited for the occupational status and income measures as well. (Berry, Kalin and Taylor, 1980, p. 275)

Similarly, groups of higher cultural status held more positive intergroup attitudes. The authors interpret these results in terms of the greater security felt by members of these privileged-status cultural groups. We expect that one's group security in the social hierarchy, especially economic security, will be related to measures of outgroup prejudice in any cultural setting.

Social influences. Considerable effort has been made in social psychology to identify the social conditions conducive to positive intergroup contact. Stephan (1985) reviewed this extensive literature and extracted 13 features of the contact situation which facilitate positive attitude change towards the out-group when individuals interact (see Box 10.1).

  This list was culled from intergroup research conducted for the most part with persons from individualist cultures who shared the same national culture. Some propositions will need to be modified in other cultural systems and across cultural lines. For example, contact across status lines (Stephan's item 2), where competence differences exist (item 4), is both normative and frequent in collectivist cultural settings. When such inter-group contact is legitimate, as in multicultural organizations, positive rather than negative outcomes could well be expected (see also Gudykunst, 1988). Stephan's (1985) list is, however, a useful starting point in developing research hypotheses and in structuring more fruitful outcomes.

Personality factors. A host of studies (e.g. Church, 1982) has examined the impact of various personality measures on various types of outcome

Box 10.1 *Stephan's list of social factors promoting intergroup harmony*

1. Co-operation within groups should be maximized and competition between groups should be minimized.
2. Members of the in-group and the out-group should be of equal status both within and outside the contact situation.
3. Similarity of group members on non-status dimensions (beliefs, values, etc.) appears to be desirable.
4. Differences in competence should be avoided.
5. The outcomes should be positive.
6. Strong normative and institutional support for the contact should be provided.
7. The intergroup contact should have the potential to extend beyond the immediate situation.
8. Individuation of group members should be promoted.
9. Non-superficial contact (e.g. mutual disclosure of information) should be encouraged.
10. The contact should be voluntary.
11. Positive effects are likely to correlate with the duration of the contact.
12. The contact should occur in a variety of contexts with a variety of in-group and out-group members.
13. Equal numbers of in-group and out-group members should be used.

Source: W. B. Gudykunst, *Bridging Differences: Effective intergroup communication*, p. 80. © Sage Publications Inc. Reprinted by permission.

measures, taken from various sources and provided by various types of sojourner interacting in various contexts with various host cultures. The consequent yield of results is understandably complex!

Given this daunting array of past work, contemporary researchers have learned to take a much broader approach, measuring a variety of predictors and a variety of outcomes within the same study. In an excellent example of this approach, Ward and Kennedy (in press) began by distinguishing two forms of adaptation. The first they labelled 'psychological', referring to intrapsychic capacities for coping with novel, demanding environments. This type of adaptation appears to overlap with Hammer's (1987) first domain of intercultural effectiveness, the ability to deal with stress. The second form of adaptation they labelled 'sociocultural', referring to capacities for negotiating interactions with members of the new, host culture. This type of adaptation appears to overlap with Hammer's second and third domains, the ability to develop intercultural relations and the ability to communicate effectively.

Ward and Kennedy (in press) discovered that in two different inter-cultural settings psychological adjustment was positively affected by an internal locus of control, a smaller number of life changes (Holmes and Masuda, 1974), greater contact with co-nationals for social support, and lower difficulty in managing daily social contacts. Sociocultural adaptation, on the other hand, was enhanced by lower degrees of difference between host and sojourner cultures, greater interaction with host nationals, extraversion and lower levels of mood disturbances. These results in both adaptive domains are consistent with most of the previous research into cross-cultural adaptation and suggest a robust set of findings.

Only some of Ward and Kennedy's predictors are personality variables, and of the available personality measures, they chose to use only a few. Despite the plethora of personality tests, there is only a limited number of personality variables (McCrae and John, 1992). As we discovered in Chapter 4, the 'Big Five' (Digman, 1990), extroversion, agreeableness, conscientiousness, emotional stability and openness to experience, prob-ably account for most of what is known about personality variation and exert their influences on a wide range of responses relevant to cross-cultural effectiveness.

The proliferation of the personality variables studied in this area could be halted if researchers would simply assess the Big Five using culturally appropriate measures. We may expect that higher extroversion, agreeable-ness, conscientiousness, emotional stability and openness would be predictive of intercultural adjustment, however assessed, with their relative degree of influence varying across the different contexts for cross-cultural contact. These personality variables will probably turn out to be related to other social factors predicting success, such as degree of host contact. In short, a simplification and organization of this confusing area could be achieved if researchers adopted a more unified approach.

Skills. Furnham (1989) has approached the problem of cross-cultural adaptation from a skill perspective. Depending on which cultural groups are involved, people will need specific knowledge about the rules of inter-action with their hosts. This can be gleaned from a variety of information sources, and may include guidance about making culturally correct attribu-tions (Brislin *et al.*, 1986) for surprising interpersonal behaviours that occur in the new cultural context, as shown in Box 10.2.

Knowledge about these normative patterns of behaviour in the new culture will then have to be put into practice. Argyle (1979) has identified seven social skills which can be developed in persons, including perspective-taking, expression, conversation, assertiveness, emotionality, anxiety control, and affiliation. Many of these skill areas involve aspects of non-verbal behaviour, which are so important in regulating interaction. Once a culture's position on these interpersonal dimensions is known,

Box 10.2   *The culture assimilator*

The culture assimilator is a resource for teaching people to improve the accuracy of their cross-cultural attributions. Brislin *et al.* (1986) developed a culture-general assimilator by collecting a variety of cross-cultural misunderstandings that arose in connection with each of 18 universal themes in social interaction (e.g. dominance–submission). Readers are presented with a number of these detailed 'critical incidents' and invited to choose the correct interpretation for the impasse between the participants. Informed commentary is then provided on each of the possible choices, so that students improve their understanding of the cultural logics involved. An example follows. Read through and work out your own answer before you look at the box on page 200.

Oh! So proper!
The English class that Martha Anderson is helping to teach is going very well. The Vietnamese, Cambodian and Central American students seem to enjoy one another and are adjusting to each other well. The men and women frequently help one another. Having very little exposure to other cultures, Martha is amazed at their ease of interaction and often asks the instructor about the different behaviour she observes in the classroom. They are all very polite to each other even when they do not seem to be able to understand each other. They are also especially polite when they are talking to her or to the other instructors, always addressing them with very formal polite titles. Martha would like to develop relationships with some of the students and to make them feel more at home. In one particular instance she is talking privately with Vien Thuy Ng. She asks him to call her by her first name, saying, 'My name is Martha. Please call me Martha!' Vien responds by acknowledging that he does indeed know her name, but 'Would it not be good to call you by your proper title?' She persists by saying that this is too formal and that they can just be good friends and go by first names. Vien just smiles and nods, but he does not return to the English class the next week.
   What could explain this kind of situation?

1. Vien Thuy Ng thought that Martha was too aggressive and forward towards him, as women do not talk to men.
2. Martha should not have singled out one individual person. Vien did not like being singled out.
3. The English class is too complicated for Vien and he does not really know what is going on.
4. Martha violated a rather intricate system of hierarchy that exists in South Asian countries.

Source: R. W. Brislin *et al.*, *Intercultural Interactions: A practical guide.* © 1986 by Sage Publications Inc. Reprinted by permission.

people with 'deficits' can learn to respond differently in various contact situations. As we saw in Chapter 6, Collett (1971) successfully taught Arab non-verbal skills to normally 'standoffish' Englishmen, thereby enhancing the impressions they gave to Arabs later. Some persons will already have culturally fitting skills through personality or training; the rest can be acquired through education.

This is a more microscopic approach to cross-cultural adaptation than the personality approach and is very useful for focused training programmes. It does, however, require accurate knowledge about the various skills required for adaptation to a specific culture.

Of course, the vast majority of cultural sojourners or immigrants will have no access to such programmes; they will have to adapt as best they can. It is here we believe that broad personality dispositions will influence their willingness and ability to learn these necessary skills during their daily encounters across cultural lines. Traits like agreeableness and extroversion will enable them to find 'culture friends' or mediators to guide them and form a support network to sustain them while they are learning to function effectively.

Cultural loss?

What is the price of cross-cultural adaptation for one's cultural identity? The historical legacy of colonialism has left many people worried about the potential of intercultural contact for the destruction of native heritages. In extreme forms there is genocide; in other forms, there is assimilation, whereby a stronger cultural group absorbs the weaker, so that the latter's distinctive organization, rituals, dress, architecture, crafts and so forth simply disappear.

At the individual level there are spirited concerns expressed about the loss of cultural identity which may arise out of intercultural contact. Alatas (1972) has identified the 'captive mind syndrome' where a person rejects his or her traditions and uncritically swallows those of another cultural group. Others (e.g. Stonequist, 1937) have lamented the rejection of their traditions by people eager to 'pass' into a different cultural group, as sometimes happens with immigrants (Taft, 1973). Park (1928) introduced the term 'marginal man' to designate a person torn between two incompatible traditions and consigned to the periphery of each. This problem is especially acute for returnees who find themselves rejected by their own cultural group when they return 'home' (Kidder, 1991).

Not all contact leads to rootlessness or cultural loss. Groups may segregate themselves from other groups and their members adopt chauvinistic, ethnocentric attitudes and stereotypes towards these other groups. In effect, their cultural identity has been reinforced through cross-

Box 10.3   *The culture assimilator: explanations*

Rationales for the alternative explanations:
1. In many south-east Asian countries, the roles of women may be restricted in some ways, such as in approaching men. However, this class is in the United States and there are some students from other countries as well as the instructors interacting together. The fact that the class is mixed and that the students seem to get along fairly well suggests that this is really not the reason for Vien's disappearance from the class. There is a better answer: please select again.
2. It is true that individuals from Asian societies do not like to be singled out. However, in this instance, this minor correction was not a singling out. Martha was talking with Vien alone so there would be no great embarrassment involved since others were not present. There is more going on: please select again.
3. This conclusion can hardly be drawn as the scenario states that all seemed to be going well in the class. Please select again.
4. This is the best answer. South-east Asians have a very intricate system of status hierarchy. Martha violated it by trying to play down her role or perceived status. Her attempt may not have been the total cause for Vien not wanting to return, however. Perhaps if she had just suggested it and left it open for Vien to choose, he might have felt more comfortable. Her persistence in the matter forced Vien into a situation where he had to relinquish a value that affected his whole world-view or life-style.

Source: R. W. Brislin *et al.*, *Intercultural Interactions: A practical guide.* © 1986 by Sage Publications Inc. Reprinted by permission.

cultural contact. That contact thereafter becomes limited to specialized persons and geographical areas in order to contain the potential for cultural degradation.

There are obvious emotional and political overtones to many of the concerns voiced about loss of cultural identity. A recent study by Rosenthal and Feldman (1992) indicates that a more dispassionate, analytic approach is required in considering this problem. They first note that ethnic identity is a multidimensional concept. It includes subjective self-evaluation (by which ethnic label does one describe oneself?); the evaluative meaning given to one's ethnic group membership (positive or negative); the cultural practices of one's group (friendship choices, language use, food preferences, attendance at festivals and so forth); and finally, the importance one attaches to these practices. If these aspects of identity are not highly correlated, then cultural contact may affect only certain aspects of ethnic identity.

To evaluate this reasoning, Rosenthal and Feldman assessed each of these elements of identity among first- and second-generation Chinese immigrants to Canada and Australia, in comparison with Chinese students in Hong Kong. As expected, they found only moderate linkage between their various measures of ethnic identity. Cultural practices and labelling oneself as Chinese declined in the first generation, but fell no further in the second. Subjective evaluation of one's identity and the importance attached to Chinese cultural practices did not decline at all. The authors conclude that external aspects of cultural identity may change slowly over time, but that the internal components are more resistant to change.

These findings suggest that many previous studies of ethnic identity have been too global in their conclusions about cultural loss. A closer examination of intercultural contact reveals a subtler, less insidious process at work, at least in some cases. It is true that both Canadian and Australian government policies explicitly endorse multiculturalism and the protection of minority rights (Humana, 1986). Perhaps for this reason Chinese immigrant adolescents there experience no more health problems or difficulties with their parents than do host adolescents (Chiu, Feldman and Rosenthal, in press). Clearly, greater attention must be paid in future research to contextual factors and to multiple measures of ethnic identification before valid conclusions can be drawn as to the possible dangers of cultural contact.

Cultural gains?

A more hopeful possibility at the group level is integration. It occurs 'when different groups maintain their cultural identity in some respects, but merge into a superordinate group in other respects (Bochner, 1982, p. 26)'. This merging typically occurs in work and political contexts and is sustained by key 'acculturation attitudes' (Berry *et al.*, 1989). The first of these attitudes asserts that it is valuable to maintain relationships with other groups; the second, that it is valuable to maintain one's cultural identity and characteristics. The attitudes promote integration and can themselves be supported by a governmental policy endorsing cultural pluralism, such as one finds in the Canadian Multiculturalism Act of 1987.

At the personal level, the response to an integrative social context is a set of open attitudes (McCrae and Costa, 1985; Sampson and Smith, 1957) that enable a person to mediate – 'select, combine and synthesize the appropriate features of different social systems without losing their cultural cores (Bochner, 1982, p. 29)'. These 'mediating persons' in effect travel on two or more passports, providing linguistic and cultural links across various traditional boundaries (Bochner, 1982). They are not chauvinistic about their own culture, but rather fully aware of the strengths of each of the various cultural groups they deal with.

The transition experience.   This balancing is not purchased at the expense of their ego integrity, but instead leads to a higher level of maturity (e.g. Adler, 1987). In describing this transition, Adler (1975) points out that it may be stimulated by the confrontation between different cultural systems:

> The dynamics of the cross-cultural experience at the personal level represents the process of positive disintegration. Such experiences can occur whenever new environments of experience and perception are encountered. Although many different reactions and responses can take place in this confrontation of cultures, the greatest shock may be the encounter with one's own cultural heritage and the degree to which one is a product of it. In the encounter with another culture, the individual gains new experiential knowledge by coming to understand the roots of his or her own ethnocentrism and by gaining new perspectives and outlooks on the nature of culture. Throughout the transitional experience the individual is presented with differences and complexity. When differences cannot be ignored, they become distorted. This distortion gives rise to emotions that each person must come to understand experientially. In so doing, learning, self-awareness and personal growth take place. (p. 22)

Anecdotal evidence suggests that such inspirational personal outcomes can emerge from the intercultural encounter (Storti, 1990). Certainly the hope of such change motivates some exploration across cultures, and fuller scientific documentation of it would be most useful in helping us to understand the cross-cultural experience.

Test case: intercultural marriage.   Fontaine (1990) argues that viable inter-cultural marriages provide a useful case study for intercultural relations generally, because 'the partners must have developed workable strategies for dealing with diversity and/or be receiving benefits that offset the greater losses (Fontaine and Dorch, 1980, p. 230)'. Fontaine maintains that such couples create 'inter-cultural microcultures' which permit them to nego-tiate a shared life. These microcultures emphasize a focus on the ecological context of the tasks at hand, as one way of avoiding a power confrontation between 'my' cultural way versus 'your' cultural way. When differences do arise, partners often attribute the difficulties to cultural background rather than to the personality of their spouse. This attributional style accords culture an external reality that becomes one feature of the task constraints to be considered and accommodated. Fontaine reports that what develops in time is an intercultural microculture that has significant departures from either spouse's cultural heritage – a creative synthesis without a sense of cultural loss.

Metacultural awareness. Fontaine's (1990) analysis of intercultural marriages identifies two key components to their success. First, partners must be cognizant of their partner's cultural heritage, and second, they must accord that heritage legitimacy in their dealings with one another. Both developments enhance the process of externalizing culture. It becomes a separable aspect of one's self, as does the cultural heritage of one's partner. When one becomes capable of considering culture as a distinct component of an individual's heritage, one has developed 'metacultural' awareness.

Such awareness arises out of personal or direct cross-cultural experience. In dealing with people from different cultural traditions, one then begins factoring in their cultural background. Their traditions can be seen to explain their 'idiosyncrasies' and their positive contributions earn them 'credits' (Hollander, 1958). One is thereby able to accommodate to the other's tradition when it is appropriate and to make allowances for otherwise 'inappropriate' behaviour from one's partner. Communication difficulties decrease and negative attributions are softened.

We believe that metacultural awareness is an important personality variable moderating successful cross-cultural outcomes. If studies of cross-cultural interaction involved those with such awareness, the typically negative outcomes could well be different. Such projects will have to be quite sophisticated, however, since metacultural awareness is a two-handed process: many have seen the cartoon of the *Japanese man's* extended hand hitting the bowing *American's* head as they first meet. Each is demonstrating his metacultural awareness and the result is a failed interaction! Since both parties are cross-culturally knowledgeable and now know that their partner is also, they will have to negotiate which culture's rules to use and when. A new layer of complexity has been added to the communication process. 'Curiouser, and curiouser', said Alice (in Wonderland)!

Improving outcomes

A cautionary note is in order here, before psychologists wrestle further with how to enhance cross-cultural interactions:

Clearly no amount of psychological engineering is going to make poverty-stricken ethnic groups inclined to welcome or even accept interactions with representatives of wealthy or powerful cultures. Nor are members of the better-placed cultures likely to feel comfortable in the presence of persons from grossly disadvantaged societies. However, psychology can make a contribution in instances where there is a minimum of realistic conflict, and yet a great deal of mutual distrust, hostility and even violence. (Bochner, 1982, p. 37)

We agree with the spirit of Bochner's assessment that certain historical, political, economic and social situations drastically limit the impact of whatever psychological knowledge can be applied to improve an intercultural encounter. These other factors often contribute to the unsupportive intergroup environment identified by Stephan (1985) and discussed earlier. They must generally be addressed politically and will not respond rapidly even where they are so addressed.

Additionally, it is a fact of life that most people's interactions across cultural lines occur without the benefit of planned input from anybody. They adapt as best they can in the laboratory of life and often do remarkably well. Nevertheless, significant groups such as the diplomatic corps, multinational corporations and international aid organizations can and do select and train their personnel for intercultural effectiveness. How can they enhance this effectiveness?

Organizational considerations

The basic issue here is whether the organization is aware that culture shapes interpersonal behaviour and institutional practices (Hofstede, Bond and Luk, in press) with consequent effects on newcomer adaptation. If so, the question then is whether the organization is willing to negotiate its policies and procedures, or whether it will expect its personnel to 'cut their toes to fit the shoe', as the Chinese adage puts it. It is probable that organizations established and maintained by people from cultures low in power distance will be more accommodating in these respects (Bond, in press).

Given a supportive organizational 'culture', how can its members be assisted to work more effectively across cultural lines? A number of factors are important (Bond, in press; Tung, 1981):

○ An organizational policy explicitly supporting cultural pluralism.
○ Top management who endorse and who model cultural accommodation.
○ Availability of fellow culture members for newcomers at work or outside work to provide social support.
○ Attention to factors important in spouse adjustment, such as consulting with them before the assignment (Black and Gregerson, 1991a).
○ Training in the effective use of the organization's common language for *both* native *and* non-native speakers.
○ In-depth pre-departure training on cultural as well as environmental features of the new posting.
○ Provision of an 'in-house' cultural mediator to advise and consult with the newcomer about issues related to cultural adjustment.
○ Use of criteria for performance evaluation that include aspects of cross-cultural effectiveness, like the ability to resolve misunderstandings.

○ Consideration of the re-entry problems facing someone after an overseas posting (Adler, 1981), especially ensuring that the posting fits the member's future career path.

Personnel selection

When organizations do have a field of candidates from which to choose, any and all of the personality factors mentioned before should be used. It is also wise to select persons whose cultural background is maximally similar to that of the new host culture, using some scheme like Schwartz's (in press) mapping of values for matching expatriates and locals. Culturally relevant skills, like language or knowledge of the host culture's history and literature, are also an asset. Finally, a track record of success in other cross-cultural postings augers well for any future assignment.

Conclusion

Our world is changing. Cross-cultural contact is increasing, as global interdependencies inexorably expand. Historically, the outcomes of inter-cultural contact are chequered at best. An enhanced set of skills and dispositions will be required of us all if, as Faulkner believed, mankind is not merely to survive, but to prevail. This chapter has identified the key outcomes interculturally and the factors which influence them. They must be carefully considered as we negotiate our future.

ELEVEN

The future of social psychology across cultures

From microscopic particles to everyday complexity, many paths now seem open.

(James Gleick, *Chaos: Making a new science*, 1987)

The world we all inhabit is changing at a dizzying pace. Economic development, political realignments, technological progress and media globalization are leading us towards greater modernity and interdependence. Some social scientists contend that these parallel processes will result in a convergence at the societal and psychological levels that will render cross-cultural psychology an irrelevant shard of intellectual history. Others perceive potential for continued, even expanding, diversity, as peoples of different cultural traditions confront the realities of development. Coupled with this belief in future diversity is a conviction about the viability of the cross-cultural contribution within social psychology. This chapter explores this debate in light of our previous chapters, especially their emphasis on the role of individualism–collectivism.

Social psychology as history?

In a seminal paper, Gergen (1973) argued that social psychologists were engaged in examining contemporary historical developments rather than discovering behavioural principles which would remain valid across time and place. Gergen asserted that 'If we scan the most prominent lines of research during the past decade, we soon realize that the observed regularities, and thus the major theoretical principles, are firmly wedded to historical circumstances (p. 315).' In discussing Festinger's (1954) theory of social comparison processes, for example, Gergen suggested that its fundamental tenet of people wishing to evaluate their opinions and abilities accurately was a historically driven disposition. 'In effect, the entire line of research appears to depend on a set of learned propensities, propensities that could be altered by time and circumstance (p.315).'

Further complicating the search for scientific regularities was the impact of our disseminating the results of work in contemporary social psychology. As such information circulated, it could become an important new element in the equation predicting behaviour. People might accept the findings as prescriptive guidelines or protect their freedom of action by reacting against the implied prescriptions. In either case, a current result could not be used to predict a future outcome, because people's knowledge of the scientific 'law' now entered the equation.

Implications

In Gergen's (1973) view, the consequences of the historical embeddedness and the reactive effects of knowledge are twofold. First, 'Principles of human interaction cannot readily be developed over time, because the facts on which they are based do not generally remain stable (p. 309).' Social psychology could not therefore aspire to the scientific status of, say, physics or biology. The future would be negotiable and open, not predicated on knowledge derived from the past.

Second, Gergen concludes that 'We must think then in terms of a *continuum of historical durability*, with phenomena highly susceptible to historical influence at one extreme and the more stable processes at the other (p. 318).' This conclusion led Gergen to encourage the study of historical and literary documents from the past, as a way of assessing the continuity of interpersonal processes and concerns. In this vein Adamopoulos and Bontempo (1986) have scanned a variety of ancient literary sources for three themes of social behaviour – association, superordination and intimacy. Adamopoulos (1988), for example, detects an early example of egocentric individualism in the exchanges between Agamemnon and Achilles documented in the *Iliad*, a 3,000-year-old classic of Greek literature.

Gergen's (1973) conclusion also led him to encourage the study of cross-cultural social psychology and is consistent with the quantum leap in the amount of cross-cultural psychology which has been undertaken in the last two decades. In his words, 'Although cross-cultural replication is fraught with difficulty, similarity in a given function from across widely divergent cultures would strongly attest to its durability (p. 318).' This book has described many of the universal patterns which have emerged from this accumulation of research. In addition, we have identified dimensions of cultural variation which can be used to bring some degree of order to the apparent discrepancies in results from different cultural systems.

Nevertheless, we are still left with Gergen's warning that our capacity to use present knowledge to predict future realities is questionable. The world is changing and social-psychological issues and possibly processes are changing as a result. How can our knowledge from the past help us to understand the interpersonal environments of tomorrow? The remainder of this chapter presents speculations and data from social scientists which bear on this issue.

How do cultures change?

In Chapter 3, we defined culture with Hofstede (1980) as the 'collective programming of the mind', with that programming being operationalized in terms of value dimensions. Hofstede argued that these cultural values originated from both external and internal factors operating within each society. The internal factors were labelled 'ecological' and included aspects of a nation's geography, economy, hygiene, demography, gene pool, history, technology, urbanization and material resources. The external influences included forces of nature, such as climate changes or environmental disasters, and forces of man, such as trade, scientific discovery and the internationalization of the media.

Hofstede (1980) maintains that societal norms and cultural values do change in response to changes in these internal and external factors. In order to anticipate future developments in the 'collective programming of the mind' and hence in social behaviour, it is important to examine the structure of these change factors and their change over time.

The 'character' of nations

Social scientists, such as economists, sociologists and political scientists are interested in the wider social factors that influence social behaviour. In order to develop a taxonomy of such factors, they have isolated a host of such macro-level variables, like gross national product per person, degree of urbanization, extent of political pluralization, proportion of the population employed in the service industries, life expectancy at birth and so forth. These nation-level variables are themselves interrelated in the same way as values are interrelated. Like values, they may be examined by factor analysis to reveal underlying dimensions on which particular nations may be ranked and compared with one another.

One of the best examples of such a study was the 'Dimensionality of Nations' project, initiated by Harold Guetzkow and reported by Rummel (1972). Two hundred and thirty-six macro-level variables from 82 nations were considered. Using factor analysis, this set of variables was simplified and grouped into seven major dimensions: economic development, size, political orientation, foreign conflict, density, Catholic culture and internal conflict. The highest loading items on the economic development factor, for example, were (per unit of population):

○ Number of telephones.
○ Non-agricultural population.
○ Number of radio receivers.
○ Gross national product.
○ Energy consumption.
○ Newsprint consumption.
○ Number of hospital beds.
○ Number employed in manufacturing.

Using each country's score on these seven dimensions, Rummel was able to present a stable and accurate map of national 'character'.

Two important conclusions may be drawn from this and similar studies. First, a factor of economic development invariably emerges, usually commanding the largest number of variables (e.g. Adelman and Morris, 1967; Marsh, 1967). Second, there are always *other* factors of variation in addition to economic development which emerge from such analyses. Both of these conclusions are relevant in considering the convergence hypothesis, which we shall now present.

The convergence hypothesis

Nations, like people, develop over time. Cattell (1953), for example, factor analyzed a number of macro-level variables descriptive of Great Britain from 1837 to 1937. He extracted ten dimensions along which Great Britain had changed over the 100 years analyzed. One of these ten he labelled 'cultural pressure', which was essentially a factor of economic modernization whose strengths increased monotonically during this period.

The diffusion of scientific discoveries and industrial technology since the eighteenth century has driven economic development in all countries of the world. Common characteristics of this global transformation are the specialization of labour, the globalization and impersonality of marketplaces, the exploitation of natural energy sources and the concentration of capital resources. Political life has also been transformed. As Yang (1988) has described it:

political modernization is composed of three major processes: the replacement of a large number of traditional authorities by a single national political authority, the emergence of new political functions that must be managed by new administrative hierarchies chosen on the basis of achievement rather than ascription, and increased participation in politics by social groups throughout society, along with the development of new institutions such as political parties and interest groups to organize this participation. (p. 67)

Similarly, Yang describes how sociocultural modernization is proceeding apace: 'Sociocultural changes are reflected in such processes as the expansion of education, the diversification of occupations, the secularization of religion, the intensification of urbanization, and the development of mass communications (pp. 67–8).'

Economic determinists maintain that the political and social changes described above are consequences of the changes in modes of production. Given the wide and increasing diffusion of such economic developments, convergency theorists conclude with Kerr *et al.* (1960) that 'the logic of industrialization will eventually lead us all to a common society where ideology will cease to matter (p. 12).' Ideology will cease to matter, presumably, because we will all share a common ideology. To the extent that ideology or values drive behaviour, then differences across people of different cultural heritages will, in time, cease to exist. Such is the putative psychological consequence of the societal convergence produced by modernization.

Convergency theorists believe, then, that given sufficient time for diffusion of technology, training and capital to occur, all countries will be drawn into the vortex of a common modernity (see Meyer, 1970). Inglehart (1977), for example, surveyed values in a variety of European countries and the United States, identifying two major factors. The first he characterized as materialist–post-materialist. This dimension spanned the transition from Maslow's (1954) security and social needs to his self-actualization needs. The wealthier the country, the higher would be the proportion of postmaterialists. Based on these sorts of results, some social scientists would argue that a gradual increase of wealth in all countries will make people similar and render our current enchantment with cross-cultural differences in behaviour an archeological curiosity – a historical digression. Interestingly, this academic assessment of contemporary development has filtered down to public awareness and generated ideological reactions from developing nations.

Modernization and westernization

The scientific aspects of the debate about convergence are complicated by a political agenda: namely, the need of people in many developing countries to maintain their cultural pride by distinguishing their culture from that of the West. Politicians in some countries can forge a unity out of disparate ethnic communities by rallying their supporters against the spectre of westernization. For their part, citizens of such emerging nations may derive some cultural pride by differentiating themselves from western traditions, as Tajfel's (1981) study would predict. So, for example, we have the following news release from the *South China Morning Post* (5 January 1991):

SINGAPORE, Fri. – Singapore outlined today five 'shared values' it said would help the country develop a national identity and combat Western influence. 'The shared values should help us develop a Singaporean identity,' a government white paper said. Schools and parents should inculcate the values in young people, it added. It identified the values as: nation before community and society above self, family as the basic unit of society, regard and community support for the individual, consensus instead of contention and racial and religious harmony.

Particularly worrisome in the minds of many political leaders is the growing self-centredness and erosion of civil harmony which they believe will follow in the wake of western-inspired modernization.

A questionable thesis?   There are many rational shortcomings to this line of argument, politically useful as it may be (Weinberg, 1969). First, the depiction of 'the West' is very broad, including a host of mostly North American and northern European countries which are themselves culturally different in many respects. We have noted earlier that the values and social organization of these nations are by no means uniform (Hofstede, 1991; Rummel, 1972; Schwartz, in press). Second, critics of the West typically identify the negative features of its social life, ignoring its many positive features, like broad social welfare, the relatively high status of women and the observance of human rights (Bond, 1991a; Naroll, 1983). Third, they confuse origin with outcome. True, the industrial revolution originated in the West and many of its refinements have developed there. As Yang has pointed out, however, modernization

is new to all societies, Western and non-Western. The major modern features created by such a new process cannot be found in traditional non-Western ones. It is in this sense that modernization is not Westernization in its strict and narrow sense – the acceptance of traditionally Western things by a non-Western society. (p. 68)

Only rigid economic determinists would conclude that grafting modernization on to Asian, African or South American societies would turn them into western clones. There is good empirical evidence that these new hosts for modernity will transform this developmental impetus in distinctive and varied ways (e.g. Tsurumi, 1992). Let us then turn to the scientific evidence regarding convergence.

The constellation of individual modernity

Effective participation in modern society is hypothesized to require a core syndrome of cognitions and motivations. To assess this core, sociologists like Kahl (1968) and Inkeles and Smith (1974) have developed comprehensive batteries of standardized questions and administered these questionnaires to adult samples in a variety of developing countries. Other researchers have focused on single countries, comparing the responses of people from groups at different presumed stages in the modernization process, such as city dwellers versus rural inhabitants (e.g. Armer and Youtz, 1971; Guthrie, 1977; and Schnaiberg, 1970).

These instruments, whether they use questions which are imposed-etic or derived-etic, show a high degree of agreement in their outcomes. This overlap suggests that a common denominator of psychological characteristics is emerging across these many studies, as may be seen in Box 11.1.

Box 11.1   *The profile of a modern person*

Yang (1988) has synthesized the results from both the cross-cultural and intracultural studies and produced the following profile of the modern person:

- A sense of personal efficacy (anti-fatalism).
- Low social integration with relatives.
- Egalitarian attitudes towards others.
- An openness to innovation and change.
- A belief in sex equality.
- High achievement motivation.
- Independence or self-reliance.
- Active participation in social organizations
- Tolerance of, and respect for, others.
- Cognitive and behavioural flexibility.
- Strong future orientation.
- Empathetic capacity.
- A high need for information.
- The propensity to take risks in life.
- Secularization in religious belief.
- A preference for urban life.
- An individualistic orientation towards others.
- Psychological differentiation.
- A non-local orientation.

Is individualism another name for modernity?. Alert readers will note some conceptual similarity between modernity and individualism as psychological profiles. Yang (1988) contends that about two-thirds of the above characteristics overlap with the profile of individualism. If individualism and collectivism are conceptualized as opposite ends of a continuum, then increasing modernization would lead to a gradual individualization of psychological processes.

One could take the economic index of gross national product per capita as a rough approximation of societal modernization. If this step is taken, then Hofstede's (1980) research shows a strong correlation between modernity (as measured by wealth) and cultural individualism of +0.82. Bond's (1988b) work demonstrates a similar link between wealth and psychological individualism. Furthermore, Hofstede's (1980) longitudinal research across a four-year span indicated that individualism was the only one of his four dimensions to increase on average across his entire sample of 40 countries during that period.

These lines of work thus suggest that economic development, which is generally increasing, goes hand in hand with a change in certain broad patterns of behaviour. These patterns are central to the contrast between collectivism and individualism which has informed and unified our presentation in this text. Should we then conclude that the content of this text may become a historical artefact, doomed to obsolescence?

Internationalism

An additional factor is emerging in conjunction with global development which may add a further homogenizing influence to cultural variation. This is the increasing awareness of humanity's interdependence. As many commentators (e.g. Brown *et al.*, 1990; Mesarovic and Pestel, 1974) have clamoured for people to realize, our growing technological sophistication has brought in its wake the potential for ecological destruction. Mankind's depletion of energy sources, over-harvesting of the oceans, assault upon the atmosphere, destruction of the rain-forests and erosion of fertile soil are bringing us closer to global disaster. Our headlong pursuit of personal and national affluence has resulted in a 'commons dilemma' (Dawes, 1980) where the very support systems of life on this planet are at risk. Many argue that nations must co-operate to avert this impending disaster (Brown, 1972).

One consequence of these recent developments is the growth of internationalism, a constellation of attitudes with important implications for behaviour towards people of different races, nations and cultures. Sampson and Smith (1957) labelled this concept 'world-mindedness' which they defined as 'a frame of reference, or value orientation favouring a world-view of the problems of humanity, with mankind, rather than the nationals of a particular country, as the primary reference group (p. 105).' They showed that within their American sample this international orientation was a coherent clustering of beliefs on social, political, economic and religious questions, a cluster which was stable within persons and negatively related to authoritarianism.

Internationalism was once the preserve of futurists, political factions and certain religious groups, but it has lately been accorded wider currency by economic developments. Given its recent emergence, it is understandable that it has received little attention from psychologists. Public awareness of mankind's ecological vulnerability is steadily growing, however, so one could anticipate an increase in the influence of internationalism as a value and a belief orientation (see, for example, Takeshita, 1990). What are its possible consequences for cultural diversity?

Schwartz's (in press) recent work, which was discussed in Chapter 3, is helpful. One of the seven culture-level types of value measured in his international survey was 'harmony', consisting of the following value components: unity with nature, protection of the environment and a world of beauty. This value-type incorporates a set of concerns that form one part of internationalism.

Teacher samples from 24 countries showed considerable variation in levels of endorsement of harmony values. Many would argue that such variation must decrease over time, as the planet's citizens become more aware of the need to sacrifice present economic demands for future environmental safety. As argued by Schwartz (see, for example, Schwartz and Bilsky, 1990), the increase in overall endorsement of 'harmony' will be purchased at the expense of the value-type which stands in opposition to it: that is, mastery. That value-type emphasizes success, ambition, independence and so forth, acquisitive values that many commentators believe have fuelled our current crisis (Laslo, 1989). The overall consequence of environmental developments, then, is likely to be a reduction in variation across one of Schwartz's major axes of value differences among nations.

This assumption is speculative, of course, but it is exactly the same sort of argument about the future as surrounded modernity in the past. Repeated administration of the Schwartz value survey will enable us to assess this hypothesis empirically. In the meantime let us look at the arguments opposing convergence.

The evidence against convergence

As is common in science, a strongly stated universal proposition begins to disintegrate upon closer scrutiny. A number of approaches to the convergence hypothesis themselves converge to suggest that the thesis must be questioned and modified. These approaches are discussed below.

Economic development and values

As mentioned earlier, Inglehart (1977) detected a trend in North American and European countries whereby citizens' values were shifting from materialist to post-materialist. As other countries modernized, Inglehart hypothesized that the values of their populace would likewise shift.

Research in other industrialized countries does not, however, support such a conclusion. If we take wealth as a rough measure of modernity, only one of Hofstede's four (1980) or five (1991) dimensions of cultural variation shows any relationship with wealth. The other multicultural studies of values which we discussed earlier likewise extract from two to seven dimensions of national variation in values, and only one of these dimensions correlates substantially with measures of economic development (Bond, 1988b; Rummel, 1972; Schwartz, in press). This frequent finding suggests that values are free to vary in a number of ways independent of a country's level of modernization. These 'modernity-free' domains of value are probably related to the other dimensions of variation in national character discussed earlier, and exert their impact on social behaviour just as does individualism.

The fate of individualism–collectivism.   Of course, the dimension which does most closely associated with wealth and therefore with modernity appears to be various formulations of individualism–collectivism. In this regard a number of points can be made. First, the strength of the relationship between wealth and individualism varies from study to study, and in some cases (e.g. Schwartz, in press) is small. Countries at the same level of economic development may thus vary considerably in their levels of individualism. Second, the only study to assess individualism–collectivism across time actually reported an *increase* in variation of country scores across a four-year span (Hofstede, 1980, Chapter 8). Third, over the last 25 years it is not a country's level of individualism that has best predicted its economic development; rather it is the unrelated measure of values called Confucian work dynamism which now relates to growth rates in gross national product (Chinese Culture Connection, 1987), whatever may have been the case in the past. A country's level of Confucian work dynamism is unrelated to its actual wealth or to its level of individualism, a finding which suggests continued variation across countries in their wealth and hence in their level of individualism–collectivism.

At the very least, then, we must conclude that there is no inexorable convergence of countries towards greater individualism in values with the march of time and of progress. Variations in individualism–collectivism will continue to be an important tool for interpreting cross-cultural differences in behaviour, just as they are an important tool for understanding individual variation within a culture (e.g. Earley, 1989).

Variability of the modernization syndrome

If modernization is a uniform, linear process, then the pattern of modernization across its many components (increased exposure to the mass media, greater secularization, etc.) should be the same from country to country. The evidence indicates that it is not. Studies of the modernization syndrome *across* cultures (e.g. Sack, 1973) and *within* cultures (e.g. Chiu, 1979) reveal a multifaceted phenomenon which takes different forms in different places. Sack, for example, borrowed 29 items tapping the modernity complex from previous studies and administered them to over a thousand Tunisians. Careful analysis did not reveal a single, underlying dimension of modernism uniting these measures. Instead, eight unrelated components of the process were revealed: activism, rejection of the white-collar syndrome, universalism, low integration with relatives, sense of personal trust and autonomy, rejection of the past, preference for urban life and family modernism. As Yang (1988) concludes: 'The evidence ... unequivocally points to the fact that modern psychological characteristics simply do not cohere to form a well-unified syndrome. Individual modernism may be composed of separate components (p. 81).' Individuals and groups within different countries can therefore modernize in different ways and with different outcomes.

Traditionalism and modernity as unrelated

The anxiety voiced by some politicians about the spread of modernism is based in part upon the worry that traditional values will be eroded. They set cultural heritage in opposition to economic progress using a zero-sum logic – more of one, less of the other.

Many social scientists, however, maintain that cultural systems are innovative and can synthesize traditional and modern elements in unique ways, so that both traditional and modern elements may co-exist without tension (e.g. Levine, 1968). Psychological data from Taiwan (Yang, 1986) and Japan (Ike, 1973) support precisely such a conclusion. In describing

Trommsdorff's (1973) survey research in Japan, Yang (1988), for example, concludes that:

strong traditional values such as group solidarity, interpersonal harmony, paternalism, and familism are coexisting with quite modern values such as achieve-ment and competition, and that along with democratic values exist beliefs in hierarchical social structures and in authority, obedience, and inequality of men and women. (p. 82)

Reports about the attitudes of lay persons towards modernity are con-sistent with a position of fruitful, supportive co-existence (Bond and King, 1985). The basic, organizing principles involved are twofold. First, a distinction is made between modernization and westernization. This contrast enables one to undertake change without feeling indebted or subservient to the West. Second, one differentiates the beneficial from the retrogressive aspects of both traditional culture and modern culture. The positive elements of the past and present are embraced; the negative, discarded. Hong Kong Chinese, for example, believe that they retain their tradition of respect for authority, but discard its fatalism; they adopt modern competitiveness, but reject its sexual promiscuity. This cognitive strategy enables one to forge a desirable identity for the future while retaining a connection to one's historical legacy, and demonstrates the operation of social creativity in the face of intergroup threat (Tajfel, 1981).

Migration and psychological change

One of the strongest challenges to one's cultural distinctiveness occurs when one emigrates to a country with different cultural traditions. The power of modernization would be demonstrated if people from less modernized countries were found to assimilate to the thought and behaviour patterns characteristic of their more modernized hosts. This is a complex problem to explore, requiring attention to such sociological and political issues as the status of the immigrants, their relative numbers and dispersion in the host country, constitutional protection for multi-culturalism, effective enforcement of legislation against discrimination and so forth. The research is difficult to do, requiring access to often closed communities and to samples across a number of generations.

One of the best examples of such work was recently completed by Feldman and Rosenthal (1990). They assessed changes in parental restrictiveness and compliance across two generations of Chinese immigrants from Hong Kong to the United States and to Australia. Expectations for autonomy in first- and second-generation teenagers were compared to those of their Anglo hosts and Chinese counterparts back in

Hong Kong. Their first conclusion was that cultural adaptation appears to be very slow, with even second-generation Chinese responding more like their Hong Kong counterparts than their host Caucasians. Second, they found that this cultural resilience was more marked in certain domains than in others. So, for example, Chinese in host countries adapted more to local norms about social activities, like spending time with friends, but not to norms for heterosexual activities, like early dating or overnight trips with mixed-sex friends. The authors conclude that:

Although Chinese family patterns undergo modest changes when Chinese families live in the West, they nonetheless remain different from their Western counterparts, in terms of the amount of structure they provide and the extent to which they use child-rearing practices which promote autonomy. (p. 277)

Parental restrictiveness is one characteristic of the collectivist family structure (Barry, Child and Bacon, 1959; Kagitcibasi, 1990). Despite the connection of independence from parental influence to the modernity syndrome, there is good evidence for the persistence of traditional socialization practices despite residence in modern, individualistic nations (see also Hines, 1973).

Of course, there are other behavioural and cognitive domains where influence can and does operate (Feldman, Mont-Reynaud and Rosenthal, in press). Pressures to adapt to local practice vary from activity to activity, just as we have seen with modernization generally. We believe that within this force-field, however, members of cultural groups placing a higher value on their own traditions (Bond, 1988b) are better enabled to resist these pressures. The net result in many immigrant societies is not the 'melting pot' so many feared, but rather the subcultural mosaic so many sought. In societies endorsing civil and political liberties (Humana, 1986) these ethnic differences will persist.

A middle way between convergence and divergence

The convergence hypothesis is slippery – adamant proponents may dismiss the opposing evidence by declaring that insufficient time has elapsed for modernizing influences to work their homogenizing effect. Given each country's unique background and different entry points into the process, the process in each is bound to be varied, but the eventual outcome will be the same.

This is a linear, simplistic stance which resists those contemporary developments in science which emphasize *systems* of influence (von Bertalanffy, 1973) and the subtle interdependencies of inputs (Gleick, 1987; Woodcock and Davis, 1981). We believe that it is more realistic to posit an openness in the modernization process. Different developing societies enter the modernization process with different traditional and contemporary inputs, making it risky to apply historical precedents to their development. Changing systems continue to be changed by the outcomes of the change process itself. The various modern cultures will themselves evolve in complex and unpredictable ways, making the notion of convergence towards some common end point implausible. More probably, we will continue to observe islands of convergence within a sea of diversity. Box 11.2 illustrates the way in which the adaptation of immigrants to four different countries proved to depend upon subtly different factors.

Specific functional convergence

Yang (1988) has argued that various behaviours and dispositions are adaptive to the imperatives of industrial societies. The value of certain characteristics in agrarian, hunting, gathering or pastoral communities will be lost, and they will be replaced by characteristics which function more easily in technological environments. Some of these characteristics have been identified in the psychological syndrome of modernization, and the

Box 11.2 *The mental health of immigrants*

Kleiner and Okeke (1991) studied the incidence of mental health problems among immigrants both within countries and internationally. Within the USA, they found that black migrants to Philadelphia from southern states had fewer mental health problems than blacks born in Philadelphia or in the north. However, in Norway, rural migrants to Oslo had more problems than those born there or coming from other cities.

Kleiner and Okeke explain this difference by showing that different values prevail in each location. In their Philadelphia sample, status striving and ambition predominated. Migrants from the south experienced the least gap between expectations and reality. In Oslo, status striving and ambition were not so highly valued, and those with the greatest mental health problems were the rural migrants who most rejected these values.

Kleiner and Okeke report further studies of migrants to Nigeria and to Israel. In the Nigerian samples status achievement was highly valued, while in Israel economic security values predominated. In all four countries, however, those with the greatest problems were those with the largest gap between their salient espoused values and the values which are actually rewarded.

increase in their frequency represents the 'kernel of truth' in the literature on psychological convergence.

However, this kernel of truth is smaller than often portrayed and it can flourish in varied cultural soils. Stylistic, expressive and goal-directed characteristics which have no functional relation to industrial–technical performance will remain and evolve in accordance with each culture's internal logic. In addition, Yang (1988) points out that 'It is of course also possible that new, unique, non-functional characteristics are formed during the process for the society to advance to its modern phase (p. 84).' So variety can continue despite modernization, and it may even be fostered by the process of growth.

There will continue to be a need to explore the impact of cultural variation on social behaviour. The dimensions of cultural variation may themselves evolve and be replaced, requiring new concepts to be identified in the quest to explain the whole range of human behaviour. One important element in that evolution will be periodic sampling of cultural groups using established value surveys (e.g. Schwartz, in press) which may be expanded. Such projects will enable social psychologists to monitor cross-cultural changes in value endorsements as humanity evolves. Emerging value dimensions, such as internationalism, may be grafted on to these established instruments in order to determine their relationship to existing dimensions.

Future contributions

Cross-cultural social psychology has a short history, one which approximately parallels that of transoceanic flight. Its primary role to date has been that of a gadfly, prodding the mainstream to be more cautious in its generalizations (Bond, 1988b) and less naive about its culturally shaped biases (Furby, 1979; Sampson, 1978). But more is possible.

A psychological theory of culture

As Whiting (1976) pointed out, the traditional concept of culture is too broad and imprecise for scientific use; it must be 'unpacked'. For psychologists, this unpacking takes the form of identifying constructs that relate to behaviour, like values, motivations, beliefs, expectancies for reinforcement, personality traits and so forth. These constructs must be quantifiable and measured in ways that are sensitive to the various cultural backgrounds of each respondent.

The outcome of such unpacking would be that individuals from *different* cultural groups could be located *vis-à-vis* one another in the same way as could individuals from within the *same* cultural group. So a person's cultural background would be 'unpacked' by locating that person at some point on a universally useful dimension that relates to behaviour. Different positionings on this dimension could then be used to explain differences in behaviour among typical people from different cultures, just as the positions could be used to explain differences in behaviour among people from the same cultural group.

A case in point.   An example may help here. Bond, Leung and Schwartz (1992) wanted to understand differences between Israeli and Hong Kong students in how they prefer to resolve conflicts. It was found that Israelis were more likely than the Chinese to endorse the use of arbitration, for example. In and of itself this categorical difference is not particularly illuminating. However, processes mediating the preferences for resolving conflicts had also been measured. It was found that the choice of arbitration was related to the belief that arbitration would lead to animosity reduction between the contending parties. This relationship obtained for both Israeli and Chinese respondents, indicating a culturally common process. The cultural difference that was detected in endorsing arbitration could then be explained by the finding that Israelis in general believed that arbitration was more likely to reduce animosity than did the Chinese in general. So the same theoretical mechanism that explained variation in arbitration preferences among respondents within a culture could be shown to explain average differences between typical respondents from different cultures.

This procedure of measuring both behaviours *and* mediating processes can be extended to other domains of social behaviour. The mediating processes which are of interest will, of course, vary from domain to domain. Because the influence of these processes has been assessed in more than one cultural group, however, one's confidence in the potential universality of the processes will increase dramatically. The benefits of this procedure will grow stronger the more dissimilar are the cultural groups involved.

Results obtained through this approach will begin to legitimize *empirically* the attempts made by social psychologists to extend their ideas and findings beyond their traditional cultural borders of North America and Europe. The mystique of culture could then 'wither away', as it becomes replaceable by specific, defined, operationalized variables of psychological interest. Only then will the field move closer towards developing general theories of social behaviour (Triandis, 1978, 1988).

Setting an example for current social psychology

The ambitious goal just outlined can equally well apply to much contemporary research in social psychology. As Clark (1987) has noted:

Education level, sex, socio-economic status, and all our other favourite demographic variables are themselves no more psychological than is culture, but we
have become so accustomed to using such variables as stand-ins for the correlated
psychological factors that progress toward understanding the underlying concepts
has virtually stopped in many areas. (p. 466)

Successful examples of cultural unpackaging could stimulate mainstream
social psychologists to examine the theoretical implications of such basic
demographic variables as these *within* their own cultures and subcultures.
Research would thus become less superficially descriptive and more
psychologically explanatory. This demand for scientific refinement is just
as pressing for within-culture studies as it is for cross-cultural studies, even
though the demand is more often levelled at cross-culturalists (see Clark,
1987, for an elaboration of this discrepancy).

Expanding our understanding

The early European explorers searched for the Spice Islands in order to
enhance their local cuisine. Cloves, pepper, cardamom, ginseng and so
forth greatly enlarged the culinary range of European chefs and were often
found to have additional uses in medical treatment. Similarly, cross-
cultural work in social psychology may unearth concepts, processes and
theories which broaden our appreciation of what factors influence
behaviour by providing a forum for psychologists from outside the mainstream. As Moghaddam (1987) expresses this hope: 'the growth of an
indigenous third-world psychology could potentially lead to fresh ideas
that could only spring from the work of third-world psychologists, with
beneficial results for all of psychology (p. 917).' A few examples will
illustrate this potential.

Conflict resolution. As described before, beliefs about *animosity reduction*
are important in determining how people choose among various strategies
for resolving conflict. This important theoretical construct was introduced
to the psychological community by a Chinese psychologist, Leung (1987).
Before then, the classical text on conflict resolution by Thibaut and Walker
(1975), two Americans, had identified *control* over the process of conflict as
the fundamental factor influencing strategy choice for resolving social
disputes.

Given our previous discussion of collectivism and individualism, it will
appear plausible that a Chinese psychologist would focus on the outcome
of the conflict for the parties concerned whereas Americans would focus on

the process of its resolution. The important consideration here is that *both* factors contribute towards explaining how people decide to resolve conflict in many national cultures, be they Dutch, Indian, Canadian, Korean, Spanish or Japanese. The combined input of psychologists from different cultural traditions has yielded theoretical synergy. Like blind and deaf travellers, we can assist one another on our way.

Models of maturity. Kagitcibasi, a Turkish social psychologist, has been in the vanguard of those pointing out the consistent value bias among western psychologists towards individualism. This bias is strongly expressed in the area of developmental psychology, where 'It is taken for granted that the development of autonomy and independence is a pre-requisite for optimal personality, cognitive, and moral development (Kagitcibasi, 1988, p. 31).' Challenging this assumption, she describes a variety of social situations and cultural milieux where people's 'innate sociality' – in the terms we are using, their interdependence – is the cornerstone to a functional, adaptive life-style. Kagitcibasi concludes that 'Such socialization values and practices cannot be adequately studied with a theoretical orientation based on Western, individualistic ideology, emphasizing autonomy and self-reliance in child development (p. 34).'

Consistent with our previous discussion on convergence, Kagitcibasi (1988) notes that 'A family culture of relatedness and interdependence ... is not incompatible with socio-economic development (p. 36).' Parading data from a variety of cultures, she asserts that 'It is possible for individual loyalties to co-exist with communal–familial loyalties and relations, in a new synthesis, rather than being mutually exclusive (p. 36).' An *inter-dependent* interpersonal perspective does not pit the individual against the group and can thus provide scientists with a fruitful base to explore the 'psychology of relatedness' (Kagitcibasi, 1990).

A psychology of relatedness would propose a different view of maturity than would a psychology of independence (see, for example, Tu, 1985). Such a theory would honour the human requirements both for 'agency' (autonomy, independence) *and* for 'communion' (relatedness, inter-dependence). Research by Kagitcibasi, Sunar and Bekman (1988) and by others (e.g. Lin and Fu, 1990) shows that *both* these orientations may be promoted simultaneously in certain cultural settings. The results of the Lin and Fu research suggest that this outcome is achieved by parental support of interdependence within the family setting, coupled with strong pres-sures for autonomy and achievement outside the family. The conception of the ideal adult that is suggested by such investigations will differ from that emphasized in individualistic cultural settings because it will accord the orientation towards relatedness a more pivotal role in the fully func-tioning person. This perspective can also contribute to currently active debates about gender roles and about cultural diversity in western societies.

Conclusion

These and other innovations are only now beginning to emerge, to be conceptualized and integrated into the psychological literature. Were such ideas slow in coming? We think not. Their emergence had to await the diffusion of 'western' psychology to different cultural milieux and the nurturing of local psychologists who are capable of challenging the biases of the discipline in its own terminology, using its established procedures.

We have now reached this stage. The development of cross-cultural social psychology is one of its manifestations. Its consequences will be an intellectual synergy that will enable us to transcend the limitations imposed by our different cultural origins. We may then be able to claim that we have a more truly universal understanding of humanity's social behaviour.

And the end of all exploring will be to arrive where we started
And know the place for the first time.

(T. S. Eliot, *The Four Quartets*)

References

Abelson, R. (1976) 'Script processing in attitude formation and decision making', in J. Carroll and J. Payne (eds.), *Cognition and Social Behavior*, Hillsdale, NJ: Erlbaum.

Abelson, R. P. (1981) 'The psychological status of the script concept', *American Psychologist*, **36**, 715–29.

Abrams, D., Wetherell, M., Cochrane, S., Hogg, M. A., and Turner, J. C. (1990) 'Knowing what to think by knowing who you are: self-categorisation and the nature of norm formation, conformity and group polarisation', *British Journal of Social Psychology*, **29**, 97–119.

Adamopoulos, J. (1988) 'Interpersonal behavior: cross-cultural and historical perspectives', in M. H. Bond (ed.), *The Cross-Cultural Challenge to Social Psychology*, Newbury Park, CA: Sage.

Adamopoulos, J., and Bontempo, R. (1986) 'Diachronic universals in interpersonal structures: Evidence from literary sources', *Journal of Cross-Cultural Psychology*, **17**, 169–89.

Adams, J. S. (1965) 'Inequity in social exchange', in L. Berkowitz (ed.), *Advances in Experimental Social Psychology*, volume 2, New York: Academic Press.

Adelman, I., and Morris, C. T. (1967) *Society, Politics and Economic Development: A quantitative approach*, Baltimore, MD: Johns Hopkins University Press.

Adler, N. J. (1981) 'Re-entry: managing cross-cultural transitions', *Group and Organization Studies*, **6**, 341–56.

Adler, P. S. (1975) 'The transitional experience: an alternative view of culture shock', *Journal of Humanistic Psychology*, **15**, 13–23.

Adler, P. S. (1987) 'Culture shock and the cross-cultural learning experience', in L. F. Luce and E. C. Smith (eds.), *Toward Internationalism: Readings in cross-cultural communication*, Cambridge, MA: Newbury House.

Adorno, T. W., Frenkel-Brunswick, E., Levinson, D. J., and Sanford, N. (1950) *The Authoritarian Personality*, New York: Harper, Row.

Ajzen, I. (1988) *Attitudes, Personality and Behavior*, Milton Keynes: Open University Press.

Alatas, S. H. (1972) 'The captive mind in development studies: some neglected problems and the need for an autonomous social science tradition in Asia', *International Social Science Journal*, **24**, 9–25.

Alcock, J. E. (1974) 'Cooperation, competition and the effects of time pressure in Canada and India', *Journal of Conflict Resolution*, **18**, 171–97.

Alcock, J. E. (1975) 'Motivation in an asymmetric bargaining situation: a cross-cultural study', *International Journal of Psychology*, **10**, 69–81.

Allport, F. H. (1924) *Social Psychology*, Boston, MA: Houghton Mifflin.

Almaney, A., and Ahwan, A. (1982) *Communicating with the Arabs*, Prospect Heights, IL: Waveland.

Altman, I., and Chemers, M. M. (1980) 'Cultural aspects of environment–behaviour relationships', in H. C. Triandis and R. W. Brislin (eds.), *Handbook of Cross-Cultural Psychology*, volume 5, Boston, MA: Allyn and Bacon.

Altman, I., and Gauvain, M. (1981) 'A cross-cultural dialectic analysis of homes', in L. Liben, A. Patterson and N. Newcombe (eds.), *Spatial Representation and Behavior across the Life-Span*, New York: Academic Press.

Al-Zahrani, S. S. A. (1991) 'Cross-cultural differences in attributions of responsibility to the self, the family, the ingroup, and the outgroup in the USA and Saudi Arabia: Western versus non-Western cultural attributional patterns of responsibility', unpublished doctoral dissertation, Michigan State University.

Amabile, T. M., and Glazebrook, A. H. (1982) 'A negativity bias in interpersonal evaluation', *Journal of Experimental Social Psychology*, **18**, 1–22.

Amir, T. (1984) 'The Asch conformity effect: a study in Kuwait', *Social Behavior and Personality*, **12**, 187–90.

Amir, Y. (1969) 'Contact hypothesis in ethnic relations', *Psychological Bulletin*, **71**, 319–42.

Amir, Y. (1976) 'The role of intergroup contact in change of prejudice and ethnic relations', in P. A. Katz (ed.), *Towards the Elimination of Racism*, New York: Pergamon.

Amir, Y., and Sharon, I. (1987) 'Are social-psychological laws cross-culturally valid?', *Journal of Cross-Cultural Psychology*, **18**, 383–470.

Ancona, L., and Pareyson, R. (1968) 'Contributo allo studio della aggressione: la dinamica della obbedienza distincttiva', *Archivio di Psicologia Neurologia e Psichiatria*, **29**, 340–72.

Andreeva, G. (1979) 'The development of social psychology in the USSR', in L. H. Strickland (ed.), *Soviet and Western Perspectives in Social Psychology*, Oxford: Pergamon.

Andreeva, G. (1982) 'Common activity as a factor of causal attribution in a small group', in H. Hiebsch (ed.), *Social Psychology*, Amsterdam: North Holland.

Andreeva, G. (1984) 'Cognitive processes in developing groups', in L. H. Strickland (ed.), *Directions in Soviet Social Psychology*, New York: Springer.

Aral, S. O., and Sunar, D. (1977) 'Interaction and justice norms: a cross-national comparison', *Journal of Social Psychology*, **101**, 175–86.

Argyle, M. (1979) 'New developments in the analysis of social skills', in A. Wolfgang (ed.), *Non-verbal Behavior*, London: Academic Press.

Argyle, M., Furnham, A., and Graham, J. A. (1981) *Social Situations*, Cambridge: Cambridge University Press.

Argyle, M., Henderson, M., Bond, M.H., Iizuka, Y., and Contarello, A. (1986) 'Cross-cultural variations in relationship rules', *International Journal of Psychology*, **21**, 287–315.

Armer, M., and Youtz, R. (1971) 'Formal education and individual modernity in an African society', *American Journal of Sociology*, **76**, 604–26.

Asch, S. (1951) 'Effects of group pressure on the modification and distortion of judgments', in H. Guetzkow (ed.), *Groups, Leadership and Men*, Pittsburgh, PA: Carnegie.

Asch, S. (1956) 'Studies of independence and conformity: a minority of one against a unanimous majority', *Psychological Monographs*, **70**, no. 9 (whole number 416).

Atsumi, T., and Sugiman, T. (1990). 'Group decision processes by majority and minority: decision and implementation', *Japanese Journal of Experimental Social Psychology*, **30**, 15–23 (English abstract).

Ayman, R., and Chemers, M. M. (1983) 'Relationship of supervisory behavior ratings to work group effectiveness and subordinate satisfaction among Iranian managers', *Journal of Applied Psychology*, **68**, 338–41.

Bales, R. F. (1951) *Interaction Process Analysis: A method for the study of small groups*, Reading, MA: Addison-Wesley.

Barker, R. C. (1968) *Ecological Psychology: Concepts and Methods for Studying the Environment of Human Behavior*, Stanford, CA: Stanford University Press.

Baron, R. A., and Byrne, D. (1986) *Social Psychology: Understanding human interaction* (5th edn), Boston, MA: Allyn and Bacon.

Baron, R. A., and Byrne, D. (1991) *Social Psychology: Understanding human interaction* (6th edn), Boston, MA: Allyn and Bacon.

Barry, H., Child, I., and Bacon, M. (1959) 'Relation of child training to subsistence economy', *American Anthropology*, **61**, 51–63.

Bateson, N. (1966) 'Familiarisation, group discussion and risk-taking', *Journal of Experimental Social Psychology*, **2**, 119–29.

Baumrind, D. (1964) 'Some thoughts on ethics of research: after reading Milgram's "Behavioral study of obedience"', *American Psychologist*, **19**, 421–3.

Becker, E. (1973) *The Denial of Death*, New York: Free Press.

Bell, P. R., and Jamieson, B. D. (1970) 'Publicity of initial decisions and the risky shift phenomenon', *Journal of Experimental Social Psychology*, **6**, 329–45.

Berger, C. R. (1987) 'Communicating under uncertainty', in M. E. Roloff and G. R. Mitter (eds.), *Interpersonal Processes*, Newbury Park, CA: Sage.

Berger, P. L., and Luckman, T. (1966) *The Social Construction of Reality*, New York: Doubleday.

Berkowitz, L. (1989) 'Frustration–aggression hypothesis: examination and reformulation', *Psychological Bulletin*, **106**, 59–73.

Berman, J. J., Murphy-Berman, V., and Singh, P. (1985) 'Cross-cultural similarities and differences in perceptions of fairness', *Journal of Cross-Cultural Psychology*, **16**, 55–67.

Bernstein, B. (1971) *Class, Codes and Control*, volume 1, London: Routledge and Kegan Paul.

Berry, J. (1967) 'Independence and conformity in subsistence-level societies', *Journal of Personality and Social Psychology*, **7**, 415–8.

Berry, J. (1969) 'On cross-cultural comparability', *International Journal of Psychology*, **4**, 119–28.

Berry, J. (1980) 'Introduction to methodology', in H. Triandis and J. Berry (eds.), *Handbook of Cross-Cultural Psychology*, volume 2, Boston, MA: Allyn and Bacon.

Berry, J. (1989) 'Imposed etics – emics – derived etics: the operationalisation of a compelling idea', *International Journal of Psychology*, **24**, 721–35.

Berry, J., and Annis, R. C. (1974) 'Ecology, culture and psychological differentiation', *International Journal of Psychology*, **9**, 173–93.

Berry, J. W., & Kalin, R. (1979) 'Reciprocity of inter-ethnic attitudes in a multi-cultural society', *International Journal of Intercultural Relations*, **3**, 99–112.

Berry, J. W., Kalin, R., and Taylor, D. M. (1977) *Multiculturalism and Ethnic Attitudes in Canada*, Ottawa: Ministry of Supplies and Services.

Berry, J. W., Kalin, R., and Taylor, D. M. (1980) 'Multiculturalism and ethnic attitudes in Canada', in J. E. Goldstein and R. M. Bienvenue (eds.), *Ethnicity and Ethnic Relations in Canada*, Toronto: Butterworth.

Berry, J. W., Kim, U., Minde, T., and Mok, D. (1987) 'Comparative studies of acculturative stress', *International Migration Review*, **21**, 491–551.

Berry, J. W., Kim, U., Power, S., Young, M., and Bujaki, M. (1989) 'Acculturation attitudes in plural societies', *Applied Psychology*, **38**, 185–206.

Bertalanffy, L. von (1973) *General Systems Theory: Foundations, developments, applications* (rev. edn), New York: Braziller.

Bethlehem, D. W. (1975) 'The effect of westernisation on cooperative behaviour in Central Africa', *International Journal of Psychology*, **10**, 219–24.

Bhawuk, D. P. S. (1990) 'Cross-cultural orientation programs', in R. W. Brislin (ed.), *Applied Cross-Cultural Psychology*, Newbury Park, CA: Sage.

Bijnen, E. J., and Poortinga, Y. H. (1988) 'The questionable value of cross-cultural comparisons with the Eysenck Personality Questionnaire', *Journal of Cross-Cultural Psychology*, **19**, 193–202.

Bijnen, E. J., van der Net, T. Z. J., and Poortinga, Y. H. (1986) 'On cross-cultural comparative studies with the Eysenck Personality Questionnaire', *Journal of Cross-Cultural Psychology*, **17**, 3–16.

Billig, M. (1976) *Social Psychology and Intergroup Relations*. London: Academic Press.

Birth, K., and Prillwitz, G. (1959) 'Führungsstile und Gruppenverhalten von Schulkindern', *Zeitschrift für Psychologie*, **163**, 230–301.

Black, J. S., and Gregerson, H. B. (1991a) 'The other half of the picture: antecedents of spouse cross-cultural adjustment', *Journal of International Business Studies*, **22**, 461–78.

Black, J. S., and Gregerson, H. B. (1991b) 'When Yankee comes home: factors related to expatriate and spouse repatriation adjustment', *Journal of International Business Studies*, **22**, 671–94.

Blackler, F. (ed.) (1983) *Social Psychology and Developing Countries*, Chichester: Wiley.

Blum-Kulka, S., House, J., and Kasper, G. (eds.) (1989) *Cross-cultural pragmatics: Requests and apologies*. Norwood, NJ: Ablex.

Bochner, S. (ed.) (1980) *The Mediating Person: Bridges between cultures*, Cambridge, MA: Schenkman.

Bochner, S. (1982) 'The social psychology of cross-cultural relations', in S. Bochner (ed.), *Cultures in Contact: Studies in cross-cultural interaction*, Oxford: Pergamon.

Bochner, S., and Orr, F. E. (1979) 'Race and academic status as determinants of friendship formation: a field study', *International Journal of Psychology*, **14**, 37–46.

Bochner, S., and Perks, R. W. (1971) 'National role evocation as a function of cross-national interaction', *Journal of Cross-Cultural Psychology*, **2**, 157–64.

Bond, M. H. (1983) 'Linking person perception dimensions to behavioral intention dimensions: the Chinese connection', *Journal of Cross-Cultural Psychology*, **14**, 41–63.

Bond, M. H. (1985) 'Language as a carrier of ethnic stereotypes in Hong Kong', *Journal of Social Psychology*, **125**, 53–62.

Bond, M. H. (1986) 'Mutual stereotypes and the facilitation of interaction across cultural lines', *International Journal of Intercultural Relations*, **10**, 259–76.

Bond, M. H. (ed.) (1988a) *The Cross-Cultural Challenge to Social Psychology*, Newbury Park, CA: Sage.

Bond, M. H. (1988b) 'Finding universal dimensions of individual variation in multicultural studies of values: the Rokeach and Chinese value surveys', *Journal of Personality and Social Psychology*, **55**, 1009–15.

Bond, M. H. (1991a) 'Chinese values and health: a cross-cultural examination', *Psychology and Health*, **5**, 137–52.

Bond, M. H. (1991b) 'Cultural influences on modes of impression management: implications of the culturally diverse organization', in R. A. Giacolone and P. Rosenfeld (eds.), *Applied Impression Management: How image-making affects managerial decisions*, Newbury Park, CA: Sage.

Bond, M. H. (in press) 'The process of enhancing cross-cultural competence in Hong Kong organizations', *International Journal of Intercultural Relations*.

Bond, M. H., and Cheung, K. V. (1991) 'Resistance to group or personal insults in an ingroup or outgroup context', *International Journal of Psychology*, **25**, 83–94.

Bond, M. H., and Cheung, M. K. (1984) 'Experimenter language choice and ethnic affirmation by Chinese trilinguals in Hong Kong', *International Journal of Intercultural Relations*, **8**, 347–56.

Bond, M. H., and Cheung, T. S. (1983) 'The spontaneous self-concept of college students in Hong Kong, Japan, and the United States', *Journal of Cross-Cultural Psychology*, **14**, 153–71.

Bond, M. H., and Dutton, D. G. (1975) 'The effect of interaction anticipation and experience as a victim on aggressive behavior', *Journal of Personality*, **43**, 515–27.

Bond, M. H., and Forgas, J. P. (1984) 'Linking person perception to behavioral intention across cultures: the role of cultural collectivism', *Journal of Cross-Cultural Psychology*, **15**, 337–52.

Bond, M. H., and Hewstone, M. (1988) 'Social identity theory and the perception of intergroup relations in Hong Kong', *International Journal of Intercultural Relations*, **12**, 153–70.

Bond, M. H., and Hwang, K. K. (1986) 'The social psychology of Chinese people', in M. H. Bond (ed.), *The Psychology of the Chinese People*, Hong Kong: Oxford University Press.

Bond, M. H., and King, A. Y. C. (1985) 'Coping with the threat of westernization in Hong Kong', *International Journal of Intercultural Relations*, **9**, 351–64.

Bond, M. H., and Lee, P. W. H. (1981) 'Face saving in Chinese culture: a discussion and experimental study of Hong Kong students', in A. Y. C. King and R. P. L. Lee (eds.), *Social Life and Development in Hong Kong*, Hong Kong: Chinese University Press.

Bond, M. H., and Shiraishi, D. (1974) 'The effect of body lean and status of an interviewer on the non-verbal behaviour of Japanese interviewees', *International Journal of Psychology*, **9**, 117–28.

Bond, M. H., and Yang, K. S. (1982), 'Ethnic affirmation versus cross-cultural accommodation: the variable impact of questionnaire language on Chinese bilinguals in Hong Kong', *Journal of Cross-Cultural Psychology*, **12**, 169–81.

Bond, M. H., Chiu, C. K., and Wan, K. C. (1984) 'When modesty fails: the social impact of group-effacing attributions following success or failure', *European Journal of Social Psychology*, **14**, 335–8.

Bond, M. H., Hewstone, M., Wan, K. C., and Chiu, C. K. (1985) 'Group-serving attributions across intergroup contexts: cultural differences in the explanation of sex-typed behaviours', *European Journal of Social Psychology*, **15**, 435–51.

Bond, M. H., Leung, K., and Schwartz, S. (1992) 'Explaining choices in procedural and distributive justice across cultures', *International Journal of Psychology*, **27**, 211–25.

Bond, M. H., Leung, K., and Wan, K. C. (1982a) 'How does cultural collectivism operate? The impact of task and maintenance contributions on reward allocations', *Journal of Cross-Cultural Psychology*, **13**, 186–200.

Bond, M. H., Leung, K., and Wan, K. C. (1982b) 'The social impact of self-effacing attributions: the Chinese case', *Journal of Social Psychology*, **118**, 157–66.

Bond, M. H., Wan, K. C., Leung, K., and Giacolone, R. A. (1985) 'How are responses to verbal insult related to cultural collectivism and power distance?' *Journal of Cross-Cultural Psychology*, **16**, 111–27.

Boski, P. (1983) 'A study of person perception in Nigeria: ethnicity and self versus other attributions for achievement-related outcomes', *Journal of Cross-Cultural Psychology*, **14**, 85–108.

Boucher, J. D., and Carlson, G. E. (1980) 'Recognition of facial expression in three cultures', *Journal of Cross-Cultural Psychology*, **11**, 263–80.

Bourhis, R. Y., Giles, H., Leyens, J. P., and Tajfel, H. (1979) 'Psycholinguistic distinctiveness: language divergence in Belgium', in H. Giles and R. N. St Clair (eds.), *Language and Social Psychology*, Baltimore, MD: University Park Press.

Bradbury, T. N., and Fincham, F. D. (1990) 'Attributions in marriage: a review and critique', *Psychological Bulletin*, **107**, 3–33.

Brehm, J. W. (1966) *A Theory of Psychological Reactance*, New York: Academic Press.

Brewer, M. B. (1988) 'A dual process model of impression formation', in R. Wyer and T. Scrull (eds.), *Advances in Social Cognition*, volume 1, New York: Erlbaum.

Brigham, J. C. (1971) 'Ethnic stereotypes', *Psychological Bulletin*, **76**, 15–38.

Brislin, R. W. (1970) 'Back-translation for cross-cultural research', *Journal of Cross-Cultural Psychology*, **1**, 185–216.

Brislin, R. W., Cushner, K., Cherrie, C., and Yong, M. (1986) *Intercultural Interactions: A practical guide*, Beverly Hills, CA: Sage.

Brislin, R. W., Lonner, W., and Thorndike, R. M. (1973) *Cross-Cultural Research Methods*, New York: Wiley.

Bronfenbrenner, U. (1961) 'The mirror image in Soviet–American relations: a social psychologist's report', *Journal of Social Issues*, **17**, 45–56.

Brown, L. R. (1972) *World Without Borders*, New York: Vintage.

Brown, L. R. *et al.* (1990) *State of the World 1990*, New York: Norton.

Burley, P. M., and McGuiness, J. (1977) 'Effects of social intelligence on the Milgram paradigm', *Psychological Reports*, **40**, 767–70.

Burgoon, J. K. (1989) 'Comparatively speaking: applying a comparative approach to non-verbal expectancy violations theory', unpublished manuscript, University of Arizona.

Burgoon, J. K., and Walther, J.B. (1990) 'Non-verbal expectancies and the evaluative consequences of violations', *Human Communication Research*, **17**, 232–65.

Buss, D. M. (1989) 'Sex differences in human mate preferences: evolutionary hypotheses tested in 37 cultures', *Behavioral and Brain Sciences*, **12**, 1–49.

Buss, D. M., and 49 co-authors (1990) 'International preferences in selecting mates: a study of 37 cultures', *Journal of Cross-Cultural Psychology*, **21**, 5–47.

Buunk, B., and Hupka, R. B. (1987) 'Cross-cultural differences in the elicitation of sexual jealousy', *Journal of Sex Research*, **23**, 12–22.

Byrne, D. (1974) *An Introduction to Personality: Research, Theory, and Applications* (2nd edn), Englewood Cliffs, NJ: Prentice Hall.

Byrne, D., and 7 co-authors (1971) 'The ubiquitous relationship: attitude similarity and attraction – a cross-cultural study', *Human Relations*, **24**, 201–7.

Cantor, N., and Mischel, W. (1978) 'Prototypes in person perception', in L. Berkowitz (ed.), *Advances in Experimental Social Psychology*, volume 12, New York: Academic Press.

Carden, A. I., and Feicht, R. (1991) 'Homesickness among American and Turkish college students', *Journal of Cross-Cultural Psychology*, **22**, 418–28.

Carlson, J., and Davis, D. M. (1971) 'Cultural values and the risky shift: a cross-cultural test in Uganda and the United States', *Journal of Personality and Social Psychology*, **20**, 392–9.

Carment, D. W. (1974) 'Indian and Canadian choice behavior in a maximising difference game and in a game of chicken', *International Journal of Psychology*, **9**, 213–21.

Carment, D. W., and Alcock, J. E. (1984) 'Indian and Canadian behavior in two person power games', *Journal of Conflict Resolution*, **28**, 507–21.

Carter, H., and Glick, P. C. (1970) *Marriage and Divorce: A social and economic study*, Cambridge, MA: Harvard University Press.

Cattell, R. B. (1953) 'A quantitative analysis of the changes in the culture pattern of Great Britain, 1837–1937, by P-technique', *Acta Psychologica*, **9**, 99–121.

Chandler, T. A., Shama, D. D., Wolf, F. M., and Planchard, S. K. (1981) 'Multiattributional causality: a five cross-national samples study', *Journal of Cross-Cultural Psychology*, **12**, 207–21.

Chandra, S. (1973) 'The effects of group pressure in perception: a cross-cultural conformity study', *International Journal of Psychology*, **8**, 37–9.

Chinese Culture Connection (1987) 'Chinese values and the search for culture-free dimensions of culture', *Journal of Cross-Cultural Psychology*, **18**, 143–64.

Chiu, H. Y. (1979) 'A test of unidimensionality and universality of individual modernity in ten Taiwanese communities', unpublished doctoral dissertation, Indiana University.

Chiu, M. I., Feldman, S. S., and Rosenthal, D. A. (in press) 'The influence of immigration on parental behavior and adolescent distress in Chinese families residing in two Western nations', *Journal of Research on Adolescence*.

Choi, S. C., and Choi, S. H. (1992) 'The conceptualisation of Korean tact, Noon-Chi', in S. Iwawaki, Y. Kashima and K. Leung (eds.), *Innovations in Cross-Cultural Psychology*, Amsterdam: Swets and Zeitlinger.

Christensen, H. T. (1973) 'Attitudes toward marital infidelity: a nine culture sampling of university student opinion', *Journal of Comparative Family Studies*, **4**, 197–214.

Christie, R., and Geis, F. (1970) *Studies in Machiavellianism*, New York: Academic Press.

Church, A. T. (1982) 'Sojourner adjustment', *Psychological Bulletin*, **91**, 540–72.

Church, A. T. (1987) 'Personality research in a non-Western culture: the Philippines', *Psychological Bulletin*, **102**, 272–92.

Church, A. T., and Katigbak, M. S. (1988) 'The emic strategy in the identification and assessment of personality dimensions in a non-Western culture', *Journal of Cross-Cultural Psychology*, **19**, 140–63.

Church, A. T., and Katigbak, M. S. (1989) 'Internal, external and self-report structure of personality in a non-Western culture: an investigation of cross-language and cross-cultural generalisability', *Journal of Personality and Social Psychology*, **57**, 857–72.

Church, A. T., and Katigbak, M. S. (1992) 'The cultural context of academic motives: a comparison of Filipino and American college students', *Journal of Cross-Cultural Psychology*, **23**, 40–58.

Claeys, W. (1967) 'Conformity behavior and personality variables in Congolese students', *International Journal of Psychology*, **2**, 13–23.

Clark, L. A. (1987) 'Mutual relevance of mainstream and cross-cultural psychology', *Journal of Consulting and Clinical Psychology*, **55**, 461–70.

Collett, P. (1971) 'On training Englishmen in the non-verbal behaviours of Arabs', *International Journal of Psychology*, **6**, 209–15.

Collett, P., and O'Shea, G. (1976) 'Pointing the way to a fictional place: a study of direction-giving in England and Iran', *European Journal of Social Psychology*, **6**, 447–58.

Costa, P. T., and Macrae, R. R. (1985) *The NEO Personality Inventory Manual*, Odessa, FL: Psychological Assessment Resources.

Coupland, J., Coupland, N., Giles, H., and Wiemann, J. (1988) 'My life in your hands: processes of self-disclosure in intergenerational talk', in N. Coupland (ed.), *Styles of Discourse*, London: Croom Helm.

Cousins, S. (1989) 'Culture and selfhood in Japan and the US', *Journal of Personality and Social Psychology*, **56**, 124–31.

Cox, T. H., Lobel, S., and McLeod, P. L. (1991) 'Effects of ethnic group cultural differences on cooperative and competitive behavior on a group task', *Academy of Management Journal*, **34**, 827–47.

Crutchfield, R. S. (1955) 'Conformity and character', *American Psychologist*, **10**, 191–8.

Cupach, W. R., Metts, S., and Hazelton, V. (1978) 'Coping with social dis-ease: remedial strategies and embarrassment', paper presented at the Western Speech Communication Association, Salt Lake City, Utah, February.

Dawes, R. M. (1980) 'Social dilemmas', *Annual Review of Psychology*, **31**, 169–93.

De Monchaux, C., and Shimmin, S. (1955) 'Some problems in experimental group psychology', *Human Relations*, **8**, 53–60.

Derlega, V. J., and Stepien, E. G. (1977) 'Norms regulating self-disclosure among Polish university students', *Journal of Cross-Cultural Psychology*, **8**, 369–76.

Deutsch, K. (1968) 'Toward a cybernetic model of man and society', in W. Buckley (ed.), *Modern Systems Theory for the Behavioral Scientist*, Chicago, IL: Aldine.

Deutsch, M., and Gerard, H. B. (1955) 'A study of normative and informational influences upon social judgment', *Journal of Abnormal and Social Psychology*, **51**, 629–36.

Diab, L. N. (1970) 'A study of intragroup and intergroup relations among experimentally produced small groups', *Genetic Psychology Monographs*, **82**, 49–82.

Digman, J. M. (1990) 'Personality structure: emergence of the five-factor model', *Annual Review of Psychology*, **41**, 417–40.

Doise, W. (1986) *Levels of Explanation in Social Psychology*, Cambridge: Cambridge University Press.

Doise, W., Csepeli, G., Dann, H., Gouge, C., Larsen, K., and Ostell, A. (1972) 'An experimental investigation into the formation of intergroup representations', *European Journal of Social Psychology*, **2**, 202–4.

Doktor, R. (1983) 'Culture and the management of time: a comparison of Japanese and American top management practice', *Asia Pacific Journal of Management*, **1**, 65–71.

Dollard, J., Doob, L. W., Miller, N. E., Mowrer, O. H., and Sears, R. R. (1939) *Frustration and Aggression*, New Haven, CT: Yale University Press.

Doms, M. (1983) 'The minority influence effect: an alternative approach', in W. Doise and S. Moscovici (eds.), *Current Issues in European Social Psychology*, volume 1, Cambridge: Cambridge University Press.

Doms, M., and van Avermaet, E. (1980) 'Majority influence, minority influence and conversion behaviour: a replication', *Journal of Experimental Social Psychology*, **16**, 283–92.

Draguns, J. (1990) 'Normal and abnormal behaviour in cross-cultural perspective: specifying the nature of their relationship', in J. J. Berman (ed.), *Nebraska Symposium on Motivation, 1989*, Lincoln, NB: Nebraska University Press.

Druckman, D., Benton, A. A., Ali, F., and Bagur, J. S. (1976) 'Cultural differences in bargaining behavior', *Journal of Conflict Resolution*, **20**, 413–49.

Durkheim, E. (1898) 'Représentations individuelles et représentations collectives', *Revue de Métaphysique et de Morale*, **6**, 273–302.

Dutton, D. G. (1973) 'Reverse discrimination: the relationship of amount of perceived discrimination toward a minority group on the behaviour of majority group members', *Canadian Journal of Behavioural Science*, **5**, 34–45.

Earley, P. C. (1989) 'Social loafing and collectivism: a comparison of the United States and the People's Republic of China', *Administrative Science Quarterly*, **34**, 565–81.

Earley, P. C. (1991) 'East meets West meets Mideast: further explorations of collectivistic and individualistic work groups', unpublished paper, Department of Strategic Management and Organization, University of Minnesota.

Earley, P. C. (in press) 'Relation of collectivistic beliefs to social processes in work groups', *Administrative Science Quarterly*.

Ebbinghaus, H. (1908) *Abriss der Psychologie*, Leipzig: Veit.

Edelmann, R. J. (1982) 'The effect of embarrassed reactions', *Australian Journal of Psychology*, **34**, 359–87.

Ekman, P., Sorenson, E. R., and Friesen, W. V. (1969) 'Pan-cultural elements in facial displays of emotion', *Science*, **164**, 86–8.

Ekman, P., and 11 others (1987) 'Universals and cultural differences in the judgments of facial expressions of emotion', *Journal of Personality and Social Psychology*, **53**, 712–17.

Elliot, G. C., and Meeker, B. F. (1984) 'Modifiers of the equity effect: group outcome and causes for individual performance', *Journal of Personality and Social Psychology*, **46**, 586–97.

Enriquez, V. (1988) 'The structure of Philippine social values: towards integrating indigenous values and appropriate technology', in D. Sinha and H. S. R. Kao (eds.), *Social Values and Development: Asian perspectives*, New Delhi: Sage.

Epstein, S., and O'Brien, E. J. (1985) 'The person–situation debate in historical and current perspective', *Psychological Bulletin*, **98**, 513–37.

Erez, M., and Earley, P. C. (1987) 'Comparative analysis of goal-setting strategies across cultures', *Journal of Applied Psychology*, **72**, 658–65.

Evans, G. W., Palsane, N., and Carrere, S. (1987) 'Type A behavior and occupational stress: a cross-cultural study of blue-collar workers', *Journal of Personality and Social Psychology*, **52**, 1002–7.

Everett, J. E., and Stening, B. W. (1987) 'Stereotyping in American, British, and Japanese corporations in Hong Kong and Singapore', *Journal of Social Psychology*, **127**, 445–60.

Eysenck, H. W. (1986) 'Cross-cultural comparisons: the validity of assessment by indices of factor comparisons', *Journal of Cross-Cultural Psychology*, **17**, 506–15.

Eysenck, H. W., and Eysenck, S. B. G. (1982) 'Recent advances in the cross-cultural study of personality', in J. N. Butcher and C. D. Spielberger (eds.), *Advances in Personality Assessment*, volume 2, Hillsdale, NJ: Erlbaum.

Farr, R. M. (1989) 'The social and collective nature of representations', in J. P. Forgas and J. M. Innes (eds.), *Recent Advances in Social Psychology: An international perspective*, Amsterdam: North-Holland.

Farris, G. F., and Butterfield, A. (1972) 'Control theory in Brazilian organizations', *Administrative Science Quarterly*, **17**, 574–85.

Faucheux, C. (1976) 'A critique of cross-cultural social psychology', *European Journal of Social Psychology*, **6**, 269–322.

Feagin, J. (1972) 'Poverty: we still believe that God helps them who help themselves', *Psychology Today*, **6**, 101–29.

Feign, L. (1986) *Fong's Aieeyaaa*, Hong Kong: Hong Kong Standard.

Feign, L. (1987) *Fong's Aieeyaaa, Not Again*, Hong Kong: Hong Kong Standard.

Feldman, R. E. (1967) 'Honesty toward compatriot and foreigner: field experiments in Paris, Athens and Boston', in W. W. Lambert and R. Weisbrod (eds.), *Comparative Perspectives on Social Psychology*, Boston, MA: Little, Brown.

Feldman, S. S., and Rosenthal, D. A. (1990) 'The acculturation of autonomy expectations in Chinese high schoolers residing in two Western nations', *International Journal of Psychology*, **25**, 259–81.

Feldman, S. S., Mont-Reynaud, R., and Rosenthal, D. A. (in press) 'The acculturation of values of Chinese adolescents residing in the United States and Australia',
International Journal of Psychology.

Felson, R. B. (1978) 'Aggression as impression management', *Social Psychology
Quarterly*, **41**, 205–13.

Festinger, L. (1954) 'A theory of social comparison processes', *Human Relations*, **7**,
117–40.

Fiedler, F. E. (1967) *A Contingency Theory of Leadership Effectiveness*, New York:
McGraw-Hill.

Fishman, J. A. (1972) *Language and Nationalism*, Rowley, MA: Newbury House.

Fiske, A. P. (1991) 'The cultural relativity of selfish individualism: anthropological
evidence that humans are inherently sociable', in M. S. Clark (ed.), *Prosocial
Behavior*, Newbury Park, CA: Sage.

Fiske, A. P. (in press) 'The four elementary forms of sociality: framework for a
unified theory of social relations', *Psychological Review*.

Fliegel, D. (1987) 'Immigrant professionals must speak American', *Boston Globe*, 16
June, p. 19.

Foley Meeker, B. (1970) 'An experimental study of cooperation and competition in
West Africa', *International Journal of Psychology*, **5**, 11–19.

Fontaine, G. (1990) 'Cultural diversity in intimate intercultural relationships', in D.
Cahn (ed.), *Intimates in Conflict: A communication perspective*, Hillsdale, NJ: Erlbaum.

Fontaine, G., and Dorch, E. (1980) 'Problems and benefits of close intercultural
relationships', *International Journal of Intercultural Relations*, **4**, 329–37.

Forgas, J. P. (1979) *Social Episodes: The study of interaction routines*, London:
Academic Press.

Forgas, J. P. (1981) 'Affective and emotional influences on episode representations',
in J. P. Forgas (ed.), *Social Cognition: Perspectives on everyday understanding*,
London: Academic Press.

Forgas, J. P., and Bond, M. H. (1985) 'Cultural influences on the perception of
interaction episodes', *Personality and Social Psychology Bulletin*, **11**, 75–88.

Frager, R. (1970) 'Conformity and anti-conformity in Japan', *Journal of Personality
and Social Psychology*, **15**, 203–10.

Fraser, C., Gouge, C., and Billig, M. (1971) 'Risky shifts, cautious shifts and group
polarisation', *European Journal of Social Psychology*, **1**, 7–30.

Freedle, R. (ed.) (1979) *New Directions in Discourse Processing*, volume 2, Norwood,
NJ: Ablex.

Freire, P. (1970) *The Pedagogy of the Oppressed*, New York: Herder and Herder.

French, J. R. P., Israel, J., and Ås, D. (1960) 'An experiment on participation in a
Norwegian factory: interpersonal dimensions of decision-making', *Human
Relations*, **13**, 3–19.

Friend, R., Rafferty, Y., and Bramel, D. (1990) 'A puzzling misinterpretation of the
Asch "conformity" study', *European Journal of Social Psychology*, **20**, 29–44.

Friesen, W. (1972) 'Cultural differences in facial expressions in a social situation: an
experimental test of the concept of display rules', unpublished Ph.D. thesis,
University of California, San Francisco.

Fry, P. S., and Ghosh, R. (1980) 'Attributions of success and failure: comparison
of cultural differences between Asian and Caucasian children', *Journal of
Cross-Cultural Psychology*, **11**, 343–63.

Furby, L. (1979) 'Individualistic bias in studies of locus of control', in A. R. Buss (ed.), *Psychology in Social Context*, New York: Irvington.

Furnham, A. (1982) 'The message, the context and the medium', *Language and Communication*, **2**, 33–47.

Furnham, A. (1989) 'Communicating across cultures: a social skills perspective', *Counselling Psychology Quarterly*, **2**, 205–22.

Furnham, A. (1990) 'Expatriate stress: the problems of living abroad', in S. Fisher and C. L. Cooper (eds.), *On the Move: The psychology of change and transition*, Chichester: Wiley.

Furnham, A., and Bochner, S. (1982) 'Social difficulty in a foreign culture: an empirical analysis of culture shock', in S. Bochner (ed.), *Cultures in Contact*, New York: Pergamon.

Furnham, A., and Bochner, S. (1986) *Culture Shock: Psychological reactions to unfamiliar environments*, London: Methuen.

Furuhata, K. (1980) *Ningenkankei no Shakaishinrigaku (Social Psychology of Interpersonal Relations)*, Tokyo: Science Publishers.

Gabrenya, W. K., Wang, Y. E., and Latané, B. (1985) 'Social loafing on an optimising task: cross-cultural differences among Chinese and Americans', *Journal of Cross-Cultural Psychology*, **16**, 223–42.

Gallois, C., Franklyn-Stokes, A., Giles, H., and Coupland, N. (1988) 'Communication accommodation in intercultural encounters', in Y. Y. Kim and W. B. Gudykunst (eds.), *Theories in Intercultural Communication*, Newbury Park, CA: Sage.

Geertz, C. (1974) 'From the native's point of view: on the nature of anthropological understanding', in K. Basso and H. Selby (eds.), *Meaning in Anthropology*, Albuquerque, NM: University of New Mexico Press.

Gerard, H. B., Wilhelmy, R. A., and Connolly, E. S. (1968) 'Conformity and group size', *Journal of Personality and Social Psychology*, **8**, 79–82.

Gergen, K. J. (1973) 'Social psychology as history', *Journal of Personality and Social Psychology*, **26**, 309–20.

Gibson, J. J. (1979) *The Ecological Approach to Visual Perception*, Boston, MA: Houghton Mifflin.

Giles, H., and Byrne, J. L. (1982) 'An intergroup approach to second language acquisition', *Journal of Multilingual and Multicultural Development*, **3**, 17–40.

Giles, H., and Johnson, P. (1981) 'The role of language in ethnic group relations', in J. Turner and H. Giles (eds.), *Intergroup Behavior*, Chicago, IL: University of Chicago Press.

Giles, H., and Johnson, P. (1986) 'Perceived threat, ethnic commitment, and interethnic language behaviour', in Y. Y. Kim (ed.), *Interethnic Communication: Current research*, Newbury Park, CA: Sage.

Giles, H., and Johnson, P. (1987) 'Ethnolinguistic identity theory: a social-psychological identity approach to language maintenance', *International Journal of the Sociology of Language*, **68**, 69–99.

Giles, H., and Ryan, E. B. (1982) 'Prolegomena for developing a social psychological theory of language attitudes', in E. B. Ryan and H. Giles (eds.), *Attitudes towards Language Variation*, London: Edward Arnold.

Giles, H., Bourhis, R. Y., and Taylor, D. M. (1977) 'Towards a theory of language in ethnic group relations', in H. Giles (ed.), *Language, Ethnicity, and Intergroup Relations*, London: Academic Press.

Giles, H., Coupland, N., and Wiemann, J. M. (1992). '"Talk is cheap ... but my word is my bond": beliefs about talk', in K. Bolton and H. Kwok (eds.), *Sociolinguistics Today: International perspectives*, London: Routledge.

Giorgi, L., and Marsh, C. (1990) 'The Protestant work ethic as a cultural phenomenon', *European Journal of Social Psychology*, **20**, 499–518.

Glass, D. C. (1977) *Behavior Patterns, Stress and Coronary Disease*, Hillsdale, NJ: Erlbaum.

Gleick, J. (1987) *Chaos: Making a new science*, New York: Viking.

Glenn, E. S., Witmeyer, D., and Stevenson, K. A. (1977) 'Cultural styles of persuasion', *International Journal of Intercultural Relations*, **1**, 52–66.

Goffman, E. (1956) 'Embarrassment and social organization', *American Journal of Sociology*, **62**, 264–271.

Goffman, E. (1959) *The Presentation of Self in Everyday Life*, New York: Doubleday.

Gologor, E. (1977) 'Group polarisation in a non-risk-taking culture', *Journal of Cross-Cultural Psychology*, **8**, 331–46.

Gouge, C., and Fraser, C. (1972) 'A further demonstration of group polarisation', *European Journal of Social Psychology*, **2**, 95–7.

Graham, J. L. (1985) 'The influence of culture on the process of business negotiations: an exploratory study', *Journal of International Business Studies*, **16**, 81–96.

Gudykunst, W. B. (1988) 'Culture and intergroup processes', in M. H. Bond (ed.), *The Cross-Cultural Challenge to Social Psychology*, Newbury Park, CA: Sage.

Gudykunst, W. B. (1991). *Bridging Differences: Effective intergroup communication*, Newbury Park, CA: Sage.

Gudykunst, W. B., Gao, G., and Franklyn-Stokes, A. (1992a) 'Self-monitoring and concern for social appropriateness in China and England', Fourth Asian regional conference, International Association for Cross-Cultural Psychology, Kathmandu, Nepal.

Gudykunst, W. B., Gao, G., Nishida, T., Nadamitsu, Y., and Sakai, J. (1992b) 'Self-monitoring in Japan and the United States', in S. Iwawaki, Y. Kashima and K. Leung (eds.), *Innovations in Cross-Cultural Psychology*, Amsterdam: Swets and Zeitlinger.

Gudykunst, W. B., and 7 others (1992c) 'The influence of individualism–collectivism, self-monitoring and predicted outcome value on communication in ingroup and outgroup relationships', *Journal of Cross-Cultural Psychology*, **23**, 196–213.

Gudykunst, W. B., and Hammer, M. R. (1988) 'Strangers and hosts: an uncertainty reduction-based theory of intercultural adaptation', in Y. Y. Kim and W. B. Gudykunst (eds.), *Intercultural Adaptation*, Newbury Park, CA: Sage.

Gudykunst, W. B., Yang, S. M., and Nishida, T. (1985) 'A cross-cultural test of uncertainty reduction theory: comparisons of acquaintance, friend, and dating relationships in Japan, Korea, and the United States', *Human Communication Research*, **11**, 407–55.

Gudykunst, W. B., Ting-Toomey, S., and Chua, E. (1988) *Culture and Interpersonal Communication*, Newbury Park, CA: Sage.

Guthrie, G. M. (1977) 'A socio-psychological analysis of modernization in the Philippines', *Journal of Cross-Cultural Psychology*, **8**, 177–206.

Hall, E. T. (1966) *The Hidden Dimension*, New York: Doubleday.

Hall, E. T. (1976) *Beyond Culture*, New York: Doubleday.

Hall, E. T. (1983) *The Dance of Life*, New York: Doubleday.

Hamilton, D. C., and Trolier, T. K. (1986) 'Stereotypes and stereotyping: an overview of the cognitive approach', in J. F. Dovidio and S. L. Gaertner (eds.), *Prejudice, Discrimination, and Racism*, Orlando, FL: Academic Press.

Hammer, M. R. (1987) 'Behavioral dimensions of intercultural effectiveness: a replication and extension', *International Journal of Intercultural Relations*, **11**, 65–88.

Harnett, D. L., and Cummings, L. L. (1980) *Bargaining Behavior: An International Study*, Houston, TX: Dame.

Harré, R., and Secord, P. F. (1972) *The Explanation of Social Behaviour*, Oxford: Basil Blackwell.

Harwood, J., Giles, H., and Bourhis, R. Y. (in press) 'The genesis of vitality theory: historical patterns and discoursal dimensions', *International Journal of the Sociology of Language*.

Haslett, B., and Ogilvie, J. (1988) 'Feedback processes in small groups', in R. Cathcart and L. Samovar (eds.), *Small Group Communication: A reader* (5th edn), Dubuque, IA: William C. Brown.

Hatcher, J. (1982) 'Arousal and conformity', in H. Brandstatter, J. H. Davis and G. Stocker-Kreichgauer (eds.), *Group Decision-Making*, London: Academic Press.

Hedge, A., and Yousif, Y. H. (1992) 'The effect of urban size, cost and urgency on helpfulness: a cross-cultural comparison between the United Kingdom and the Sudan', *Journal of Cross-Cultural Psychology*, **23**, 107–15.

Heelas, P., and Lock, A. (eds.) (1981) *Indigenous Psychologies: The Anthropology of the Self*, London: Academic Press.

Heider, F. (1958) *The Psychology of Interpersonal Relations*, New York: Wiley.

Herman, S., and Shield, E. (1961) 'The stranger group in a cross-cultural situation', *Sociometry*, **24**, 165–74.

Herzlich, C. (1973) *Health and Illness: A social psychological analysis*, London: Academic Press.

Hewitt, J. P. (1991) *Self and Society: A symbolic interactionist social psychology* (5th edn), Boston, MA: Allyn and Bacon.

Hewstone, M. (1989) 'Changing stereotypes with disconfirming information', in D. Bar-Tal, C. F. Graumann, A. W. Kruglanski and W. Stroebe (eds.), *Stereotyping and Prejudice: Changing conceptions*, New York: Springer Verlag.

Hewstone, M., and Brown, R. (1986) 'Contact is not enough: an intergroup perspective on the contact hypothesis', in M. Hewstone and R. Brown (eds.), *Contact and Conflict in Intergroup Encounters*, Oxford: Basil Blackwell.

Hewstone, M., and Ward, C. (1985) 'Ethnocentrism and causal attribution in Southeast Asia', *Journal of Personality and Social Psychology*, **48**, 614–23.

Hewstone, M., Stroebe, W., Codol, J. P., and Stephenson, G. (1988) *Introduction to Social Psychology: A European perspective*, Oxford: Blackwell.

Hines, G. H. (1973) 'The persistence of Greek achievement motivation across time and culture', *International Journal of Psychology*, **8**, 285–8.

Hinkle, S., and Brown, R. (1990) 'Intergroup comparisons and social identity: some links and lacunae', in D. Abrams and M. Hogg (eds.), *Social Identity Theory: Constructive and critical advances*, Hemel Hempstead: Harvester.

Hinkle, S., Brown, R., and Ely, P. G. (1990) 'Individualism/collectivism, group ideology and intergroup processes', paper presented at British Psychological Society conference, London, December.

Ho, D. Y. F. (1976) 'On the concept of face', *American Journal of Sociology*, **81**, 867–84.

Hobart, C. W. (1958) 'The incidence of romanticism during courtship', *Social Forces*, **36**, 362–7.

Hofstede, G. (1980) *Culture's Consequences: International differences in work-related values*, Beverly Hills, CA: Sage.

Hofstede, G. (1983) 'Dimensions of national cultures in fifty countries and three regions', in J. Deregowski, S. Dzuirawiec and R. Annis (eds.), *Explications in Cross-Cultural Psychology*, Lisse: Swets and Zeitlinger.

Hofstede, G. (1991) *Cultures and Organizations: Software of the mind*, London: McGraw-Hill.

Hofstede, G., Bond, M. H., and Luk, C. L. (in press) 'Individual perceptions of organizational cultures', *Organization Studies*.

Hogg, M. A., and Sunderland, J. (1991) 'Self-esteem and intergroup discrimination in the minimal group paradigm', *British Journal of Social Psychology*, **30**, 51–62.

Hollander, E. P. (1958) 'Conformity, status and idiosyncrasy credit', *Psychological Review*, **65**, 117–27.

Holmes, T. H., and Masuda, M. (1974) 'Life change and illness susceptibility', in B. S. Dohrenwend and B. P. Dohrenwend (eds.), *Stressful Life Events: Their nature and effects*, New York: Wiley.

Hui, C. H., and Triandis, H. C. (1989) 'Effects of culture and response format on extreme response style', *Journal of Cross-Cultural Psychology*, **20**, 296–309.

Hui, C. H., Triandis, H. C., and Yee, C. (1991) 'Cultural differences in reward allocation: is collectivism the explanation?', *British Journal of Social Psychology*, **30**, 145–57.

Hullos, M. (1980) 'Collective education in Hungary: development of competitive–cooperative and role-taking behaviours', *Ethos*, **8**, 3–23.

Humana, C. (1986) *World Human Rights Guide*, London: Pan.

Ichheiser, G. (1943) 'Misunderstandings of personality in everyday life and the psychologist's frame of reference', *Character and Personality*, **12**, 145–60.

Ike, N. (1973) 'Economic growth and intergenerational change in Japan', *American Political Science Review*, **67**, 1194–1203.

Inglehart, R. (1977) *The Silent Revolution: Changing values and political styles among western publics*, Princeton, NJ: Princeton University Press.

Inkeles, A., and Smith, D. H. (1974) *Becoming Modern: Individual change in six developing countries*, Cambridge, MA: Harvard University Press.

Israel, J., and Tajfel, H. (eds.) (1982) *The Context of Social Psychology: A critical assessment*, London: Academic Press.

Izard, C. (1971) *The Face of Emotion*, New York: Appleton-Century-Crofts.

Izard, C. (1980) 'Cross-cultural perspectives on emotion and emotion communication', in H. C. Triandis and W. Lonner (eds.), *Handbook of Cross-Cultural Psychology: Volume 3, Basic Processes*, 185–221, Boston, MA: Allyn and Bacon.

Jaffe, Y., and Yinon, Y. (1983) 'Collective aggression: the group–individual paradigm in the study of collective antisocial behaviour', in H. H. Blumberg, A. P. Hare, V. Kent and M. F. Davies (eds.), *Small Groups and Social Interaction*, volume 1, 267–75, Chichester: Wiley.

Jahoda, G. (1979) 'A cross-cultural perspective on experimental social psychology', *Personality and Social Psychology Bulletin*, **5**, 142–8.

Jahoda, G. (1982) *Psychology and Anthropology: A psychological perspective*, London: Academic Press.

Jahoda, G. (1984) 'Do we need a concept of culture?', *Journal of Cross-Cultural Psychology*, **15**, 139–52.

Jamieson, B. D. (1968) 'The risky shift phenomenon with a heterogeneous sample', *Psychological Reports*, **23**, 203–6.

Jesuino, J. C. (1986) 'Influence of leadership processes on group polarisation', *European Journal of Social Psychology*, **16**, 413–24.

John, O. P., Goldberg, L. R., and Angleitner, A. (1984) 'Better than the alphabet: taxonomics of personality descriptive terms in English, Dutch, and German', in H. Bonarius, G. van Heck and N. Smid (eds.), *Personality Psychology in Europe: Theoretical and empirical developments*, Lisse: Swets and Zeitlinger.

Jones, E. E., and Gerard, H. B. (1967) *Foundations of Social Psychology*, New York: Wiley.

Juralewicz, R. S. (1974) 'An experiment in participation in a Latin American factory', *Human Relations*, **27**, 627–37.

Kagan, S., and Madsen, M. C. (1972) 'Experimental analyses of cooperation and competition of Anglo-American and Mexican children', *Developmental Psychology*, **6**, 49–59.

Kagan, S., Knight, G.P., and Martinez Romero, S. (1982) 'Culture and the development of conflict resolution style', *Journal of Cross-Cultural Psychology*, **13**, 43–58.

Kagitcibasi, C. (1970) 'Social norms and authoritarianism: a Turkish–American comparison', *Journal of Cross-Cultural Psychology*, **4**, 157–74.

Kagitcibasi, C. (1988) 'Diversity of socialization and social change', in P. R. Dasen, J. W. Berry and N. Sartorius (eds.), *Health and Cross-Cultural Psychology*, Newbury Park, CA: Sage.

Kagitcibasi, C. (1990) 'Family and socialization in cross-cultural perspective: a model of change', in J. Berman (ed.), *Nebraska Symposium on Motivation, 1989*, Lincoln, NB: Nebraska University Press.

Kagitcibasi, C. (1992) 'A critical appraisal of individualism–collectivism: toward a new formulation', in U. Kim, H. C. Triandis and G. Yoon (eds.), *Individualism and Collectivism: Theoretical and methodological issues*, Newbury Park, CA: Sage.

Kagitcibasi, C., Sunar, D., and Bekman, S. (1988) *Comprehensive Preschool Education Project Final Report*, Ottawa: IDRC.

Kahl, J. A. (1968) *The Measurement of Modernism: A study of values in Brazil and Mexico*, Austin, TX: University of Texas Press.

Kahn, A., Lamm, H., and Nelson, R. (1977) 'Preferences for an equal or equitable allocation', *Journal of Personality and Social Psychology*, **35**, 837–44.

Kakimoto, T. (1992) 'Cognitive distraction and the effect of social categorisation', paper presented at the 25th International Congress of Psychology, Brussels.

Kashima, Y., and Triandis, H. C. (1986) 'The self-serving bias in attributions as a coping strategy: a cross-cultural study', *Journal of Cross-Cultural Psychology*, **17**, 83–97.

Kashima, Y., Siegal, M., Tanaka, K., and Isaka, H. (1988) 'Universalism in lay conceptions of distributive justice: a cross-cultural examination', *International Journal of Psychology*, **23**, 51–64.

Kashima, Y., Siegal, M., Tanaka, K., and Kashima, E. S. (1992) 'Do people believe behaviours are consistent with attitudes? Towards a cultural psychology of attribution processes', *British Journal of Social Psychology*, **31**, 111–24.

Katriel, T. (1986) *Talking Straight: Dugri speech in Israeli sabra culture*, Cambridge: Cambridge University Press.

Katz, D., and Braly, K. W. (1933) 'Verbal stereotypes and racial prejudice', *Journal of Abnormal and Social Psychology*, **28**, 280–90.

Keating, C. F. (1985) 'Human dominance signals: the primate in us', in S. L. Ellyson and J. F. Dovidio (eds.), *Power, Dominance and Non-Verbal Behavior*, New York: Springer-Verlag.

Kelley, H. H. (1967) 'Attribution theory in social psychology', in D. Levine (ed.), *Nebraska Symposium on Motivation*, Lincoln, NB: Nebraska University Press.

Kelley, H. H. (1973) 'The processes of causal attribution', *American Psychologist*, **28**, 107–28.

Kelley, H. H., and 7 co-authors (1970) 'A comparative experimental study of negotiation behaviour', *Journal of Personality and Social Psychology*, **16**, 411–38.

Kelley, K., and 5 co-authors (1986) 'Chronic self-destructiveness and locus of control in cross-cultural perspective', *Journal of Social Psychology*, **126**, 573–7.

Kerr, C., Dunlop, J. T., Harbison, F. H., and Myers, C. A. (1960) *Industrialism and Industrial Man: The problems of labor and management in economic growth*, London: Heinemann.

Kerr, S., and Jermier, J. M. (1978) 'Substitutes for leadership: their meaning and measurement', *Organizational Behavior and Human Performance*, **22**, 375–403.

Kidder, L. H. (1991) 'Japanese returnees: loose threads in a tight culture', unpublished manuscript, Temple University.

Kiesler, C. A., Kiesler, S. B., and Pallak, M. S. (1967) 'The effect of commitment to future interaction on reactions to norm violations', *Journal of Personality*, **35**, 585–600.

Kilham, W., and Mann, L. (1974) 'Level of destructive obedience as a function of transmitter and executant roles in the Milgram obedience paradigm', *Journal of Personality and Social Psychology*, **29**, 696–702.

Kim, K. I., Park, H. J., and Suzuki, N. (1990) 'Reward allocations in the United States, Japan and Korea: a comparison of individualistic and collectivistic cultures', *Academy of Management Journal*, **33**, 188–98.

Kleiner, R. J., and Okeke, B. I. (1991) 'Advances in field theory: new approaches and methods in cross-cultural research', *Journal of Cross-Cultural Psychology*, **22**, 509–24.

Kluckhohn, C., and Murray, H. A. (1948) *Personality in Nature, Culture and Society*, New York: Knopf.

Kogan, N., and Doise, W. (1969) 'Effects of anticipated delegate status on level of risk-taking in small decision-making groups', *Acta Psychologica*, **29**, 228–43.

Koomen, W. (1988) 'The relationship between participation rate and liking ratings in groups', *British Journal of Social Psychology*, **27**, 127–32.

Korte, C., and Ayvalioglu, N. (1981) 'Helpfulness in Turkey: cities, towns and urban villages', *Journal of Cross-Cultural Psychology*, **12**, 123–41.

Korte, C., Ympa, I., and Toppen, A. (1975) 'Helpfulness in Dutch society as a function of urbanisation and environmental input level', *Journal of Personality and Social Psychology*, **32**, 996–1003.

Korten, F. F. (1974) 'The influence of culture and sex on the perception of persons', *International Journal of Psychology*, **9**, 31–44.

Koseki, Y. (1989) 'A study of the influence of deviant minority on visual judgments within a small group', *Japanese Psychological Research*, **31** (4), 149–60.

Kravitz, D. A., and Martin, B. (1986) 'Ringelmann rediscovered: the original article', *Journal of Personality and Social Psychology*, **50**, 936–41.

Krichevskii, R. L. (1983) 'The phenomenon of the differentiation of the leadership role in small groups', in H. H. Blumberg, A. P. Hare, V. Kent and M. Davies (eds.), *Small Groups and Social Interaction*, volume 1, Chichester: Wiley.

LaFrance, M., and Mayo, C. (1976) 'Racial differences in gaze behaviour during conversations: two systematic observational studies', *Journal of Personality and Social Psychology*, **33**, 547–52.

Lamb, T. A., and Alsifaki, M. (1980) 'Conformity in the Asch experiment: inner–other directedness and the "defiant subject"', *Social Behaviour and Personality*, **8**, 13–16.

Lambert, W. E. (1967) 'The social psychology of bilingualism', *Journal of Social Issues*, **23**, 91–109.

Lamm, H., and Kogan, N. (1970) 'Risk-taking in the context of intergroup negotiation', *Journal of Experimental Social Psychology*, **6**, 351–63.

Landau, S. F. (1984) 'Trends in violence and aggression: a cross-cultural analysis', *International Journal of Comparative Sociology*, **24**, 133–58.

Langer, E. (1989) *Mindfulness*, Reading, MA: Addison-Wesley.

L'Armand, K., and Pepitone, A. (1975) 'Helping to reward another person: a cross-cultural analysis', *Journal of Personality and Social Psychology*, **31**, 189–98.

L'Armand, K., Pepitone, A., and Shanmugam, T. E. (1981) 'Attitudes toward rape: a comparison of the role of chastity in India and the US', *Journal of Cross-Cultural Psychology*, **12**, 284–303.

Larsen, K. (1974) 'Conformity in the Asch experiment', *Journal of Social Psychology*, **94**, 303–4.

Larsen, K., Triplett, J. S., Brant, W. D., and Langenberg, D. (1979) 'Collaborator status, subject characteristics and conformity in the Asch paradigm', *Journal of Social Psychology*, **108**, 259–63.

Laslo, E. (1989) *The Inner Limits of Mankind*, London: Oneworld.

Latané, B., Williams, K., and Harkins, S. (1979) 'Many hands make light the work: causes and consequences of social loafing', *Journal of Personality and Social Psychology*, **37**, 822–32.

Lazarus, R. S. (1981) 'Little hassles can be hazardous to health', *Psychology Today*, **58**, 60–2.

Lerner, M. J. (1980) *The Belief in a Just World*, New York: Plenum.

Leung, K. (1987) 'Some determinants of reactions to procedural models for conflict resolution: a cross-national study', *Journal of Personality and Social Psychology*, **53**, 898–908.

Leung, K. (1989) 'Cross-cultural differences: individual-level and cultural-level analysis', *International Journal of Psychology*, **24**, 703–19.

Leung, K., and Bond, M. H. (1982) 'How Chinese and Americans reward task-related contributions: a preliminary study', *Psychologia*, **25**, 32–9.

Leung, K., and Bond, M. H. (1984) 'The impact of cultural collectivism on reward allocation', *Journal of Personality and Social Psychology*, **47**, 793–804.

Leung, K., and Bond, M. H. (1989) 'On the empirical identification of dimensions for cross-cultural comparison', *Journal of Cross-Cultural Psychology*, **20**, 133–51.

Leung, K., Bond, M. H., Carment, D. W., Krishnan, L., and Liebrand, W. B. G. (1990) 'Effects of cultural femininity on preference for methods of conflict processing: a cross-cultural study', *Journal of Experimental Social Psychology*, **26**, 373–88. Correction to this paper (1991) *Journal of Experimental Social Psychology*, **27**, 201–2.

Leung, K., Bond, M. H., and Schwartz, S. H. (1991) 'How to explain cross-cultural differences: values, valences and expectancies?', submitted paper.

Leung, K., and Iwawaki, S. (1988) 'Cultural collectivism and distributive behavior: a cross-cultural study', *Journal of Cross-Cultural Psychology*, **19**, 35–49.

Leung, K., and Lind, E. A. (1986) 'Procedural justice and culture: effects of culture, gender and investigator status on procedural preferences', *Journal of Personality and Social Psychology*, **50**, 1134–40.

Leung, K., and Park, H. J. (1986) 'Effects of interactional goal on choice of allocation rules: a cross-national study', *Organizational Behavior and Human Decision Processes*, **37**, 111–20.

Levine, D. N. (1968) 'The flexibility of traditional culture', *Journal of Social Issues*, **24**, 129–41.

LeVine, R. A., and Campbell, D. T. (1972) *Ethnocentrism: Theories of conflict, ethnic attitudes and group behavior*, New York: Wiley.

Levine, R. V., and Bartlett, C. (1984) 'Pace of life, punctuality and coronary heart disease in six countries', *Journal of Cross-Cultural Psychology*, **15**, 233–55.

Levine, R. V., West, L. J. and Reis, H. T. (1980) 'Perceptions of time and punctuality in the US and Brazil', *Journal of Personality and Social Psychology*, **38**, 541–50.

Levy, L. (1960) 'Studies in conformity', *Journal of Psychology*, **50**, 39–41.

Lewin, K. (1947) 'Group decision and social change', in T. M. Newcomb and E. L. Hartley (eds.), *Readings in Social Psychology*, New York: Holt.

Lewin, K., Lippitt, R., and White, R. K. (1939) 'Patterns of aggressive behavior in experimentally created "social climates"', *Journal of Social Psychology*, **10**, 271–99.

Leyens, J-P., and Fraczek, A. (1984) 'Aggression as an interpersonal phenomenon', in H. Tajfel (ed.), *The Social Dimension*, volume 1, Cambridge: Cambridge University Press.

Lin, C. Y. C., and Fu, V. R. (1990) 'A comparison of child rearing practices among Chinese, immigrant Chinese, and Caucasian-American parents', *Child Development*, **61**, 429–33.

Lind, E. A., Erickson, B. E., Friedland, N., and Dickenberger, M. (1978) 'Reactions to procedural models for adjudicative conflict resolution', *Journal of Conflict Resolution*, **22**, 318–41.

Little, K. B. (1968) 'Cultural variations in social schemata', *Journal of Personality and Social Psychology*, **10**, 1–7.

Lonner, W. (1980) 'The search for psychological universals', in H. C. Triandis and W. W. Lambert (eds.), *Handbook of Cross-Cultural Psychology: Volume 1, Perspectives*, 143–204, Boston, MA: Allyn and Bacon.

Lonner, W. (1989) 'The introductory psychology text: beyond Ekman, Whorf and biassed IQ tests', in D. M. Keats, D. Munro and L. Mann (eds.), *Heterogeneity in Cross-Cultural Psychology*, Amsterdam: Swets and Zeitlinger.

Loveday, L. (1982) *The Sociolinguistics of Learning and Using a Non-native Language*, Oxford: Pergamon.

Luk, C. L., and Bond, M. H. (1992) 'Chinese lay beliefs about the causes and cures of psychological problems', *Journal of Clinical and Social Psychology*, 11, 140–57.

Maass, A., and Clark, R. D. (1984) 'Hidden impact of minorities: fifteen years of minority influence research', *Psychological Bulletin*, 95, 428–50.

McArthur, L. Z., and Baron, R. M. (1983) 'Toward an ecological theory of social perception', *Psychological Review*, 90, 215–38.

McArthur, L. Z., and Berry, D. S. (1987) 'Cross-cultural agreement in perceptions of baby-faced adults', *Journal of Cross-Cultural Psychology*, 18, 165–192.

McClelland, D. C. (1961) *The Achieving Society*, New York: Free Press.

McClintock, C. G., and McNeel, C. P. (1966) 'Cross-cultural comparisons of interpersonal motives', *Sociometry*, 29, 406–27.

McCrae, R. R., and Costa, P. T., Jr (1985) 'Openness to experience', in R. Hogan and E. H. Jones (eds.), *Perspectives in Personality*, volume 1, Greenwich, CT: JAI Press.

McCrae, R. R., and Costa, P. T., Jr (1987) 'Validation of the five-factor model of personality across instruments and observers', *Journal of Personality and Social Psychology*, 52, 81–90.

McCrae, R. R., and John, O. P. (1992) 'An introduction to the five factor model and its applications', *Journal of Personality*, 60, 175–215.

McDougall, W. (1908) *Introduction to Social Psychology*, London: Methuen.

McGuire, W. J., McGuire, C. V., Child, P., and Fujioka, T. (1978) 'Salience of ethnicity in the spontaneous self-concept as a function of one's ethnic distinctiveness in the social environment', *Journal of Personality and Social Psychology*, 36, 511–20.

Mackie, M. (1973) 'Arriving at "truth" by definition: the case of stereotype inaccuracy', *Social Problems*, 20, 431–47.

McNeel, C. P., McClintock, C. G., and Nuttin, J. (1972), 'Effects of sex-role in a two-person mixed-motive game', *Journal of Personality and Social Psychology*, 24, 372–8.

Madsen, M. (1967) 'Cooperative and competitive motivation of children in three Mexican sub-cultures', *Psychological Reports*, 20, 1307–20.

Madsen, M. (1971) 'Developmental and cross-cultural differences in the cooperative and competitive behavior of young children', *Journal of Cross-Cultural Psychology*, 2, 365–71.

Madsen, M., and Lancy, D. F. (1981) 'Cooperative and competitive behavior: experiments related to ethnic identity and urbanization in Papua New Guinea', *Journal of Cross-Cultural Psychology*, 12, 389–408.

Madsen, M., and Shapira, A. (1970) 'Cooperative and competitive behavior of urban Afro-American, Anglo-American, Mexican-American and Mexican village children', *Developmental Psychology*, 3, 16–20.

Madsen, M., and Yi, S. (1975) 'Co-operation and competition of urban and rural children in the republic of South Korea', *International Journal of Psychology*, **10**, 269–75.

Mahler, I., Greenberg, L., and Hayashi, H. (1981) 'A comparative study of rules of justice: Japanese versus Americans', *Psychologia*, **24**, 1–8.

Makita, M. (1952) 'Comparative study on lecture and group decision in motivating a desired behavior', *Japanese Journal of Educational Psychology*, **1**, 84–91.

Mann, L. (1980) 'Cross-cultural studies of small groups', in H. C. Triandis and R. W. Brislin (eds.), *Handbook of Cross-Cultural Psychology*, vol. 5, Boston, MA: Allyn and Bacon.

Mann, L., Radford, M., and Kanagawa, C. (1985) 'Cross-cultural differences in children's use of decision rules: a comparison of Japan and Australia', *Journal of Personality and Social Psychology*, **49**, 1557–64.

Mantell, D. M. (1971). 'The potential for violence in Germany', *Journal of Social Issues*, **27**, 101–12.

Manz, C. C. (1983) *The Art of Self-Leadership*, Englewood Cliffs, NJ: Prentice-Hall.

Marin, G. (1981) 'Perceiving justice across cultures: equity vs. equality in Colombia and in the United States', *International Journal of Psychology*, **16**, 153–9.

Marin, G. (1983) 'The Latin American experience in applying social psychology to community change', in F. Blackler (ed.), *Social Psychology and Developing Countries*, Chichester: Wiley.

Marin, G. (1985) 'Validez transcultural del principio de equidad: el colectivismo–individualismo come una variable moderatora', *Revista Interamericana de Psicologia Occupational*, **4**, 7–20.

Marin, G., and Marin, B. V. (1982) 'Methodological fallacies when studying Hispanics', in L. Bickman (ed.), *Applied Social Psychology Annual*, **3**, 99–118.

Marin, G., Mejia, B., and Oberle, C. (1975) 'Cooperation as a function of place of residence among Colombian children', *Journal of Social Psychology*, **95**, 127–8.

Markus, H., and Kitayama, S. (1991) 'Culture and the self: implications for cognition, emotion and motivation', *Psychological Review*, **98**, 224–53.

Markus, H., and Kitayama, S. (in press) 'Cultural variation in the self-concept', in G. R. Goethals and J. Strauss (eds.), *Multidisciplinary Perspectives on the Self*, New York: Springer-Verlag.

Markus, H., and Zajonc, R. B. (1985) 'The cognitive perspective in social psychology', in G. Lindzey and E. Aronson (eds.), *Handbook of Social Psychology*, volume 1, New York: Random House.

Marrow, A. J. (1964) 'Risks and uncertainties in action research', *Journal of Social Issues*, **20** (3), 5–20.

Marsella, A. J., De Vos, G., and Hsu, F. L. K. (1985) *Culture and Self: Asian and western perspectives*, London: Tavistock.

Marsh, R. M. (1967) *Comparative Sociology: A codification of cross-societal analysis*, New York: Harcourt Brace Jovanovich.

Marwell, G., and Schmitt, D. R. (1972) 'Cooperation and interpersonal risk: cross-cultural and cross-procedural generalisations', *Journal of Experimental Social Psychology*, **8**, 594–9.

Marwell, G., Schmitt, D. R., and Boyesen, B. (1973) 'Pacifist strategy and cooperation under interpersonal risk', *Journal of Personality and Social Psychology*, **28**, 12–20.

Maslow, A. H. (1954) *Motivation and Personality*, New York: Harper.

Matsuda, N. (1985) 'Strong, quasi- and weak conformity among Japanese in the modified Asch procedure', *Journal of Cross-Cultural Psychology*, **16**, 83–97.

Matsui, T., Kakuyama, T., and Onglatco, M. L. (1987) 'Effects of goals and feedback on performance in groups', *Journal of Applied Psychology*, **72**, 407–15.

Matsumoto, D. (1989) 'Cultural influences of the perception of emotion', *Journal of Cross-Cultural Psychology*, **20**, 92–105.

Matsumoto, D. (1992) 'American–Japanese cultural differences in the recognition of universal facial expressions', *Journal of Cross-Cultural Psychology*, **23**, 72–84.

Matsumoto, D., Kudoh, T., Scherer, K., and Wallbot, H. G. (1988) 'Emotion antecedents and reactions in the US and Japan', *Journal of Cross-Cultural Psychology*, **19**, 267–86.

Mazur, A. (1977) 'Interpersonal spacing on public benches in "contact" versus "non-contact" cultures', *Journal of Social Psychology*, **101**, 53–8.

Mead, G. H. (1934) *Mind, Self and Society*, Chicago, IL: University of Chicago Press.

Mead, M. (1935) *Sex and Temperament in Three Primitive Societies*, New York: Morrow.

Meade, R. D. (1967) 'An experimental study of leadership in India', *Journal of Social Psychology*, **72**, 35–43.

Meade, R. D. (1972) 'Future time perspectives of Americans and subcultures in India', *Journal of Cross-Cultural Psychology*, **3**, 93–100.

Meaning of Working International Team (1987) *The Meaning of Work: An international view*, New York: Academic Press.

Meeus, W. H. J., and Raaijmakers, Q. A. W. (1986) 'Administrative obedience: carrying out orders to use psychological-administrative violence', *European Journal of Social Psychology*, **16**, 311–24.

Mesarovic, M., and Pestel, E. (1974) *Mankind at the Turning Point: The second report to the Club of Rome*, New York: Dutton.

Mesquita, B., and Frijda, N. H. (1992) 'Cultural variations in emotions: a review', *Psychological Bulletin*, **112**, 179–204.

Meyer, A. G. (1970) 'Theories of convergence', in C. Johnson (ed.), *Change in Communist Systems*, Berkeley, CA: University of California Press.

Mikula, G. (1974) 'Nationality, performance and sex as determinants of reward allocation', *Journal of Personality and Social Psychology*, **29**, 435–40.

Milgram, S. (1961) 'Nationality and conformity', *Scientific American*, **205**, 45–51.

Milgram, S. (1963) 'Behavioral study of obedience', *Journal of Abnormal Psychology*, **67**, 371–8.

Milgram, S. (1974) *Obedience to Authority: An experimental view*, New York: Harper and Row.

Mill, J. S. (1872/1973) *A System of Logic*, volumes 7 and 8 in J. M. Robson (ed.), *Collected Works of John Stuart Mill*, Toronto: University of Toronto Press.

Miller, A. G., and Thomas, R. (1972) 'Cooperation and competition among Blackfoot Indian and urban Canadian children', *Child Development*, **43**, 1104–10.

Miller, J. G. (1984) 'Culture and the development of everyday social explanation', *Journal of Personality and Social Psychology*, **46**, 961–78.

Miller, J. G., Bersoff, D. M., and Harwood, R. L. (1990) 'Perceptions of social responsibilities in India and in the United States: moral imperatives or personal decisions?', *Journal of Personality and Social Psychology*, **58**, 33–47.

Milner, D. (1975) *Children and Race,* Harmondsworth: Penguin.

Miranda, F. S. B., Caballero, R. B., Gomez, M. N. G., and Zamorano, M. A. M. (1981) 'Obediencia a la autoridad', *Psiquis,* **2,** 212–21.

Mischel, W. (1968) *Personality and Assessment,* New York: Wiley.

Misra, S. (1981) 'Excursion from the pure to the applied in experimental social psychology', in J. Pandey (ed.), *Perspectives on Experimental Social Psychology in India,* New Delhi: Concept.

Misra, S., and Kalro, A. (1979) 'Triangle effect and the connotative meaning of trust in prisoner's dilemma', *International Journal of Psychology,* **14,** 1–35.

Misumi, J. (1985) *The Behavioral Science of Leadership: An interdisciplinary Japanese research program,* Ann Arbor, MI: University of Michigan Press.

Misumi, J., and Haraoka, K. (1958) 'An experimental study of group decision (1)', *Research Bulletin of the Faculty of Education,* Kyushu University, **5,** 61–81.

Misumi, J., and Haraoka, K. (1960) 'An experimental study of group decision (11)', *Japanese Journal of Educational and Social Psychology,* **1,** 136–53.

Misumi, J., and Nakano, S. (1960) 'A cross-cultural study of the effects of democratic, authoritarian and laissez-faire atmosphere in children's groups', *Japanese Journal of Educational and Social Psychology,* **1,** 10–22 and 119–35.

Mizokawa, D. T., and Ryckman, D. B. (1990) 'Attributions of academic success and failure: a comparison of six Asian-American ethnic groups', *Journal of Cross-Cultural Psychology,* **21,** 434–51.

Moede, W. (1920) *Experimentelle Massenpsychologie,* Leipzig: Hirzel.

Moghaddam, F. M. (1987) 'Psychology in the three worlds', *American Psychologist,* **42,** 912–20.

Moghaddam, F. M. (1990) 'Modulative and generative orientations in psychology: implications for psychology in the three worlds', *Journal of Social Issues,* **46,** 21–41.

Montepare, J. M., and Zebrowitz McArthur, L. (1987) 'Perceptions of adults with child-like voices in two cultures', *Journal of Experimental Social Psychology,* **23,** 331–49.

Moscovici, S. (1976) *Social Influence and Social Change,* London: Academic Press.

Moscovici, S. (1981) 'On social representation', in J. P. Forgas (ed.), *Social Cognition: Perspectives on everyday life,* London: Academic Press.

Moscovici, S., and Faucheux, C. (1972) 'Social influence, conformity bias and the study of active minorities', in L. Berkowitz (ed.), *Advances in Experimental Social Psychology,* volume 6, New York: Academic Press.

Moscovici, S., and Personnaz, B. (1980) 'Studies in social influence: v Minority influence and conversion behaviour in a perceptual task', *Journal of Experimental Social Psychology,* **16,** 270–82.

Moscovici, S., and Zavalloni, M. (1969) 'The group as a polariser of attitudes', *Journal of Personality and Social Psychology,* **12,** 125–35.

Moscovici, S., Mugny, G., and van Avermaet, E. (eds.) (1985) *Perspectives on Minority Influence,* Cambridge: Cambridge University Press.

Mugny, G., and Papastomou, S. (1980) 'When rigidity does not fail: individualisation and psychologisation as resistance to the diffusion of minority innovations', *Journal of Social Psychology,* **10,** 43–61.

Mummendey, A., and Schreiber, H. J. (1984) '"Different" just means "better": some obvious and some hidden pathways to in-group favouritism', *British Journal of Social Psychology*, **23**, 363–8.

Munro, B., and Adams, G. (1978) 'Love American style: a test of role structure theory on changes in attitudes toward love', *Human Relations*, **31**, 215–28.

Munro, D. (1979) 'Locus of control attribution: factors among blacks and whites in Africa', *Journal of Cross-Cultural Psychology*, **10**, 157–72.

Munro, D. (1986) 'Work motivation and values: problems and possibilities in and out of Africa', *Australian Journal of Psychology*, **38**, 285–96.

Munroe, R. L., and Munroe, R. H. (1977) 'Cooperation and competition among East African and American children', *Journal of Social Psychology*, **101**, 145–6.

Murphy-Berman, V., Berman, J. J., Singh, P., Pachauri, A., and Kumar, P. (1984) 'Factors affecting allocation to needy and meritorious recipients: a cross-cultural comparison', *Journal of Personality and Social Psychology*, **46**, 1267–72.

Naisbitt, J., and Aburdene, P. (1990) *Megatrends 2000: Ten new directions for the 1990's*, New York: Avon.

Nakane, C. (1970) *Japanese Society*, London: Weidenfeld and Nicolson.

Naroll, R. (1983) *The Moral Order*, Beverly Hills, CA: Sage.

Needham, J. (1978) *The Shorter Science and Civilisation of China*, Cambridge: Cambridge University Press.

Needham, R. (1981) 'Inner states as universals: sceptical reflections on human nature', in P. Heelas and A. Lock (eds.), *Indigenous Psychologies: The anthropology of the self*, London: Academic Press.

Nicholson, N., Cole, S. G., and Rocklin, T. (1985) 'Conformity in the Asch situation: a comparison between contemporary British and US university students', *British Journal of Social Psychology*, **24**, 59–63.

Nisbett, R. E., and Ross, L. (1980) *Human Inference: Strategies and shortcomings of social judgments*, Englewood Cliffs, NJ: Prentice Hall.

Noesjirwan, J. (1977) 'Contrasting cultural patterns of interpersonal closeness in doctors' waiting rooms in Sydney and Jakarta', *Journal of Cross-Cultural Psychology*, **8**, 357–68.

Norman, W. T. (1963) 'Toward an adequate taxonomy of personality attributes: replicated factor structure in peer nomination personality ratings', *Journal of Abnormal and Social Psychology*, **66**, 574–83.

Oatey, H. (1992) 'Conceptions of social relations and pragmatics research', unpublished manuscript, University of Lancaster.

Oberg, K. (1960) 'Cultural shock: adjustment to a new cultural environment', *Practical Anthropology*, **7**, 177–82.

Oksenberg, L. (1971) 'Machiavellianism in traditional and Westernised Chinese students', in W. W. Lambert and R. Weisbrod (eds.), *Comparative Perspectives on Social Psychology*, Boston, MA: Little, Brown.

Pandey, J. (1979) 'Effect of status of benefactor and recipient on helping behaviour', *Journal of Social Psychology*, **15**, 303–11.

Pandey, J. (ed.) (1981) *Perspectives on Experimental Social Psychology in India*, New Delhi: Concept.

Pandey, J. (1981) 'Ingratiation as social behaviour', in J. Pandey (ed.), *Perspectives on Experimental Social Psychology in India*, New Delhi: Concept.

Pandey, J. (1986) 'Socio-cultural perspectives on ingratiation', in B. A. Maher and W. B. Maher (eds.), *Progress in Experimental Personality Research*, volume 14, Orlando, FL: Academic Press.

Pandey, J., Sinha, Y., Prakash, A., and Tripathi, R. C. (1982) 'Right–left political ideologies and attribution of the causes of poverty', *European Journal of Social Psychology*, **12**, 327–31.

Park, R. E. (1928) 'Human migration and the marginal man', *American Journal of Sociology*, **33**, 881–93.

Payne, M., and Vandewiele, M. (1987) 'Attitudes toward love in the Caribbean', *Psychological Reports*, **60**, 715–21.

Pepitone, A., and 7 co-authors (1967) 'The role of self-esteem in competitive choice behavior', *International Journal of Psychology*, **2**, 147–59.

Pepitone, A., and 10 co-authors (1970) 'Justice in choice behavior: a cross-cultural analysis', *International Journal of Psychology*, **5**, 1–10.

Perrin, S., and Spencer, C. P. (1981) 'Independence or conformity in the Asch experiment as a reflection of cultural and situational factors', *British Journal of Social Psychology*, **20**, 205–10.

Pettigrew, T. (1958) 'Personality and sociocultural factors in intergroup attitudes: a cross-national comparison', *Journal of Conflict Resolution*, **2**, 29–42.

Pettigrew, T. F. (1979) 'The ultimate attribution error: Extending Allport's cognitive analysis of prejudice', *Personality and Social Psychology Bulletin*, **5**, 461–76.

Philbrick, J. L. (1987) 'Sex differences in romantic attitudes toward love in engineering students', *Psychological Reports*, **61**, 482.

Philbrick, J. L., and Opolot, J. A. (1980) 'Love style: comparison of African and American attitudes', *Psychological Reports*, **46**, 286.

Pierson, H. D., and Bond, M. H. (1982) 'How do Chinese bilinguals respond to variations of interviewer language and ethnicity?', *Journal of Language and Social Psychology*, **1**, 123–39.

Poortinga, Y. H. (1990) 'Towards a conceptualisation of culture for psychology', *Cross-Cultural Psychology Bulletin*, **24**, 2–10.

Porat, A. (1970) 'Cross-cultural differences in resolving union-management conflict through negotiations', *Journal of Applied Psychology*, **54**, 441–51.

Potter, J., and Wetherell, M. (1987) *Discourse and Social Psychology*, London: Sage.

Pratto, F., and Bargh, J. A. (1991) 'Stereotyping based on apparently individuating information: trait and global components of sex stereotypes under attention overload', *Journal of Experimental Social Psychology*, **27**, 26–47.

Pyszczynski, T. A., and Greenberg, J. (1981) 'Role disconfirmed expectancies in the instigation of attributional processing', *Journal of Personality and Social Psychology*, **40**, 31–8.

Quattrone, G. A., and Jones, E. E. (1980) 'The perception of variability within ingroups and outgroups: implications for the law of small numbers', *Journal of Personality and Social Psychology*, **38**, 141–52.

Rabbie, J. (1982) 'Are groups more aggressive than individuals?', Henri Tajfel lecture, conference of the British Psychological Society, Social Psychology section.

Ramirez, M. (1967) 'Identification with Mexican family values and authoritarianism in Mexican-Americans', *Journal of Social Psychology*, **73**, 3–11.

Rapoport, A., Guyer, M., and Gordon, D. (1971) 'A comparison of performance of Danish and American students in a "threat" game', *Behavioral Science*, **16**, 456–66.

Rim, Y. (1964) 'Personality and group decisions involving risk', *Psychological Reports*, **14**, 37–45.

Rodrigues, A. (1982) 'Replication: a neglected type of research in social psychology', *Interamerican Journal of Psychology*, **16**, 91–109.

Rodriguez, A., and Seoane, J. (eds.) (1989) *Creencias, Actitudes y Valores*, volume 7 of J. Mayor and J. L. Pinillos (eds.), *Tratado de Psicologia General*, Madrid: Alhambra University Press.

Rohner, R. (1984) 'Toward a conception of culture for cross-cultural psychology', *Journal of Cross-Cultural Psychology*, **15**, 111–38.

Rosenthal, D. A., and Feldman, S. S. (1992) 'The nature and stability of ethnic identity in Chinese youth: effects of length of residence in two cultural contexts', *Journal of Cross-Cultural Psychology*, **23**, 214–27.

Rosenzweig, M. R. (1992) *International Psychological Science: Progress, problems and prospects*, Washington, DC: American Psychological Association.

Ross, E. A. (1908) *Social Psychology*, New York: Macmillan.

Ross, L. (1977) 'The intuitive psychologist and his shortcomings: distortions in the attribution process', in L. Berkowitz (ed.), *Advances in Experimental Social Psychology*, volume 10, 173–220.

Rothbart, M., Evans, M., and Fulero, S. (1979) 'Recall for confirming events: memory processes and the maintenance of social stereotypes', *Journal of Experimental Social Psychology*, **15**, 343–55.

Rotter, J. (1966) 'Generalised expectancies for internal versus external control of reinforcement', *Psychological Monographs*, **80** (Whole No. 609).

Ruben, B. (1976) 'Assessing communication competency for intercultural adaptation', *Group and Organization Studies*, **1**, 334–54.

Ruben, B. D., and Kealey, D. J. (1979) 'Behavioral assessment of communication competency and the prediction of cross-cultural adaptation', *International Journal of Intercultural Relations*, **3**, 15–47.

Rummel, R. J. (1972) *The Dimensions of Nations*, Beverly Hills, CA: Sage.

Rumelhart, D. E. (1984) 'Schemata and the cognitive system', in R. S. Wyer and T. K. Scrull (eds.), *Handbook of Social Cognition*, volume 1, Hillsdale, NJ: Erlbaum.

Russell, J. A. (1991) 'Culture and the categorisation of emotions', *Psychological Bulletin*, **110**, 426–50.

Sack, R. (1973) 'The impact of education on individual modernity in Tunisia', *International Journal of Comparative Sociology*, **14**, 245–72.

Sampson, D. L., and Smith, H. P. (1957) 'A scale to measure world-minded attitudes', *Journal of Social Psychology*, **45**, 99–106.

Sampson, E. E. (1978) 'Personality and the location of identity', *Journal of Personality*, **46**, 552–68.

Sampson, E. E. (1981) 'Cognitive psychology as ideology', *American Psychologist*, **36**, 730–43.

Sampson, E. E. (1985) 'The decentralization of identity: toward a revised concept of personal and social order', *American Psychologist*, **40**, 1203–11.

Sanders, J. L., Hakky, U. M., and Brizzolara, M. M. (1985) 'Personal space amongst Arabs and Americans', *International Journal of Psychology*, **20**, 13–17.

Sanders, J. L., McKim, W., and McKim, A. (1988) 'Personal space among Batswana and American students', *Journal of Social Psychology*, **128**, 559–61.

Schachter, S. (1951) 'Deviation, rejection and communication', *Journal of Abnormal and Social Psychology*, **46**, 190–207.

Schachter, S., and 7 co-authors (1954) 'Cross-cultural experiments on threats and rejection', *Human Relations*, **7**, 403–39.

Scherer, K. R. (1979) 'Personality markers in speech,' in K. R. Scherer and H. Giles (eds.), *Social Markers in Speech*, Cambridge: Cambridge University Press.

Scherer, K. R., Wallbot, H. G., and Summerfield, A. B. (eds.) (1986) *Experiencing Emotion: A cross-cultural study*, Cambridge: Cambridge University Press.

Schnaiberg, A. (1970) 'Measuring modernism: theoretical and empirical explorations', *American Journal of Sociology*, **76**, 399–425.

Schneider, D. J., Hastorf, A. H., and Ellsworth, P. C. (1979) *Person Perception* (2nd edn), Reading, MA: Addison-Wesley.

Schurz, G. (1985) 'Experimentelle Überprüfung des Zusammenhangs zwischen Persönlichkeitsmerkmalen und der Bereitschaft zum destruktiven Gehorsam gegenüber Autoritäten', *Zeitschrift für Experimentelle und Angewandte Psychologie*, **32**, 160–77.

Schwartz, J. (1980) 'The negotiation for meaning', in D. Larsen-Freeman (ed.), *Discourse Analysis in Second Language Research*, Rowley, MA: Newbury House.

Schwartz, S. H. (1992) 'The universal content and structure of values: theoretical advances and empirical tests in 20 countries', in M. Zanna (ed.), *Advances in Experimental Social Psychology*, volume 25, 1–65, New York: Academic Press.

Schwartz, S. H. (in press) 'Cultural dimensions of values: towards an understanding of national differences', in U. Kim, H. C. Triandis and G. Yoon (eds.), *Individualism and Collectivism: Theoretical and Methodological Issues*, Newbury Park, CA: Sage.

Schwartz, S. H., and Bilsky, W. (1987) 'Towards a psychological structure of human values', *Journal of Personality and Social Psychology*, **53**, 550–62.

Schwartz, S. H., and Bilsky, W. (1990) 'Toward a theory of the universal content and structure of values: extensions and cross-cultural replications', *Journal of Personality and Social Psychology*, **58**, 878–91.

Schwartzwald, J., and Yinon, Y. (1977) 'Symmetrical and asymmetrical interethnic perception in Israel', *International Journal of Intercultural Relations*, **1**, 40–7.

Scott, W. A. (1965) 'Psychological and social correlates of international images', in H. C. Kelman (ed.), *International Behaviour: A social-psychological analysis*, New York: Holt, Rinehart and Winston.

Seaborne, R. (1962) 'Group influence on the perception of ambiguous stimuli', *British Journal of Psychology*, **53**, 287–98.

Segall, M. H., Dasen, P. R., Berry, J. W., and Poortinga, Y. H. (1990) *Human Behavior in Global Perspective: An introduction to cross-cultural psychology*, New York: Pergamon.

Semin, G. R. (1975) 'Two studies on polarisation', *European Journal of Social Psychology*, **5**, 121–31.

Semin, G. R., and Rubini, M. (1990) 'Unfolding the concept of person by verbal abuse', *European Journal of Social Psychology*, **20**, 463–74.

Serrano-Garcia, I., and Lopez-Sanchez, G. (1991) 'Community interventions in Puerto Rico: the impact of social-community psychology', *Applied Psychology: An International Review*, **40**, 201–18.

Shanab, M. E., and Yahya, K. A. (1978) 'A cross-cultural study of obedience', *Bulletin of the Psychonomic Society*, **11**, 267–9.

Shapira, A. (1976) 'Developmental differences in competitive behavior of kibbutz and city children in Israel', *Journal of Social Psychology*, **98**, 19–26.

Shapira, A., and Lomranz, J. (1972) 'Cooperative and competitive behavior of rural Arab children in Israel', *Journal of Cross-Cultural Psychology*, **3**, 353–9.

Shapira, A., and Madsen, M. (1969) 'Cooperative and competitive behavior of kibbutz and urban children in Israel', *Child Development*, **40**, 609–17.

Sherif, M., and Sherif, C. W. (1953) *Groups in Harmony and in Tension: An integration of studies on intergroup relations*, New York: Octagon.

Sherif, M., Harvey, O. J., White, B. J., Hood, W. R., and Sherif, C. W. (1961) *Intergroup Conflict and Cooperation: The robber's cave experiment*, Norman, OK: University of Oklahoma Press.

Shirakashi, S. (1984–5) 'Social loafing of Japanese students', *Hiroshima Forum for Psychology*, **10**, 35–40.

Shuter, R. (1976) 'Proxemics and tactility in Latin America', *Journal of Communication*, **26**, 46–52.

Shuter, R. (1977) 'A field study of non-verbal communication in Germany, Italy and the United States', *Communication Monographs*, **44**, 298–305.

Shweder, R. (1990) 'Cultural psychology: what is it?', in J. W. Stigler, R. A. Shweder and G. Herdt (eds.), *Cultural Psychology: Essays on comparative human development*, Cambridge: Cambridge University Press.

Shweder, R. A., and Bourne, E. J. (1982) 'Does the concept of the person vary cross-culturally?', in A. J. Marsella and G. M. White (eds.), *Cultural Conceptions of Mental Health and Therapy*, Dordrecht, Holland: D. Riedel.

Simmel, G. (1950) 'The stranger', in K. Wolff (ed. and trans.), *The Sociology of George Simmel*, New York: Free Press.

Simmons, C. H., von Kolke, A., and Shimizu, H. (1986) 'Attitudes toward romantic love among American, German and Japanese students', *Journal of Social Psychology*, **126**, 327–36.

Simmons, C. H., Wehner, E. A., and Kay, K. A. (1989) 'Differences in attitudes toward romantic love of French, and American college students', *Journal of Social Psychology*, **129**, 793–9.

Simon, B., and 6 co-authors (1990) 'The effects of in-group and out-group homogeneity on in-group favouritism, stereotyping and overestimation of relative in-group size', *European Journal of Social Psychology*, **20**, 519–23.

Singh, R. (1981) 'Prediction of performance from motivation and ability: an appraisal of the cultural difference hypothesis', in J. Pandey (ed.), *Perspectives on Experimental Social Psychology in India*, New Delhi: Concept.

Sinha, D. (1986) *Psychology in a Third World Country: The Indian experience*, New Delhi: Sage.

Sinha, D. (1989) 'Cross-cultural psychology and the process of indigenisation: a second view from the third world', in D. M. Keats, D. Munro and L. Mann (eds.), *Heterogeneity in Cross-Cultural Psychology*, Amsterdam: Swets and Zeitlinger.

Sinha, D. (1992) 'Appropriate indigenous psychology: The Indian trend', in S. Iwawaki, Y. Kashima and K. Leung (eds.), *Innovations in Cross-Cultural Psychology*, Amsterdam: Swets and Zeitlinger.

Sinha, D., and Tripathi, R. C. (in press) 'Individualism in a collectivist culture: a case of coexistence of opposites', in U. Kim, H. C. Triandis and G. Yoon (eds.), *Individualism and Collectivism: Theoretical and methodological issues*.

Sinha, J. B. P. (1981) *The Nurturant Task Manager: A model of the effective executive*, Atlantic Highlands, NJ: Humanities Press.

Sinha, J. B. P. (1992) 'The bulk and the front of Indian psychology', paper presented at the 25th International Congress of Psychology, Brussels.

Sloan, T., and Montero, M. (eds.) (1990) 'Psychology for the third world: a sampler', *Journal of Social Issues*, **46**(3), 1–165.

Smith, P. B. (1963) 'Differentiation between sociometric rankings: a test of four theories', *Human Relations*, **16**, 335–50.

Smith, P. B., and Misumi, J. (1989) 'Japanese management: a sun rising in the west?', in C. L. Cooper and I. T. Robertson (eds.), *International Review of Industrial and Organizational Psychology*, volume 4, Chichester: Wiley.

Smith, P. B., and Peterson, M. F. (1988) *Leadership, Organizations and Culture*, London: Sage.

Smith, P. B., and Tayeb, M. (1988) 'Organisational structure and processes', in M. H. Bond (ed.), *The Cross-Cultural Challenge to Social Psychology*, Newbury Park, CA: Sage.

Smith, P. B., Misumi, J., Tayeb, M., Peterson, M. F., and Bond, M. H. (1989) 'On the generality of leadership styles across cultures', *Journal of Occupational Psychology*, **62**, 97–100.

Smolicz, J. J. (1979) *Culture and Education in a Plural Society*, Canberra: Curriculum Development Centre.

Snyder, C. R., and Fromkin, H. L. (1980) *Uniqueness: The human pursuit of difference*, New York: Plenum.

Snyder, M. (1979) 'Self-monitoring processes', in L. Berkowitz (ed.), *Advances in Experimental Social Psychology*, **12**, 85–128.

Sommerlad, E., and Bellingham, W. P. (1972) 'Cooperation–competition: a comparison of Australian, European and Aboriginal school children', *Journal of Cross-Cultural Psychology*, **3**, 149–57.

Sorrentino, R. M., King, G., and Leo, G. (1980) 'The influence of the minority on perception: a note on a possible alternative explanation', *Journal of Experimental Social Psychology*, **16**, 293–301.

Sperber, D. (1985) 'Anthropology and psychology: toward an epidemiology of representations', *Man*, **20**, 73–89.

Stening, B. W. (1979) 'Problems in cross-cultural contact: a literature review', *International Review of Intercultural Relations*, **3**, 269–313.

Stephan, W. G. (1977) 'Stereotyping: role of ingroup–outgroup differences in causal attribution of behaviour', *Journal of Social Psychology*, **101**, 255–66.

Stephan, W. G. (1985) 'Intergroup relations', in G. Lindzey and E. Aronson (eds.), *Handbook of Social Psychology* (3rd edn), volume 2, New York: Random House.

Stephan, W. G., and Stephan, C. W. (1985) 'Intergroup anxiety', *Journal of Social Issues*, **41**, 157–76.

Stevenson, H. W., Stigler, J. W., Lee, S. Y., Lucker, G. W., Kitamura, S., and Hsu, C. C. (1985) 'Cognitive performance and academic achievement of Japanese, Chinese, and American children', *Child Development*, **56**, 713–34.

Stigler, J. W., Shweder, R. A., and Herdt, G. (eds.) (1990) *Cultural Psychology: Essays on comparative human development*, Cambridge: Cambridge University Press.

Stipek, D., Weiner, B., and Li, K. (1989) 'Testing some attribution–emotion relations in the People's Republic of China', *Journal of Personality and Social Psychology*, **56**, 109–16.

Stone Feinstein, B. E., and Ward, C. (1990) 'Loneliness and psychological adjustment of sojourners: new perspectives on cultural shock', in D. M. Keats, D. Munro and L. Mann (eds.), *Heterogeneity in Cross-Cultural Psychology*, Lisse: Swets and Zeitlinger.

Stonequist, E. V. (1937) *The Marginal Man*, New York: Scribner.

Stoner, J. A. F. (1961) 'A comparison of individual and group decisions involving risk', unpublished master's thesis, Massachusetts Institute of Technology.

Stones, C. R., and Philbrick (1991) 'Attitudes toward love of a small fundamentalist community in South Africa', *Journal of Social Psychology*, **131**, 219–23.

Storti, C. (1990) *The Art of Crossing Cultures*, Yarmouth, ME: Intercultural Press.

Strickland, L. H. (ed.) (1984) *Directions in Soviet Social Psychology*, New York: Springer.

Stroebe, W., Lenkert, A., and Jonas, K. (1988) 'Familiarity may breed contempt: the impact of student exchange on national stereotypes and attitudes', in W. Stroebe, A. Kruglanski, D. Bar-Tal and M. Hewstone (eds.), *The Social Psychology of Intergroup Conflict: Theory, research and applications*, New York: Springer.

Strube, M. J. (1981) 'Meta-analysis and cross-cultural comparison: sex differences in child competitiveness', *Journal of Cross-Cultural Psychology*, **12**, 3–20.

Sueda, K., and Wiseman, R. L. (1992) 'Embarrassment remediation in Japan and the United States', *International Journal of Intercultural Relations*, **16**, 159–74.

Sumner, W. G. (1940) *Folkways*, Boston, MA: Ginn.

Sundberg, N. D., Poole, M. E., and Tyler, L. E. (1983) 'Adolescents' expectations of future events: a cross-cultural study of Australians, Americans and Indians', *International Journal of Psychology*, **18**, 415–27.

Sussman, N., and Rosenfeld, H. (1982) 'Influence of culture, language and sex on conversational distance', *Journal of Personality and Social Psychology*, **42**, 66–74.

Taft, R. (1973) 'Migration: problems of adjustment and assimilation in immigrants', in P. Watson (ed.), *Psychology and Race*, Harmondsworth: Penguin.

Tajfel, H. (1972) 'Experiments in a vacuum', in J. Israel and H. Tajfel (eds.), *The Context of Social Psychology: A critical assessment*, London: Academic Press.

Tajfel, H. (ed.) (1978) *Differentiation between Social Groups: Studies in intergroup behaviour*, London: Academic Press.

Tajfel, H. (1981) *Human Groups and Social Categories*, Cambridge: Cambridge University Press.

Tajfel, H., Billig, M., Bundy, R.P., and Flament, C. (1971) 'Social categorisation and intergroup behaviour', *European Journal of Social Psychology*, **1**, 149–78.

Takata, T. (1987) 'Self-deprecative tendencies in self-evaluation through social comparison', *Japanese Journal of Experimental Social Psychology*, **27**, 27–36.

Takeshita, T. (1990) 'Global consciousness on five continents', paper presented at the 22nd conference of the International Association of Applied Psychology, Kyoto, Japan, 22–7 July.

Taylor, D. M. (1981) 'Stereotypes and intergroup relations', in R. C. Gardner and R. Kalin (eds.), *A Canadian Social Psychology of Ethnic Relations*, Toronto: Methuen.

Taylor, D. M., and Doria, J. R. (1981) 'Self-serving and group-serving bias in attributions', *Journal of Social Psychology*, **113**, 201–11.

Taylor, D. M., and Jaggi, V. (1974) 'Ethnocentrism and causal attribution in a South Indian context', *Journal of Cross-Cultural Psychology*, **5**, 162–71.

Taylor, S. E., Fiske, S. T., Etcoff, N. L., and Ruderman, A. J. (1978) 'Categorical and contextual bases of person memory and stereotyping', *Journal of Personality and Social Psychology*, **36**, 778–93.

Thakerar, J. N., Giles, H., and Cheshire, J. (1982) 'Psychological and linguistic parameters of speech accommodation theory', in C. Fraser and K. R. Scherer (eds.), *Advances in the Social Psychology of Language*, Cambridge: Cambridge University Press.

Thibaut, J., and Walker, L. (1975) *Procedural Justice: A psychological analysis*, Hillsdale, NJ: Erlbaum.

Thomas, D. (1975) 'Cooperation and competition among Polynesian and European children', *Child Development*, **46**, 948–53.

Timaeus, E. (1968) 'Untersuchungen zum sogennanten konformen Verhalten', *Zeitschrift für Experimentelle und Angewandte Psychologie*, **15**, 176–94.

Ting-Toomey, S. (1988) 'A face-negotiation theory', in Y. Kim and W. B. Gudykunst (eds.), *Theory in Intercultural Communication*, Newbury Park, CA: Sage.

Ting-Toomey, S. (1991) 'Intimacy expressions in three cultures: France, Japan and the United States', *International Journal of Intercultural Relations*, **15**, 29–46.

Townsend, P. (1979) *Poverty in the United Kingdom*, Harmondsworth: Penguin.

Trafimow, D., Triandis, H. C., and Goto, S. G. (1991) 'Some tests of the distinction between the private self and the collective self', *Journal of Personality and Social Psychology*, **60**, 649–55.

Triandis, H. C. (1978) 'Some universals of social behavior', *Personality and Social Psychology Bulletin*, **4**, 1–16.

Triandis, H. C. (1988) 'Cross-cultural contributions to theory in social psychology', in M. H. Bond (ed.), *The Cross-Cultural Challenge to Social Psychology*, Newbury Park, CA: Sage.

Triandis, H. C. (1989) 'The self and social behaviour in different cultural contexts', *Psychological Review*, **96**, 506–20.

Triandis, H. C. (1990) 'Cross-cultural studies of individualism and collectivism', in J. J. Berman (ed.), *Nebraska Symposium on Motivation, 1989*, Lincoln, NB: Nebraska University Press.

Triandis, H. C. (in press) 'Cross-cultural industrial and organizational psychology', in M. R. Dunnette (ed.), *Handbook of industrial and organizational psychology*, 2nd edn, Chicago, IL: Rand McNally.

Triandis, H. C., Brislin, R., and Hui, C. H. (1988) 'Cross-cultural training across the individualism–collectivism divide', *International Journal of Intercultural Relations*, **12**, 269–89.

Triandis, H. C., Leung, K., Villareal, M., and Clack, F. L. (1985) 'Allocentric vs. idiocentric tendencies: convergent and discriminant validation', *Journal of Research in Personality*, **19**, 395–415.

Triandis, H. C., Lisanski, J., Setiadi, B., Chang, B. H., Marin, G., and Betancourt, H. (1982) 'Stereotyping among Hispanics and Anglos: the uniformity, intensity, direction, and quality of auto- and heterostereotypes', *Journal of Cross-Cultural Psychology*, **13**, 409–26.

Triandis, H. C., Marin, G., Lisansky, J., and Betancourt, H. (1984) 'Simpatia as a cultural script for Hispanics', *Journal of Personality and Social Psychology*, **47**, 1363–75.

Triandis, H. C., McCusker, C., and Hui, C. H. (1990) 'Multimethod probes of individualism and collectivism', *Journal of Personality and Social Psychology*, **59**, 1006–20.

Trimble, J. E. (1990) 'Ethnic specification, validation prospects, and the future of drug use research', *International Journal of the Addictions*, **25**, 149–170.

Tripathi, R. C. (1981) 'Machiavellianism and social manipulation', in J. Pandey (ed.), *Perspectives on Experimental Social Psychology in India*, New Delhi: Concept.

Triplett, N. D. (1898) 'The dynamogenic factor in pace-making and competition', *American Journal of Psychology*, **9**, 507–33.

Trommsdorff, G. (1973) 'Value change in Japan', *International Journal of Intercultural Relations*, **7**, 337–60.

Trubisky, P., Ting-Toomey, S., and Lin, S-L. (1991) 'The influence of individualism–collectivism and self-monitoring on conflict styles', *International Journal of Intercultural Relations*, **15**, 65–84.

Tsurumi, K. (1992) 'Aspects of endogenous development in contemporary China and Japan', paper presented at joint symposium, International Associations of Comparative Sociology and of Sociology of Organizations, Kurashiki, Japan, 4–7 July.

Tu, W. M. (1985) 'Selfhood and otherness in Confucian thought', in A. J. Marsella, G. DeVos and F. L. K. Hsu (eds.), *Culture and Self: Asian and western perspectives*, New York: Tavistock.

Tung, R. (1981) 'Selection and training of personnel for overseas assignments', *Columbia Journal of World Business*, **1**, 68–78.

Turner, J. C. (1975) 'Social comparison and social identity: some prospects for intergroup behavior', *European Journal of Social Psychology*, **5**, 5–34.

Tyerman, A., and Spencer, C. (1983) 'A critical test of the Sherifs' Robber's Cave experiments', *Small Group Behavior*, **14**, 515–31.

Valdes, J. M. (ed.) (1986) *Culture Bound*, New York: Cambridge University Press.

Vanbeselaere, N. (1983) 'Mere exposure: a search for an explanation', in W. Doise and S. Moscovici (eds.), *Current Issues in European Social Psychology*, volume 1, Cambridge: Cambridge University Press.

Vandewiele, M., and Philbrick, J. L. (1983) 'Attitudes of Senegalese students toward love', *Psychological Reports*, **52**, 915–18.

van Knippenberg, A. F. M., and van Oers, H. (1984) 'Social identity and equity concerns in intergroup perceptions', *British Journal of Social Psychology*, **23**, 351–62.

Van Lange, P. A. M., and Liebrand, W. B. G. (1991) 'Social value orientation and intelligence: a test of the goal prescribe rationality principle', *European Journal of Social Psychology*, **21**, 273–92.

VanYperen, N. W., and Buunk, B. P. (1991) 'Equity theory and exchange and communal orientation from a cross-national perspective', *Journal of Social Psychology*, **131**, 5–21.

Vidmar, N. (1970) 'Group composition and the risky shift', *Journal of Experimental Social Psychology*, **6**, 153–66.

Vlaander, G., and van Rooijen, L. (1985) 'Independence and conformity in Holland: Asch's experiment in Holland three decades later', *Gedrag*, **13**, 49–55.

Vroom, V. H., and Yetton, P. W. (1973) *Leadership and Decision-making*, Pittsburgh, PA: University of Pittsburgh Press.

Wallbot, H. G., and Scherer, K. R. (1986) 'How universal and specific is emotional experience? Evidence from 27 countries on five continents', *Social Science Information*, **25**, 763–95.

Wallendorf, M., and Arnould, E. J. (1988) '"My favourite things": a cross-cultural inquiry into object attachment, possessiveness and social linkage', *Journal of Consumer Research*, **14**, 531–47.

Wan, K. C., and Bond, M. H. (1982) 'Chinese attributions for success and failure under public and anonymous conditions of rating', *Acta Psychologica Taiwanica*, **24**, 23–31.

Ward, C., and Kennedy, A. (in press) 'Psychological and socio-cultural adjustment of foreign students in Singapore and New Zealand', *Journal of Cross-Cultural Psychology*.

Watkins, D., and Regmi, M. (1990) 'Self-serving bias: a Nepalese investigation', *Journal of Social Psychology*, **130**, 555–6.

Watson, O. M. (1970) *Proxemic Behavior: A cross cultural study*, The Hague: Mouton.

Watson, O. M., and Graves, T. D. (1966) 'Quantitative research in proxemic behavior', *American Anthropologist*, **68**, 971–85.

Watzlawick, P., Beavin, J. H., and Jackson, D. D. (1967) *The Pragmatics of Human Communication*, New York: Norton.

Wehmann, P., Goldstein, M. A., and Williams, J. R. (1977) 'Effects of different leadership styles on individual risk-taking in groups', *Human Relations*, **30**, 249–59.

Weinberg, I. (1969) 'The problem of the convergence of industrial societies: a critical look at the state of a theory', *Comparative Studies in Society and History*, **11**, 1–15.

Wetherell, M. (1982) 'Cross-cultural studies of minimal groups: implications for the social identity theory of intergroup relations', in H. Tajfel (ed.), *Social Identity and Intergroup Relations*, Cambridge: Cambridge University Press.

Wheeler, L., Reis, H. T., and Bond, M. H. (1989) 'Collectivism–individualism in everyday social life: the Middle Kingdom and the melting pot', *Journal of Personality and Social Psychology*, **57**, 79–86.

White, M. J., and Li, Y. (1991) 'Second language fluency and person perception in China and the United States', *Journal of Language and Social Psychology*, **10**, 99–114.

Whiting, B. B. (1976) 'The problem of the packaged variable', in K. F. Reigel and J. A. Meacham (eds.), *The Developing Individual in a Changing World*, The Hague: Mouton.

Whittaker, J. O., and Meade, R. D. (1967) 'Social pressure in the modification and distortion of judgment: a cross-cultural study', *International Journal of Psychology*, **2**, 109–13.

Whittaker, J. O., Rosenau, C. D., Farnsworth, H., and Grosz, R. (1957) 'A repetition of Asch's "Effects of group pressure on modification and distortion of judgment"', *Perceptual and Motor Skills*, **7**, 245.

Whorf, B. L. (1956) *Language, Thought and Reality*, New York: Wiley.

Wible, D. S., and Hui, C. H. (1985) 'Perceived language proficiency and person perception', *Journal of Cross-Cultural Psychology*, **16**, 206–22.

Williams, J., and Best, D. (1982) *Measuring Sex Stereotypes: A thirty nation study*, Beverly Hills, CA: Sage.

Williams, J., and Best, D. (1990) *Sex and Psyche: Gender and Self Viewed Cross-Culturally*, Newbury Park, CA: Sage.

Williams, J., and Best, D. (1992) 'Psychological factors associated with cross-cultural differences in individualism–collectivism', in Y. Kashima (ed.), *Psychological Factors Associated with cross-cultural Differences in Individualism/Collectivism*, Newbury Park, CA: Sage.

Williams, R. (1961) *The Long Revolution*, London: Chatto and Windus.

Williams, T. P., and Sogon, S. (1984) 'Group composition and conforming behavior in Japanese students', *Japanese Psychological Research*, **26**, 231–4.

Wilpert, B. (ed.) (1991) 'Special issue: Latin America', *Applied Psychology: An International Review*, **40**, 111–236.

Wish, M. (1979) 'Dimensions of dyadic communication', in S. Weitz (ed.), *Nonverbal communication*, New York: Oxford.

Wish, M., Deutsch, M., and Kaplan, S. J. (1976) 'Perceived dimensions of interpersonal relations', *Journal of Personality and Social Psychology*, **33**, 409–20.

Witkin, H.A. (1950) 'Individual differences in the case of perception of embedded figures', *Journal of Personality*, **19**, 1–15.

Witkin, H. A., and Berry, J. (1975) 'Psychological differentiation in cross-cultural perspective', *Journal of Cross-Cultural Psychology*, **6**, 4–87.

Witkin, H. A., Dyk, R. B., Faterson, H. F., Goodenough, D. R., and Karp, S. A. (1962) *Psychological Differentiation*, New York: Wiley.

Won-Doornink, M. (1985) 'Self-disclosure and reciprocity in conversation: a cross-national study', *Social Psychology Quarterly*, **48**, 97–107.

Woodcock, A., and Davis, M. (1981) *Catastrophe Theory*, Harmondsworth: Penguin.

Worchel, S., and Austin, W. G. (eds.) (1979) *The Social Psychology of Intergroup Relations*, Monterey, CA: Brooks-Cole.

Wubbels, T., and Levy, J. (1991) 'A comparison of interpersonal behavior of Dutch and American teachers', *International Journal of Intercultural Relations*, **15**, 1–18.

Yamagishi, T. (1988) 'Exit from the group as an individualistic solution to free rider problem in the United States and Japan', *Journal of Experimental Social Psychology*, **24**, 530–42.

Yamagishi, T., and Sato, K. (1986) 'Motivational basis of the public goods problem', *Journal of Personality and Social Psychology*, **50**, 67–73.

Yang, K. S. (1986) 'Chinese personality and its change', in M. H. Bond (ed.), *The Psychology of the Chinese People*, Hong Kong: Oxford University Press.

Yang, K. S. (1988) 'Will societal modernization eventually eliminate cross-cultural psychological differences?', in M. H. Bond (ed.), *The Cross-Cultural Challenge to Social Psychology*, Newbury Park, CA: Sage.

Yang, K. S., and Bond, M. H. (1990) 'Exploring implicit personality theories with indigenous and imported constructs: the Chinese case', *Journal of Personality and Social Psychology*, **58**, 1087–95.

Yoshiyama, N. (1988) 'A time series analysis of minority influence on majority in a group', *Japanese Journal of Experimental Social Psychology*, **28**, 27–54 (English abstract).

Yuen, S. (1991) 'The concern for "face": a cross-cultural examination between subjects from Hong Kong and England', unpublished manuscript, University of Oxford.

Yukl, G. (1989) *Leadership in Organizations* (2nd edn), Englewood Cliffs, NJ: Prentice Hall.

Zajonc, R. B. (1968) 'Attitudinal effects of mere exposure', *Journal of Personality and Social Psychology*, **9** (Monograph Supplement 2), 1–27.

Zarate, M. A., and Smith, E. R. (1990) 'Person categorization and stereotyping', *Social Cognition*, **8**, 161–85.

Zebrowitz, L. A., Montepare, J., and Lee, H. K. (1991) 'Differentiating same versus other race individuals', manuscript submitted for publication.

Zebrowitz-McArthur, L. (1988) 'Person perception in cross-cultural perspective', in M. H. Bond (ed.), *The Cross-Cultural Challenge to Social Psychology*, Newbury Park, CA: Sage.

Zhurvalev, A. L., and Shorokhova, E. V. (1984) 'Social psychological problems of managing the collective', in L. H. Strickland (ed.), *Directions in Soviet Social Psychology*, New York: Springer.

Zimbardo, P. G. (1970) 'The human choice: individuation, reason and order versus deindividuation, impulse and chaos', in W. J. Arnold and D. Levine (eds.), *Nebraska Symposium on Motivation, 1969*, Lincoln, NB: Nebraska Univesity Press.

Name Index

Subject Index